Getaway &
Namibia
MIKE COPELAND

SUNBIRD
PUBLISHERS

First published in 2007
Reprinted in 2008
Second edition 2009

Sunbird Publishers (Pty) Ltd
PO Box 6836, Roggebaai, Cape Town, 8012

www.sunbirdpublishers.co.za

Registration number: 1984/003543/07

Copyright published edition © Sunbird Publishers 2007
Copyright text © Mike Copeland 2009
Copyright maps © Sunbird Publishers 2009
Copyright photographs © Mike Copeland 2007 and
individual photographers as credited

Editor: Sean Fraser
Design and layout: Chris Agenbag
Cartographer: John Hall
Editorial adviser: David Bristow

Reproduction by Resolution Colour (Pty) Ltd, Cape Town
Printed by Star Standard Industries (Pte) Ltd, Singapore

All rights reserved. No part of this publication may be reproduced, stored in a retrieval system or transmitted, in any form or by any means, electronic, mechanical, photocopying, recording or otherwise, without the prior written permission of the copyright owner(s).

ISBN: 978 1 920289 18 8

While every effort has been made to check that the information in this guide is correct at the time of going to press, the author, the publisher and its agents will not be held liable for any damages incurred through any inaccuracies.

PHOTOGRAPHIC CREDITS: (l = left, r = right, t = top, b = bottom, br = bottom right)
All photographs by the author except for: Ingeborg Peltzer p3, Justin Fox pp67,75, 77;
Rob House pp47, 60, 66, 117, 120, 123, 145, 153, 177, 178; Stephen Mulholland pp27, 35, 41, 63;
Scott Ramsay pp6, 46.
Main cover photograph (donkey cart) and insets of church and warthog by Rob House; cover microlight, title page and dedication page photographs by Dana Allen, (c) PhotoSafari

Namibia is a vast country to research and visit and I could not have written this guidebook without plenty of assistance. I am especially grateful to the owners, management and staff of all the wonderful places we stayed at and activities we enjoyed. The Namibia Tourism Board was very helpful, and Toyota supplied my tough, dependable transport. Pats was again companion and partner on all my visits to Namibia, offering constant support and helping to take reams of notes. And my publisher, Ceri, is the support behind all my books. May there be many more!

Mike Copeland,
Paarl, July 2009

I dedicate this book to Nicola, Matthew, James and Joseph,
who know and love Africa almost as much as their dad does.

Contents

INTRODUCTION
1 Facts, figures and highlights — 9
2 History and economy — 13
3 People and culture — 17
4 The natural world — 21
5 On the road — 27
6 What to pack — 35
7 Eating and sleeping — 41
8 Health and safety — 47
9 Getting there and getting around — 51
10 Practical information — 59

WINDHOEK AND THE SOUTHWEST
11 Windhoek — 67
12 Noordoewer to Windhoek — 79
13 The B4 to Lüderitz — 89
14 Ai-Ais and the Fish River Canyon — 99

THE CENTRAL WEST
15 The Namib-Naukluft — 103
16 Walvis Bay — 111
17 Swakopmund — 117
18 Henties Bay and the Skeleton Coast — 129

THE SOUTHEAST AND THE KALAHARI
19 Gobabis and south to the Kalahari — 133

THE NORTHERN REGIONS
20 North to Etosha — 139
21 Etosha National Park — 147
22 Tsumeb, Otavi and Grootfontein — 153
23 Rundu, Bushmanland and the Kaudom — 159

THE FAR NORTH
24 The Caprivi — 167
25 Katima Mulilo — 173
26 Rundu to Ruacana — 179

THE NORTHWEST
27 Kaokoland — 185
28 Damaraland — 195

INDEX — 204

MAPS

Namibia	8
Windhoek	69
Southwestern Namibia	81
Keetmanshoop	84
Lüderitz	91
Ai-Ais and the Fish River Canyon	98
Namib-Naukluft	105
Walvis Bay	113
Swakopmund	119
Gobabis	135
Otjiwarongo	142
Etosha National Park	149
Tsumeb	155
Grootfontein	157
Rundu	161
Kaudom Game Park	163
Tsumkwe	164
Eastern Caprivi	169
Katima Mulilo	174
Kaokoland	186
Damaraland	197

MAP KEY

Note: Some maps are not to scale.

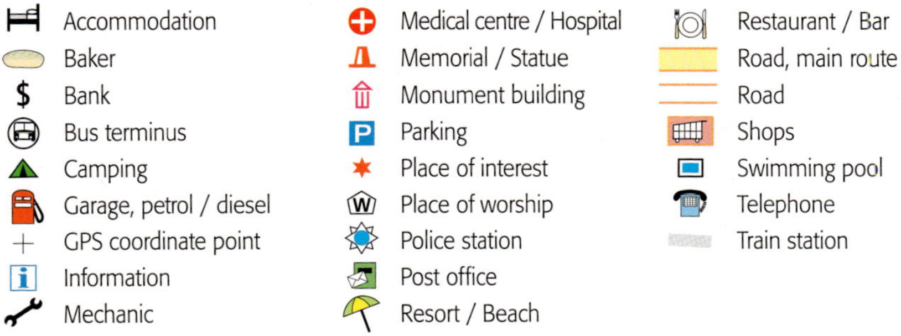

Accommodation
Baker
Bank
Bus terminus
Camping
Garage, petrol / diesel
GPS coordinate point
Information
Mechanic
Medical centre / Hospital
Memorial / Statue
Monument building
Parking
Place of interest
Place of worship
Police station
Post office
Resort / Beach
Restaurant / Bar
Road, main route
Road
Shops
Swimming pool
Telephone
Train station

HOW TO USE THIS BOOK

The first 10 chapters of this book are filled with information on Namibia, its history, people and natural environment, with notes on planning your trip, getting to your destination, staying safe and other practical aspects of travelling around Namibia. Some of the suggestions and recommended equipment are only applicable for the wilder parts of the country and should not be necessary if you are staying in and around the larger towns.

Chapter 11 explores the capital Windhoek and chapters 12 to 14 the southwest of the country. The central western parts are covered in chapters 15 to 18. Chapter 19 looks at the southeast of the country, the area that stretches into the Kalahari. Chapters 20 to 23 are devoted to the northern regions, while chapters 24 to 26 cover the far north of Namibia and chapters 27 and 28 take you inland to explore Kaokoland and Damaraland.

This guide can be used to plan a trip to or travel throughout Namibia, on-road or off-road, either with your own vehicle or a hired one, and even on public transport. Bus routes, road conditions and fuel availability, accommodation and food – it's all there. Namibia is so vast and its sights so spread out that there is no one, ideal route through the country. This has kept me from outlining a single round trip – so choose your own route and then work your way through those particular chapters here.

Prices quoted are in Namibian dollars (N$), which are on a par with South African rands (R) and are generally for residents of South Africa and other southern African countries. Locals are sometimes charged less – and foreigners often more! Please note that, while every effort has been made to list the latest prices, these could have escalated by the time you visit.

Telephone numbers are listed as you would dial them within Namibia, including the area codes. All other numbers (including South African) are preceded by the international and area dialling codes.

Introduction

Many holiday destinations slip in and out of fashion, but Namibia is always popular. With its magnificent scenery, abundant wildlife, hot-water springs, rugged hiking and 4x4 trails, birding, fishing and hunting, it's no wonder that tourists keep returning – and with good roads and communications, it's easy to get around safely in this well-organised land of wide-open spaces. In fact, it's probably the wide-open spaces that attract visitors to the country. Instead of the long distances between towns being a drawback, the vast panoramas and empty horizons mesmerise you with their stark beauty. Once you've visited the game parks, driven the 4x4 trails and fished the icy waters of the Atlantic, you'll be drawn back just to be there again, to experience the warm desert days and the cool, star-filled nights. To call it a tonic for body and soul sounds clichéd, but that's what it is.

Namibia welcomes all tourists, no matter what your budget – from the cash-strapped student couple in an old Golf, to Mum, Dad and the kids in a well-equipped Land Rover, to the well-heeled, retired European couple flying from one luxury lodge to the next, they'll all have the time of their lives and return home with memories that never seem to fade – it's a vivid country.

Fortunately, as popular as the country is, there is no mass tourism. Namibia is an individual country for individual travellers – and it's relatively cheap too. Prices are charged in Namibian dollars, not US dollars. Food, drink, accommodation and fuel are widely available and the people are honest and friendly, all of which makes Namibia a pleasant and easy introduction to travelling on the continent of Africa.

But nothing stays the same, and Namibia is growing and developing all the time. Guidebooks generally struggle to keep up with the changes, so I would welcome feedback from you, the reader. If you want to travel further into Africa, then look out for my other Getaway Guides to Botswana and Mozambique. And if you want to drop me a line, my address is mcopeland@telkomsa.net.

Namibia's flag is rich in symbolism
Blue represents the sky, ocean, precious water resources and the importance of rain. The sun symbolises life and energy. The colour red represents the Namibian people, while white refers to peace and unity. The colour green signifies the country's vegetation and agricultural resources.

Facts, figures and highlights 1

Namibia is a large, chunky country that stretches up the west coast of Africa, with a long, narrow panhandle (the Caprivi) in the north, extending eastward to the Zambezi River. Bordered in the east by Botswana, the south by South Africa, the west by the Atlantic Ocean and the north by Angola, it also manages to share a short border with Zambia at the far end of the Caprivi Strip.

A quiver tree stands in full bloom after heavy rains in the south of Namibia.

Size

At 824 300 square kilometres, Namibia is a big country – even bigger than Botswana, which is only 581 700 square kilometres, but way smaller than South Africa, at 1 221 000 square kilometres. You could fit the UK and France into Namibia if you were allowed to or two Californias, but you'd end up with a lot of very bewildered people.

Topography

The backbone of Namibia is the 2 000-metre-high central plateau, which runs from south to north, with the highest region around Windhoek. To the west lies the spectacular Namib Desert, which follows the coast all the way from South Africa to Angola. This ancient, dry and barren strip of sand, sea and gravel plains is a formidable barrier, but hosts an amazing variety of adapted flora and fauna. Running down the east of the country is the arid savanna of the Kalahari, with waves of dunes that disappear into the sands of Botswana.

Climate

With such a vast arid landscape, the climate can be pretty harsh. During the summer months (October to April), the average daily temperatures in the interior range from 20°C to 34°C, but can reach 45°C in the extreme north and south, relieved only by the rains that fall in thunderstorms. The average annual rainfall varies from less than 50 millimetres along the coast to 350 millimetres in the central interior, and 700 millimetres in the Caprivi. Winters (from May to September) are dry and much more pleasant, with cool daytime temperatures (18°C to 20°C average), but often below freezing, with frost at night. The coast is influenced by the cold Benguela current, which keeps the average temperature at a pretty stable 15°C to 25°C, but also causes regular heavy fog.

Cities and towns

Windhoek is the country's administrative, judicial and legislative capital. It is also Namibia's largest city with 240 000 inhabitants – in other words, 15% of the total population. Centrally situated, it is ideally positioned to serve and distribute to all the country's 13 regions. Swakopmund, Walvis Bay and Lüderitz are on the coast, while Keetmanshoop and Mariental cater to the needs of the south. North of Windhoek, the more fertile regions boast the towns of Grootfontein, Okahandja, Otjiwarongo, Oshakati and Tsumeb, and the Caprivi claims Rundu and Katima Mulilo. Gobabis, another large town, is situated east of Windhoek on the Trans-Kalahari Highway and serves as the gateway to Botswana.

Population

For its size, Namibia has a rather small population of around two million – that's just two and a half people per square kilometre! The largest ethnic group is the Owambo, who generally come from the north and make up just over half the population. Herero, Kavango and Damara make up about another 30%, while Rehoboth Basters, San (Bushman), Caprivians, Nama, Himba and white Namibians complete this rich cultural mix. The literacy rate is

The Spitzkoppe in southern Damaraland is famous for San paintings and challenging rock climbs.

an impressive 85% (15 years and over) as 94% of children attend school. Life expectancy is 51 years, but with a growth rate of 2.9% and an estimated adult HIV infection rate of 15%, the demographics of the country are bound to change.

Language
While English is the official language and gaining ground, Afrikaans is more widely spoken throughout Namibia. German is also spoken by the many expatriates and visitors from Germany, while the main ethnic languages are Oshiwambo and Otjiherero.

Currency
The Namibian dollar is the currency of Namibia. It has the same value as the South African rand and both currencies are legal tender in the country. The exchange rate with other foreign currencies is the same as that of the rand, and there is no black market. But remember that although you can use rands in Namibia, you cannot use the Namibian dollar in South Africa.

The exchange rate at the time of writing was around N$8,10 to the US dollar, N$11,30 to the Euro and N$13,20 to the British pound. Traveller's cheques are not popular, but they can be exchanged at banks and Bureaux de Change. International funds can also be transferred between Namibian and foreign banks using the SWIFT system.

Most credit cards are accepted, except in remote areas. Automatic teller machines (ATMs) are attached to banks and can be found in shopping malls.

An island in the Kunene River near the Epupa Falls.

Time

Time in Namibia is Universal Time (UT) plus 2 hours – the same as all its neighbours – from October to March, and UT plus 1 hour from April to September (except the Caprivi, where they remain at UT+2).

Visa requirements

Hardly anyone needs a holiday visa for Namibia. Citizens from the following countries are exempt for a period of 90 days: Austria, Australia, Angola, Britain, Botswana, Brazil, Belgium, Canada, Cuba, Denmark, France, Finland, Germany, Italy, Ireland, Iceland, Japan, Kenya, Liechtenstein, Lesotho, Luxembourg, Mozambique, Malawi, Malaysia, Netherlands, New Zealand, Norway, Portugal, Russian Federation, Switzerland, Sweden, Spain, Singapore, Swaziland, South Africa, Tanzania, USA, Zimbabwe and Zambia. Work permits are required if you plan on seeking employment in Namibia, so be sure to check with your nearest Namibian embassy.

Government

After a long period of administration by South Africa and a bitter struggle for independence, the Namibian people voted in November 1989 for a new National Assembly. With the South West African People's Organisation (Swapo) winning the majority, a new democratic constitution was written and in March 1990 the newly independent Republic of Namibia was born. A president is voted in directly by the electorate for a five-year term and is supported by a prime minister and cabinet. Parliament has two houses: one is elected directly and the other indirectly by the country's regions. Sam Nujoma was Namibia's first president and went on to serve three terms, stepping down in 2005 to make way for the present incumbent, Hifikepunye Pohamba.

Tourist highlights

If you really want to see the best Namibia has to offer and you are starting from the south, I would suggest you check out the Fish River Canyon and Ai-Ais hot springs, Lüderitz and Kolmanskop, Sossusvlei, Sesriem and the Namib-Naukluft Park, Walvis Bay and Swakopmund, the rock art of Brandberg and Twyfelfontein, the Skeleton Coast, Kaokoland and Epupa Falls, Etosha National Park, and Poppa Falls and the wonderfully remote game parks of the Caprivi. Quite a list – and then you'd still have to return via Bushmanland, the Waterberg and down to Windhoek. Read on and I'll show you how!

History and economy 2

The history of Namibia is similar to that of many other African countries – migration and battles for supremacy by local tribes and nations, the coming of European powers and their colonial domination, independence struggles and strife, and eventually self-government. The difference is that Namibia works – unlike many other African countries, there are regular free and fair elections, presidents stand down when their terms of office come to an end and democracy rules.

The lonely graves of Dorsland trekkers near Swartbooisdrif in northern Kaokoland.

History

The early prehistory of Africa's southwestern coast was much the same as it was elsewhere on the continent. Over the centuries, the Stone Age gave way to the Iron Age and hunter-gatherers eventually made way for pastoralists. These groups included the San, Damara and Nama, who all spoke a Khoisan language and became more settled as they began cultivating the land.

The first Bantu-speaking peoples to arrive on the scene were the Herero, part of a general movement down from the north. Being a stronger group, they quickly influenced the original inhabitants who had to adapt or, as in the case of the San, were marginalised.

This monument to the Dorsland trekkers overlooks the Kunene River and Angola beyond.

Being positioned far from the East's and West's seafaring nations and cursed with an inhospitable coastline meant that this part of Africa had no outside contact from across the sea. But in 1485 all this changed when the Portuguese seafarer Diego Cão stepped ashore at Cape Cross on the Skeleton Coast and erected a stone cross. The Portuguese were on a quest to find a route to the East and two years later sent Bartholomeu Diaz, who put in at Walvis Bay and Lüderitz. Diaz, however, found nothing of interest, so the Portuguese by and large ignored this part of Africa.

By the end of the 18th century, American, British and French whalers had settled around the protective bays of Walvis and Lüderitz. This prompted the Dutch, who were occupying the Cape at the time, to consolidate their position and annex Walvis Bay. When England took control of the Cape in 1806 they inherited this small piece of southwest African coast.

The stage was now set for confrontations between the indigenous population and traders, missionaries and hunters, outside influences who had slowly crept up from the Cape and inland from Walvis. Adding to the confusion was the Oorlams group, which had also drifted up from the Cape. Led by Jonker Afrikaner, they were a mixed band of Khoisan, outlaws, deserters and people of mixed blood. Throw guns and booze into the mix and you had a pretty confused and explosive situation in the mid-1800s.

By the late 19th century the 'Scramble for Africa' was in full swing and Germany annexed Lüderitzbucht, which soon

Walvis Bay's oyster beds contribute to the country's economy – and national cuisine.

developed into their colony of German South West Africa. In the subsequent parcelling up of Africa, the borders of Portugal's Angola, Britain's Bechuanaland (Botswana) and Germany's South West Africa (Namibia) were drawn. Germany, however, was determined to gain access to the Zambezi, and in 1890 'swopped' the island of Heligoland in the North Sea for the Caprivi Strip.

By the 1890s German soldiers, the *Schutztruppe*, had built a fort in Windhoek and settlers soon followed. Angry about the loss of land, the Herero organised an uprising in 1904, which was brutally put down by General Von Trotha and his troops. This set the stage for more German settlement and the colony began to grow economically. Farms increased production, new towns sprang up and a railway network was developed.

At the beginning of the 20th century diamonds were discovered around Lüderitz, and the rich copper and other minerals of Tsumeb were mined. Things were going well for German South West Africa up until the outbreak of the First World War.

South Africa sided with Britain in this war against Germany, and in 1915 sent a force north to defeat and take control of South West Africa. After the war South Africa was assigned South West Africa (SWA) as a trust territory by the League of Nations and a new period of colonisation began.

South Africa ran SWA as its own and treated the territory more or less as her fifth province. More farms were settled, an infrastructure of roads and communications began to develop and all was integrated into the larger South African economy. Mining and farming were the backbone of the local economy and South West Africa prospered.

But the aspirations of the Namibian people for independence were strong and Swapo championed the cause. An armed liberation struggled started in 1966 and developed into war, which ended in a negotiated settlement in 1989. Free and fair elections were held and, in March 1990, the independent Republic of Namibia was born.

Economy

With a per capita GDP of around N$40 000, the sectors that contribute most to the Namibian economy are mining, fishing, tourism and agriculture. Mining makes the largest contribution (8% of GDP and over 50% of exports) with reserves of uranium, lead, zinc, tin, silver, copper, tungsten and diamonds. Diamonds are the largest earner of foreign exchange as Namibia's gemstones have the highest per carat value in the world. As onshore reserves dwindle, offshore operations have been stepped up and huge barges suck gravel off the seabed to be processed on board.

Agriculture is the country's largest employer (50% of the workforce) although only 2% of the country is regarded as arable and another 46% suitable for permanent pasture. From these figures, it's easy to understand that cattle, sheep and goat farming are the main activities. The importance of agriculture lies in its contribution to the livelihoods of rural communities, and about 70% of the population is directly or indirectly dependent on the agricultural sector.

Namibia's main trading partners are South Africa, Germany, Switzerland and the UK. Walvis Bay is the country's main harbour, with Lüderitz playing a smaller role. The road system is extensive (approximately 5 500 kilometres are tarred and 37 000 kilometres gravel) and well maintained, and Windhoek's Hosea Kutako International Airport serves as the country's air gateway.

As Namibia exports mainly primary resources and imports consumer goods, there is great scope in manufacturing. Special incentives are offered and an Export Processing Zone is in place at Walvis Bay.

The mighty Kunene squeezes through the narrow gorge at Epupa.

> **Tourism is the fastest** growing sector of the economy, with community-based tourism an important component. The Namibia Community Based Tourism Association (NACOBTA) is a donor-funded organisation with the objective of benefiting more rural communities through tourism. It is hoped that a new appreciation for wildlife and ecology can be promoted through this.

People and culture 3

In contemporary Africa, tribal and ethnic differences have blurred somewhat. Ease of travel and migration, urbanisation, education and modern entertainment have made us less individual and more international. Namibia has not escaped this trend and it would be wrong to pretend that the country is peopled by tribes of distinctly different cultures. I feel that it is also insulting to compartmentalise people into groups and allocate them labels that might be inaccurate or unpopular. Fortunately, government policy seems to encourage the retention of interesting and positive aspects of the nation's different cultures and ignore the devisive ones. That said, however, we do need to look at the different cultural patterns that help make up this fascinating tapestry, even if we do have to resort to broad generalisations.

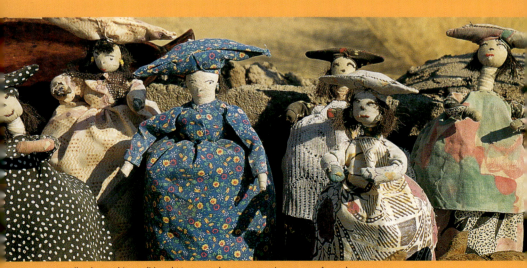

Dolls, dressed in traditional Herero style, tempt tourists at a craft market.

Culture and customs

Owambo This group, the largest in the country, speaks a Bantu-based language commonly known as Oshiwambo. Their traditional home territory is in the extreme north, between the Etosha National Park and the Angolan border, the most densely populated area in Namibia. Cattle and traditional food crops are farming mainstays, but the Owambo are generally also good traders and businessmen. A feature of traditional Owambo craftwork is the ekipa. These are carved buttons, made from ivory or bone, worn on a leather band to denote a woman's status and a measure of her husband's wealth. Today ekipas are often incorporated into modern jewellery and make a unique Namibian souvenir.

Kavango Closely related to the Owambo, many of the Kavango people also live on the northern border with Angola. Their numbers have been greatly increased over the years as their Angolan brothers fled across the border to escape the poverty and strife in that country. In addition to subsistence farming, they are also good fishermen and known for their beautiful woodcarvings.

Herero Comprising about 10% of the population, the Herero tend to be more centrally based and spill over into western Botswana. They love their cattle and the men are expert pastoralists. The women stand out in their fancy headdresses and distinctive long, flowing Victorian-style gowns, supported and puffed out with multiple layers of voluminous petticoats. Not surprisingly, they are good leatherworkers and also make and dress dolls in the traditional Herero style.

Damara The Damara are of the Khoisan family (they, too, speak a 'click' language), and one of the oldest groups in the country (along with the Nama and San). Traditionally from the arid area adjacent to the Skeleton Coast, the

Woodcarving is a traditional craft perfected by Namibians.

The San left a legacy of remarkable rock art wherever they roamed.

Damara were hunters who dabbled in mining. Look out for metalwork or wire art to take away as souvenirs.

Himba Although not a large group, traditional Himba (cattle herders who originate in the remote Kaokoland) have a very distinctive look. Often wearing no more than a small leather apron, they cover their bodies in a mixture of clay and animal fat. To have made your way into the remote mountains of Kaokoland and seen the Himba living their natural, proud lifestyle is a rare and unique travel experience. Try to find a traditional leather apron, embroidered in copper beads, as a memento of the trip.

San Also known as the Bushmen, these people were the original inhabitants of southern Africa and have remained amazingly distinct as a group as some still maintain a traditional hunter-gatherer lifestyle. Unfortunately, this inability or unwillingness to adapt to change has caused their numbers to dwindle. As farms were fenced in, the San – and the game they hunted – were forced out into the marginal land that no one else wanted. Today small groups can still be found in the Tsumeb, Otavi and Grootfontein districts and Bushmanland in the extreme northeast of the country. Traditional San jewellery made from ostrich eggshells and porcupine quills is worth looking out for when you are buying souvenirs.

> ### Racial delineations
> remain a hotly debated issue in much of Africa, and there is still much controversy about the naming of traditional peoples. The terms 'San' and 'Bushmen', for example, continue to create ongoing debate – some historians believe that the word 'San' implies a far broader delineation than the Bushmen are entitled to, while others argue that the term 'Bushmen' smacks of the Dutch colonists who referred, somewhat disparagingly, to these nomadic folk as 'people of the bush'. Equally, many query whether the people of Rehoboth should still be referred to as *basters* (the Dutch for 'bastards'). For want of a better term, I have opted to retain the colloquial nomenclature here.

People and culture | **19**

Basters Making up about 3% of the population, this Afrikaans-speaking group has an interesting history. Originally from the Cape, they are the descendants of indigenous Khoi (referred to in colonial history books as 'Hottentot') women and the Dutch settlers who first arrived in the mid-17th century. Feeling rejected by both the white and black communities, they banded together and trekked north, ending up as a well-organised mini-state in the area around present-day Rehoboth. Still a fairly close-knit group, they farm the land and produce sheepskin products such as bedspreads, rugs and warm slippers.

Caprivians The marshy eastern end of the Caprivi, between the Chobe and Zambezi rivers, is the traditional home to the Caprivians who farm and fish in this fertile little piece of paradise. Basket-weaving and woodwork are their thing.

The modest Victorian influence may still be seen in everyday dress.

Food and drink

It seems strange to have to say that the local cuisine is mainly German, but considering the abundance of meats, sausages and polonies, cakes, pastries and confectionery, the influence is obvious. Namibian meat is very good, so a South African-styled braai (barbecue) is another tasty tradition. With Namibia's long coastline, fish is good and plentiful, too, and if you are down in Swakop, Walvis or Lüderitz, look out for the exquisite oysters cultivated in the cold, unpolluted local waters. All this wonderful food can be washed down with excellent Namibian beer or even a bottle of local wine produced in Omaruru – I think I'll break for lunch now!

> ## Modern-day politics
> and an era of political correctness has meant that certain groups of people often tend to slip between the cracks – simply because one feels uncomfortable 'naming' them according to their skin colour. Nevertheless, two other important groups deserve mention in an analysis of Namibia's population: the 'coloured' people of mixed race who speak mainly English and Afrikaans and live mostly in the urban areas, where they work in trade and industry; and white Namibians (originally from South Africa or Germany), who – in broad terms – farm, own businesses and play a large part in the tourism industry.

The natural world 4

Namibia is a land of wide-open spaces and, with a small population, there is little human impact on the environment. Fortunately, the government realises the importance of ecotourism and has adopted a policy of quality, rather than quantity, tourism. Seventeen national parks and reserves (comprising 14% of the country's land area) protect habitats that range from deserts to wetlands, and include unique flora and fauna that have adapted to these different environments. From insects to elephants, lichens to baobabs, Namibia has it all. Avifauna is well represented, too, with 630 species of birds identified.

What better way to end a game drive than with a sundowner …

Namibia's 17 reserves and game parks are operated by the Ministry of Environment and Tourism (MET) who charges entrance fees to these conservation areas. Etosha National Park, Namib-Naukluft Park (Sesriem entrance), Waterberg Plateau Park, Ai-Ais Transfrontier Park and the Skeleton Coast Park all charge N$60 per person plus N$10 for your car, while other parks charge N$30 per person plus N$10 for your car. Accommodation in these reserves is operated by the independent Namibia Wildlife Resorts (NWR) and you are charged separately.

Cape Cross Seal Reserve

This 60-square-kilometre reserve is situated 130 kilometres to the north of Swakopmund and was proclaimed to protect the large colony of Cape fur seals that breeds here. Named after the stone cross that was erected here by Portuguese navigator Diego Cão in 1486, it also includes a small lichen reserve nearby and some bird islands off the coast. Breeding season for the seals is November and December, when over 200 000 can come ashore. The reserve is open daily from 10h00 to 17h00.

Caprivi Game Park

This 5 700-square-kilometre park lies in central Caprivi, between the Kavango and Kwando rivers, and runs the full width of the Caprivi strip between the Angolan and Botswanan borders. Protected but undeveloped, the only access is the B8 highway that connects Rundu to Katima Mulilo. You might see elephant or antelope crossing the road, but will find birdwatching far more rewarding with over 330 species recorded in the area. As the main road runs right through the middle of this reserve, there are no entry fees, closing times or amenities.

Daan Viljoen Game Park

About 25 kilometres west of Windhoek on the C28 lies this 40-square-kilometre park in the rolling hills of the Khomas Hochland. More of a picnic and camping spot for Windhoekers and tourists than a real game park, it does have a circular drive from which you can spot zebra, wildebeest and various antelope. Rather explore the park on foot – that way you can spot some of the interesting endemic bird species, such as Ruppell's parrot and Carp's black tit. This game park was closed at the time of writing, pending a decision on possible privatisation.

Etosha National Park

The flagship of Namibia's park system, Etosha is a gem of a park. Set in the north of Namibia around the vast Etosha Pan, the park was once the largest in the world. At 22 270 square kilometres, it is still one of the largest in Africa, and home to all the wildlife you could wish to see – lion, leopard, cheetah, rhino, elephant, giraffe, hyena, a large variety of antelope in huge herds, and 340 species of birds (big and small, raptors, migrators and flightless). With 30 waterholes and springs, the visitor has only to park and wait for the game to come to drink. Three well-equipped and well-run rest camps provide accommodation ranging from plain camping to luxury bungalows. See also page 147.

Fish River Canyon and Ai-Ais Resort

Set in the dry, barren south of the country, this natural wonder is 160 kilometres long, up to 27 kilometres wide and over 500 metres deep – the second largest gorge in Africa, after the Blue Nile Gorge in Ethiopia. Towards the southern end is a natural hot spring around which a resort has been built. Animals and birds can be seen, but most visitors come to hike the tough 90-kilometre trail through the canyon, which takes four or five days to complete. See also page 99.

Hardap Game Reserve

This 250-square-kilometre reserve and resort is situated around the Hardap Dam, Namibia's largest. Just north of Mariental, off the B1 highway, it serves as a handy overnight stop for many motorists heading up to savour Namibia's more famous game reserves. There is some game to be seen, and the dam also provides birding, watersport and angling opportunities.

Kaudom Game Park

This wild, isolated park lies in the north-eastern corner of the country and borders Botswana. Relatively new – proclaimed in 1989 – it protects the flora and fauna of the Kalahari sandveld biome. The rough, sandy conditions are suitable for 4x4s only and the rough terrain means that it would be wise to travel in convoys of at least two vehicles per group. Conditions are so tough and the elephants so mean, that the NWR have given up maintaining the two campsites that were in the park (although they are still open).

All the big and small game are here, as well as rare bird species such as Senegal coucals and Bradfield's hornbills – all unfenced and in your face. If you love the outdoors and can mount a properly equipped 4x4 trip, then I urge you to go and enjoy this wild, unspoilt wilderness. See also page 162.

Mahango Game Park

Lying along the western bank of the Kavango River, just north of the Botswana border, this smallish park (244 square kilometres) was proclaimed in 1989 to protect rare game species, such as buffalo, sable and roan antelope, Chobe bushbuck, reedbuck, tsessebe and sitatunga. There are no overnight facilities in the park, but these are available just outside at the Popa Falls resort and at several guest lodges nearby. See also page 170.

Mudumu National Park

Further east in the Caprivi, along the eastern bank of the Kwando River, lies the 1 000-square-kilometre expanse of savanna and mopane woodlands. Spotted-necked otters, hippos and crocs lurk in the waterways, while all the usual suspects can be spotted in the bush. But the eastern Caprivi is really a birdwatcher's paradise, with 70% of all Namibia's birds to be found there. Accommodation is in private guest lodges or camping. See also page 172.

Mamili National Park

Mamili lies just below Mudumu, in the southwest corner of eastern Caprivi. A swampy wetland area of channels, reed beds and islands, it is home to a similar variety of animals and birds as found up

the road in Mudumu. With only rough camping facilities and a few 4x4 tracks (impassable in the wet season), a visit to this park is for the adventurous only. See details on page 172.

> **The Mangetti Game Camp**, situated in the Kavango region, is not open to the public, but is used by the Department of Nature Conservation for game-breeding purposes.

Namib-Naukluft Park

A vast wilderness running up the coast from Lüderitz to Swakopmund and stretching about 150 kilometres inland, the Namib-Naukluft Park is one of Namibia's major tourist destinations. The proximity of attractions such as Sossusvlei, Sesriem, the Welwitschia Trail, Sandwich Harbour, Kuiseb Canyon and Naukluft mountains make it a must for every visitor to the country. **Sossusvlei** was formed when the monumentally high dunes of the Namib blocked the course of the Tsauchab River from reaching the coast. Dry most of the time, it fills on average about once every 10 years. Surrounded by mountains of sand and the odd thorn tree, the area is a favourite with photographers who love to capture the sunrise or sunset igniting the dunes with reds and oranges. Nearby Dead Pan, with its ancient bare thorn trees (dated at 500 to 600 years old), is another evocative spot. Access is restricted to between sunrise and sunset and there is no accommodation on site. The entrance gate is 65 kilometres away at Sesriem, where there is a campsite. **Sesriem** is also the name of a nearby deep, narrow gorge where pools of water form and birds seek a cool escape from the harsh sun. See also page

Escarpments and arid plains are the two most important features of Namibia's landscapes.

104. Camping and picnic sites dot the northern section of the park, particularly along the Kuiseb and Swakop rivers and east of Swakopmund, along the Welwitschia Trail (see also page 110). About 50 kilometres south of Walvis Bay lies the silted-up **Sandwich Harbour**, now a lagoon that attracts large numbers of coastal and freshwater birds (see also page 112).

The **Naukluft** mountains, near Solitaire, serve as a sanctuary for the Hartmann's mountain zebra while the steep cliffs offer perfect nesting sites for black eagles (see page 107).

National West Coast Tourist Recreation Area

This 200-kilometre coastal stretch (almost as long as its name, it seems!) between Swakopmund and the mouth of the Ugab River looks barren, but is an angler's idea of paradise. Henties Bay and Cape Cross are the only features along this coast and the best fishing spots are marked by their distance in miles from Swakopmund.

> **The Naute Recreational Resort** is a peaceful spot, situated around the Naute Dam. The resort lies about 50 kilometres southwest of Keetmanshoop, but with only a picnic site and little game, it is mainly of interest for birding, angling and watersports.

Skeleton Coast Park

A 500-kilometre continuation of the National West Coast Tourist Recreation Area, this park protects the forbidding landscape and hardy flora and fauna of one of the driest and most dangerous coastlines in the world. Shipwrecks and the bones of their unfortunate sailors

The natural world

litter beaches where even lichens and the tenacious welwitschias struggle to survive. The southern section is accessible to the general public staying at Terrace Bay and Torra Bay (see page 131), but the northern section, which stretches all the way up to the Kunune River, is best visited by using fly-in tours.

Von Bach Game Reserve

Just south of Okahandja, this is another resort set around a dam and popular with watersport and angling enthusiasts. The picnic sites are available for day visitors and camping and bungalows for overnight stays.

Waterberg Plateau Park

The Waterberg Plateau rises 200 metres above the surrounding plains to form a lush island sanctuary for over 25 species of game and 200 bird species. Situated 60 kilometres east of Otjiwarongo, the park can be explored by vehicle or on foot along a four-day wilderness trail. Comfortable accommodation is available in bungalows or at campsites. See also page 141.

Conservancies and private game reserves

A relatively new development (initiated in 1992) has seen some commercial farmers forming groups to manage and protect the environment by proclaiming conservancies over their lands. Residents of certain communal areas have done the same. Other landowners have turned their farms into private game reserves. Both communal and commercial farmers have established campsites and built accommodation to earn extra income from what would otherwise be marginal land. At present there are over 50 conservancies and about 200 private game reserves in Namibia.

Transfrontier parks

The Namibian government is firmly committed to the transfrontier concept and has already concluded a number of cross-border agreements.

Ai-Ais Richtersveld Transfrontier Park This park was created in 2003 to combine the Fish River Canyon, Ai-Ais hot springs and Hunsberg Conservancy of Namibia with the Richtersveld National Park of South Africa. The park will also include the loop of the Orange River below Noordoewer and a new ferry and border post is operating across the river at Sendelingsdrif.

Iona Skeleton Coast Transfrontier Conservation Area Also established in 2003 with an agreement signed by Namibia and Angola, this 31 500-square-kilometre TFP links the Namibian Skeleton Coast Park with Angola's Parque Nacional do Iona across the Kunene. Very isolated and desert-like, this area will probably not be developed anytime soon.

Kgalagadi Transfrontier Park The Namibian government has expressed interest in extending the Kgalagadi Transfrontier Park, which already includes South Africa's Kalahari Gemsbok National Park and Botswana's Gemsbok National Park, into Namibia to embrace privately owned farmland on its western boundary. A new border post at Mata Mata has opened up a new route for travellers wanting to enter Namibia from South Africa through this wonderful wilderness area.

On the road 5

Because of its excellent and extensive road system, Namibia makes a great motoring holiday destination. Whether you arrive in your own vehicle, or fly in and hire one, the feeling of freedom when you hit the open, uncrowded highways and byways is already worth the visit. Namibia is Road-Trip Country! As it is easily accessible by road from all its neighbours – South Africa, Botswana, Zambia and Angola – it's also possible to organise an extended round trip of southern Africa, taking in some of these countries. But you'll need time!

By main tarred roads or dusty back roads, Namibia is a biker's heaven.

From South Africa

Two main routes lead to Namibia from South Africa: the N7, which runs up north from Cape Town to cross into Nam at Noordoewer (open 24 hours), and the N10, which runs west from Upington in the Northern Cape to the border at Ariamsvlei (also open 24 hours). Both routes meet at Grünau to head north to Windhoek on the B1. But beware, these routes can be crowded at the start of the South African winter school holidays (June/July) and long delays can be experienced at the borders. The bridge across the mouth of the Orange River from Alexander Bay in South Africa to the Namibian mining town of Oranjemund is not a regular border post, as it may only be crossed if you have a permit to visit the diamond diggings in the Sperrgebiet. Upstream at Sendelingsdrif there is a new ferry that also allows border crossings, and east of Noordoewer, there is a little-used bridge and border post at Onseepkans. North of Ariamsvlei, in the sands of the Kalahari, is the lonely border post of Rietfontein, and finally the border at Mata Mata in the Kgalagadi Transfrontier Park has been opened, but only to *bona fide* visitors who must spend at least two nights in the park. All these routes and border crossings from South Africa give easy access to the attractions of southern Namibia – the Fish River Canyon and Ai-Ais, Lüderitz, Sossusvlei, Sesriem and the Namib-Naukluft Park, as well as the wide-open spaces of the Kalahari.

From Botswana

Traffic through the main border with Botswana at Buitepos has increased dramatically since the construction of the Trans-Kalahari Highway. Starting in Walvis Bay, passing through Windhoek, via Buitepos into Botswana and then down to the South African border at Lobatse, this new tarred highway allows goods landed at the port of Walvis to be in Johannesburg within a few days. Understandably, it is also popular with holidaymakers from the Gauteng area in South Africa as a shortcut to Windhoek and northern Namibia. Other border posts with Botswana include the little-known Dobe post near Tsumkwe in Bushmanland, Mohembo in central Caprivi, which links up to the Okavango Delta, and Ngoma at the far eastern end of the Caprivi, from where you can travel to Kasane in northern Bots and on into Zimbabwe or Zambia.

From Zambia

The only border post between Namibia and Zambia is Wanela, just outside the town of Katima Mulilo. The new Zambian bridge across the Zambezi here gives you the option of either heading east along a new tarred road to Livingstone or north along the rough track up the western bank of the Zambezi to Barotseland and Mongu.

From Angola

Traffic between Namibia and Angola is mainly commercial, but should become more touristy as conditions in Angola improve. The most westerly border post is the crossing of the Kunene River at Ruacana, where there is a waterfall and hydroelectric scheme. Both sides of the Kunene between here and the sea are wild and undeveloped, with Kaokoland in Namibia and the Parque Nacional do Iona in Angola. Further east, above the Etosha National Park, is the main border crossing at Oshikango. Here the Namibian B1 highway, which runs the entire length of the country, links up with the Angolan main south–north road to Luanda.

Travelling around

With a good solid car and up-to-date map you can go just about anywhere in Nam. The number of road graders per capita must be the highest in the world, and I think the ratio of total road miles per vehicles owned must be one of the highest too, which makes Namibia a pleasure in which to drive. Unlike some of its northern neighbours, you will not encounter roadblocks and the traffic cops do their duty without bribery and corruption. Nam must be one of the last countries in Africa where you can still hope to hitch a free ride from a friendly motorist and, of course, public transport is also an option (see pages 56 to 57), so you don't have to have your own vehicle to visit the country.

Namibia's roads are all numbered with a B, C or D prefix. B roads are the main tarred highways that connect the country's largest towns. The B1, for example, runs the entire length of the country from Noordoewer in the south to Oshikango in the north. High speeds can be maintained and long distances covered in a day. C roads are sometimes tarred, but mostly good, wide gravel surfaces that connect the smaller towns. Quite high speeds can also sometimes be reached on these roads, but rather keep your speed down to around 100 kilometres per hour, as sharp corners and blind rises are common. Check first before tackling the D roads as they are often just farm tracks and may require a 4x4.

Road travel

Many visitors to Namibia bring their 4x4s to experience the off-road adventures that are unique to the country. Whether tackling the deserts of the south, mountains of the Kaokoveld or swamps of the eastern Caprivi, you will need to know your vehicle and brush up on your driving skills.

Driving in sand Because a large proportion of Namibia is covered by desert, you will encounter sandy roads. Ideally, you should have a 4x4 vehicle, but no matter what you are driving, deflate your tyres for best traction. Tyre pressures of around 1.2 kPa should do the trick, but as low as 0.8 kPa might be necessary. Although this makes them more vulnerable to increased wear and tear, it gives the tyre a larger footprint and allows it to 'pancake' instead of digging in when the going gets tough.

The very sandy sections should be approached at a slightly higher speed to let your momentum carry you through, instead of trying to power your way through. Keep the vehicle's steering wheel pointed straight ahead in order to minimise frontal resistance, and select the correct gear before tackling a bad section, because changing gears causes a drop in momentum and sometimes even a full stop.

Your vehicle should have sufficient ground clearance to negotiate the *middelmannetjie* (central ridge) found on some sandy roads. And stay in the tracks – heading off a well-worn track seldom gives you better traction, and only degrades the environment by creating more scars on the landscape.

> In the heat, tiny pockets of air between sand particles expand, making it fluffier and softer, so tackle long stretches across sand during the cooler periods of the day.

Driving at night Driving after dark should be avoided where possible. Bad visibility, animals on the road and tiredness all contribute to a higher risk. Extra spotlights will help you see further, but if you must drive at night, slow right down and take great care. Kudus, particularly, tend to try to jump over your vehicle at night on the road, often crashing through your windscreen and causing damage, injury or even death.

Dust on Namibia's gravel roads poses something of a challenge too. Drive with your headlights on, even if they don't help you to see better – with any luck, oncoming traffic will see you.

Negotiating mud and water If you are not sure of the depth of the mud or water, get out and check, and if it is too deep, reverse out to safety. Move slowly through water so as not to create a bow wave and, if the fan belt is in danger of spraying the electronics of your vehicle, remove the fan belt.

Driving over rocks and stones Tyre pressure is important on rough stony ground – too soft and you will cut the sidewalls, too hard and sharp stones could push right through the tread. There are different opinions on tyre pressures, but I like to drive at readings recommended for normal highway driving.

Driving in game parks Drive slowly and quietly and, most importantly, stay on the road. Never get too close to

The deep, sandy tracks of the Kaudom Game Reserve require deflated tyres and four-wheel-drive.

animals, especially if they are with their young. Don't get out of your vehicle and never feed the animals. Littering is a cardinal sin; carry all refuse with you until you find an appropriate place to dump it. Remember that this is the animals' natural habitat and you are the intruder here.

What to do if you get stuck ...

To avoid getting stuck in the first place, engage your free-wheel hubs and four-wheel-drive long before you need them and keep them engaged even after they are no longer needed. But use your diff-lock sparingly and only if absolutely necessary. If you do get stuck and you haven't broken anything, the first option is to drive out. If you are in mud or sand, try to reverse out of trouble. Stay in the tracks you made going in and, if you manage some movement, go forward and then back, reversing out a little further each time. A strong push from passengers or bystanders will obviously help a lot. If in soft sand, deflate your tyres as much as you dare (0.8 kPa) and clear a smooth path in front of the tyres in the direction you intend travelling. If the diff or chassis is resting on the ground, dig it free so that your wheels have weight on them and can grip again.

You will simply sink deeper if you race the engine and spin the wheels. Rather go for option two – being towed out (sometimes, it's the first option). If you're driving in convoy, or someone stops to offer help, have a thick, strong towrope or strap ready. If it's long enough, your rescuer won't get stuck too. A rope with a bit of

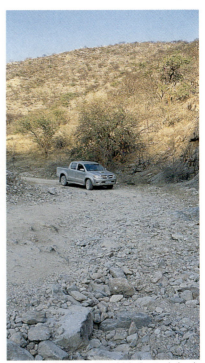

Travellers need a sturdy vehicle for Kaokoland.

give in it is better than a steel cable, for example.

Option three is 'jack and pack'. A high-lift jack on a wide base is your best bet to get the wheels up and out of trouble. Pack anything – sand, rocks and branches – under all four wheels and lower them back onto solid traction. Sand tracks and mats are useful, but they're bulky to carry, so use what you can find.

Another trick is to jack the whole back or front of the vehicle free of the ground and simply push it sideways off the high-lift jack, so that the wheels land on firmer ground. A winch (manual or mechanical) is another

In remote areas, breakdowns may pose a very real problem, so go prepared.

option but often there is little to which to attach it. Burying the spare wheel with the winch cable tied to it is hard work, but if you're desperate …

Breakdowns, punctures and accidents

In case of a breakdown, I have listed tow-in services and repair workshops in as many towns as possible. If you are planning to venture off-road, then I would recommend you take two spare tyres. In most rugged regions where you are likely to puncture a tyre, roadside entrepreneurs have set up shop, doing a fine job and providing an essential service. In the unfortunate event of an accident, you will need all the above services – and notify the police as well as your insurer as soon as possible. Emergency numbers for ambulance and medical assistance are listed on page 49, or under the entry for the nearest town.

> **VEHICLE MAINTENANCE**
> Have your vehicle fully serviced before you go and replace engine oil, spark plugs (petrol engines), air filter, oil filter and fuel filter. Along the way, check the following regularly: engine oil, coolant, transfer case oil, differential oil, gearbox oil, brake and clutch fluid and battery water. Also remove dry grass from the radiator and chassis.

VEHICLE SPARES AND TOOLS
Cut back on this list if you are not straying too far off the beaten track.

- Workshop manual for your vehicle
- Full set of socket, ring and open spanners (compatible with your vehicle)
- Selection of screwdrivers (large and small, Phillips and flat)
- Pliers and vice grip
- Set of Allen keys (compatible with your vehicle)
- Shifting spanner and monkey wrench
- Hammer
- Spade
- Axe or saw
- Hacksaw
- File
- Wheel spanner
- 2 jacks (one high-lift)
- Tyre levers (long and strong)
- Puncture repair kit (including patches, plugs, gaiters and solution)
- Tyre pump or on-board compressor
- Pressure gauge, valves and valve tool
- 2 spare tyres and tubes
- Battery jumper cables
- Fanbelts (one universal)
- Engine oil, gearbox oil and brake fluid
- Q20 spray and grease
- Gasket silicon and contact adhesive
- Towrope
- Jerry cans (if no on-board auxiliary tank)
- Siphon pump or funnel for water and fuel
- Selection of nuts, bolts, washers and self-tapping screws
- Assortment of rope, string and wire
- Selection of plastic cable ties
- Electric wire, fuses, connectors and light bulbs
- Set of spark plugs (and spanner), points and condenser (petrol vehicles only)
- Set of fuel, air and oil filters
- Spare radiator and fuel hoses with clamps
- Insulation, masking and filament tape
- Pair of warning/hazard triangles (legal requirement)
- Fire extinguisher (a good one, no toys!)
- Spare set of keys (do not keep these inside the vehicle)
- And if you know your vehicle has a particular weakness, make sure you carry the appropriate replacement parts.

What to pack 6

With so many different activities to keep you busy and large fluctuations in daily temperatures, you will have to plan carefully to be sure you take what you need and yet not overload yourself. Photography can be a wafer-thin point-and-shoot digital camera or a bulky 35mm SLR with lenses and boxes of film. Take good maps and a guidebook (this one, obviously!), clothing and personal gear, and don't forget the most important items – your documents.

Some travellers (above) even pack microlight planes for their trip to Namibia. The red dunes of the Namib (opposite) are halted by the dry Kuiseb river valley.

Documents

All visitors to Namibia need a passport that is valid for at least six months after entry. The countries whose nationals do not require a visa to enter Nam as bona fide tourists for up to 90 days are listed on page 12. If you do need a visa, it will cost N$140 and probably take a day or two to process. Apply to any one of the following places:

Ministry of Home Affairs, Cohen Building, Kasino Street, Windhoek, tel: 061-292-2111, fax: 061-292-2185

Namibian Tourism Board, Pinnacle Building, Burg Street, Cape Town, tel: +27-(0)21-422-3298, fax: +27-(0)21-422-5132, e-mail: namibia@saol.com

Namibian Tourism Board, Grosvenor Corner, 195 Jan Smuts Avenue, Rosebank, Johannesburg, tel: +27-(0)11-785-4626, fax: +27-(0)11-785-4601, e-mail: namibia@netdial.co.za

Or at one of Namibia's foreign embassies or High Commissions:

Angola: Rua Dos Conqueiros, Luanda, tel: +244-2-39-5483, fax: +244-2-33-9234, e-mail: embnam@netangola.com

Botswana: PO Box 987, Gaborone, tel: +267-390-2181, fax: +267-390-2248, e-mail: nhc.gabs@info.bw

France: 80 Avenue Foch 17, Square de L'Avenue Foch, Paris, tel: +33-144-17-3265, fax: +33-144-17-3293, e-mail: namparis@club-internet.fr

Germany: 5 Wichmannstrasse, 10787, Berlin, tel: +49-30-254-0950, fax: +49-30-254-0949, e-mail: namibiaberlin@aol.com

South Africa: PO Box 29806, Sunnyside, Pretoria, tel: +27-(0)12-481-9100, fax: +27-(0)12-343-7294, e-mail: secretary@namibia.org.za

UK: 6 Chandos Street, London, WIG 9 LU, tel: +44-207-636-6244, fax: +44-207-637-5694, e-mail: namibia-high-comm@btconnect.com

USA: 1605 New Hampshire Avenue, Washington, DC, tel: +1-202-986-0540, fax: +1-202-986-0443, e-mail: embnamibia@aol.com

It's a good idea to travel with a **yellow fever certificate**. Although they're not required when travelling between Namibia and South Africa, other countries might require you to show one.

When it comes to **vehicle documentation**, a South African driver in his own South African-registered vehicle needs only the vehicle's registration papers or a certified copy thereof. If you are driving a vehicle that is not registered in your name, a letter of authority from the owner, on an official letterhead, is required. Visitors from non-neighbouring countries will need a **carnet de passage**. This internationally recognised document (issued by your local automobile association) facilitates custom formalities when crossing borders with a vehicle, and guarantees the payment of duties in the event of the vehicle not leaving the country again. The motoring organisation that issues it will then have to pay the duties, and demand reimbursement from you. If you are a South African and need a carnet for countries further north, contact:

Automobile Association (AA) of South Africa, tel: +27-(0)861-11-1994, e-mail: aasa@aasa.co.za, website: www.aa.co.za

If coming from South Africa, vehicle **insurance** that covers you for damage to or loss of your vehicle should be valid in Namibia, but check to be sure. Drivers' licences issued in neighbouring countries are valid in Nam, but if you're coming from further afield, bring an international driver's licence issued by your local automobile association.

Maps and guidebooks

People who travel without guidebooks miss a lot. It isn't that writers know it all, but a book allows you to structure your trip and is a good base on which to build your holiday. In this book, *Getaway Guide to Namibia*, I've tried to be as inclusive and comprehensive as possible. Maps are just as important, which is why I've included good up-to-date ones here too. Look out for the excellent new map published by Sunbird and the perennial favourite published by Projects and Promotions in Windhoek (e-mail: proprom@iafrica.com.na). This fold-up map is updated every year and is very detailed. And then there is the relatively new Namibia Tour Planning Map, endorsed by the Directorate of Survey and Mapping and distributed free by the Namibia Tourism Board.

GPS and navigation

A GPS is not generally necessary for holidays in Namibia if you intend sticking to the well-worn tourist routes. However, having GPS confirmation that you are turning off at the right spot in the middle of nowhere is very reassuring, and it is even more useful for tackling the wilds of Kaokoland or Bushmanland. I have, therefore, included GPS coordinates for those not-so-easy-to-find places. A small hand-held unit that runs off the vehicle's power is sufficient, as it will give your position anywhere on earth to within 5 metres. You're probably smarter than me, and able to plot courses and create waypoints with your GPS, but I'm just happy to know that I'm on the right track.

Photography

With so much to see and do in Namibia, you should go home with many happy photographic memories of your trip. However, unless you are a professional, don't overload yourself with equipment – just lots of film or memory sticks. Namibia has beautiful early-morning and late-afternoon light, tinged orange and red by the dust particles in the air. Take your photos while the sun is low to capture that colour in your subjects – in the middle of the day, the harsh sun washes out these colours. Try to take your photographs with the sun behind you and get up close, using a flash for fill-in light on dark subjects.

Always make sure that people are comfortable with you photographing them. Engage them in conversation first, then motion with the camera that you want to take a shot of them and gauge their reaction. Usually, if you have just bought something from them, or they are showing off something of which they are proud, they won't mind.

Although you might want to give sweets or pens to the people you photograph, you will sometimes also be asked for money. Try to resist this, as it encourages begging and creates the impression that tourists are an easy source of income.

For good close-ups of animals or birds, you will need a powerful telephoto lens. Get as close as possible with your vehicle, without leaving the road or disturbing the animal; switch off the engine to avoid camera vibrations and wait patiently for something interesting to happen. If you are hoping to sell your photographs, some publications still prefer slides, but others will accept high-quality digital images. For your own enjoyment, digital or print film is fine. So, basically all you need is a camera (with a 28–90-mm lens on a 35-mm camera), memory sticks or film (100 ASA is good for all-round work) and spare batteries.

Travellers are urged to make sure documents are all in order.

Clothing and personal gear

Namibia's weather is prone to extremes – hot days and cold nights. You might also have to prepare for drenching thunderstorms and soaking coastal mists, so pack accordingly. The country is dusty, too, so you will be better off with clothes that don't show the dirt and wash and dry easily.

A useful tip to make the chore of laundry a little easier (if travelling in your own vehicle) is to seal dirty clothes with water and soap in a bucket with a lid. Stashed aboard a bouncing vehicle all day will have them as clean as the proverbial whistle and they will just need a good rinse before hanging out to dry.

If you have forgotten to pack something important, don't worry – Namibia is a well-organised and well-stocked country where most of what you need can be bought locally. One of the best shops for camping, hunting, fishing, off-roading and the like is **Cymot Greensport**. The main shop is in central Windhoek (60 Mandume Ndemufayo Avenue), but they have branches all over the country.

> To operate a two-radio in the country, it is necessary to obtain a permit from the Namibian Communications Commission: 56 Robert Mugabe Avenue, Windhoek, tel: 061-222-666, fax: 061-222-790. Permits cost N$48 and take 7–14 days to process.

TRAVEL WARDROBE

Here is a suggested clothing list:

- 2 pairs trousers or skirts: light cotton is comfortable and washable, and trousers with zip-off legs can double as shorts. Denim jeans are difficult to wash and even more difficult to dry quickly.
- 4 shirts: I prefer collared shirts to T-shirts – they're smarter, cooler and have pockets
- 2 pairs shorts: it gets hot during the day in Namibia
- Socks and underwear: they're light and easy to pack, so take at least 4 sets
- Sweater: take a lightweight sweater for summer evenings, but a warm one for the winter
- Jacket: take a light, waterproof jacket for the summer and a thick, warm one for the cold winter nights
- Shoes: a pair of light boots or walking shoes, as well as a pair of sandals
- Cap or hat: essential as the sun can burn in Namibia
- Towel and swimming costume: in the cold Atlantic for the brave or hot-water springs for the sensible!

Toiletries

- Soap and shampoo
- Toothbrush and toothpaste
- Hairbrush and nail clippers
- Toilet paper
- Sanitary towels and/or condoms
- Shaving kit
- Sunblock
- Mosquito repellent

Extras

- Backpack (a good, strong internal-framed one if you are tackling a long hike, or a smaller daypack for short excursions)
- Multipurpose tool or Swiss army knife (but don't carry this in your hand luggage if you are flying)
- Torch and spare batteries (a head-mounted one is ideal)
- Matches or lighter
- Notebook and pen
- Travel guidebooks and maps
- Cellphone and recharger (South African and Namibian networks are compatible)
- Alarm clock (probably a feature of your cellphone)
- Pocket calculator (probably a feature of your cellphone)
- Reading material (bird and other reference books, and some recreational reading)
- Plugs and adaptors (to run or recharge electrical gear)
- Sunglasses and reading glasses
- Contact-lens cleaner and spare spectacles
- Binoculars
- Photographic gear

Eating and sleeping 7

The outdoors beckon in Namibia and camping is a pleasure. The weather is usually fine and there are many beautiful places to stay. And if you're camping, why not cook outdoors as well. What could be better than braaiing under the stars with the sounds of Africa all around you? But if roughing it is not your style, don't worry – there are plenty of other options to suit your pocket, pillow and palate.

Accommodation (above and opposite) comes in all shapes and sizes, catered or self-catering.

Accommodation

Namibia's popularity as a destination is the lure of the wilds. Tourists don't come to gamble at casinos, view old cathedrals or laze about on the beach – they come for the bush experience, and Nam dishes it up in spadefuls. Campsites, tented camps, bungalows and lodges are at all the major sites. The level of accommodation covers all grades of luxury and price ranges, and is never grotty. In fact, Namibia has a very high standard of hospitality thanks to both the Hospitality Association of Namibia (HAN) and the Bed-and-Breakfast Association (B&BA). All accommodation establishments must also be registered with the National Tourism Board (NTB), which carries out regular inspections to enforce the maintenance of high standards.

Luxury hotels and lodges can offer levels of opulence only required by film stars and dictators, with prices up around the N$2 500 per person per night mark. More affordable establishments range from N$400 to N$700 per night, B&Bs average around N$300 a night and camping can be as cheap as N$50. Prices quoted here are for South Africans and residents of other SADC countries, and I have tried to always include the 15% VAT and 2% bed levy in accommodation rates (Namibians are sometimes charged less and foreigners often more). The anomaly in Nam's accommodation choices is that often a beautifully situated and highly priced lodge will also offer camping at less than a tenth of its room rate. See, it pays to camp! Please note that while every effort has been made to list the latest prices, these could have escalated by the time you visit.

Camping in permanent tents is a luxury option.

There is no way I could list all the accommodation establishments in Namibia – there are just too many – but I have tried to list the places that are pleasant to stay in and that will endure. Some places are owned by foreigners who come and go, or change ownership and managers, and many guest farms are too far off the beaten track. I apologise if I have missed a few good ones – please tell me about them for the next edition. Most places have websites and e-mail addresses and you can book over the internet. Credit cards are accepted almost everywhere. There are some good accommodation groups that represent establishments of a similar standard and price. Some even offer discounts if more than one of their hotels or lodges are used. Check them out:

Namibian Wildlife Resorts, Erkrath Building, 189 Independence Avenue, Windhoek, tel: 061-285-7200, fax: 061-224-900, e-mail: reservations@nwr.com.na, website: www.nwr.com.na

Namibia Country Lodges,
tel: 061-374-750, fax: 061-256-598,
e-mail: reservations@ncl.com.na,
website: www.namibialodges.com

Protea Hotels Namibia,
tel: +27-(0)21-430-5000, fax: +27-(0)21-430-5320, e-mail: info@proteahotels.com, website: www.proteahotels.com

The Gondwana Desert Collection,
tel: 061-230-066, fax: 061-251-863,
e-mail: info@gondwana-desert-collection.com, website: www.gondwana-desert-collection.com

Wilderness Safaris,
tel: 061-274-500, fax: 061-239-455,
e-mail: info@nts.com.na,
website: www.wilderness-safaris.com

CAMPING CHECKLIST
The following is a very basic list so try not to be too influenced by my Spartan choice.
- Tent with built-in ground sheet and mosquito net (vehicle rooftop tents are easy and safe)
- Camp stretcher and/or foam mattress
- Sleeping bag and inner sheet
- Pillow
- Light, folding camp chairs and table
- Lamp (first choice should be a fluorescent type that works off your vehicle's battery)
- Clothesline and pegs
- Washbasin and soap

OUTDOOR COOKING CHECKLIST
- Cooker and fuel
- Ice-box or small fridge (the compressor type is best)
- Barbecue grid in a bag
- Sack of wood or charcoal
- Firelighters and matches
- Pot (a traditional black, cast-iron pot is ideal for over a fire)
- Frying pan and kettle
- Plates and bowls
- Chopping board and a sharp knife
- Mugs and/or glasses
- Cutlery and can opener
- Washing-up bowl, soap and cloth
- Paper towels and refuse bags

On the menu

Vegetarians struggle in Namibia. This is Red Meat Country – beef and game mostly. It's so bad (or good) that cattle farmers have a name for chicken – salad! But the meat is magnificently tender, succulent and tasty and the hotels and restaurants know how to prepare it well. Off course, you can cook it yourself, too – it is difficult to beat a braai over hot *doringhout* coals, but please don't denude the area around a campsite of firewood.

Windhoek offers the most cosmopolitan eating experiences. History dictates that German cuisine dominates, with everything from eisbein to Black Forest cake, but you will also find African, Cuban, Indian, Italian, Portuguese and Argentinean. Namibian fish is excellent, with freshly caught linefish such as kabeljou, galjoen and steenbras gracing the country's restaurant tables, while the oysters from the icy waters of Lüderitz and Walvis are to die for, doll! It is difficult to define 'cuisine Namibienne', but I think it could be anything that is a product of the country. A good local chef will use wild mushrooms from the north, truffles from the Kalahari, asparagus from Swakopmund, and don't forget the biltong in the salad (sorry, vegetarians!).

Importing animal products into Namibia

Very strict regulations apply to the importation of animal products into Namibia and veterinary import permits (at a cost of N$50 each) are issued by the Directorate of Veterinary Services in Windhoek: tel: 061-208-7503, fax: 061-208-7779. The exceptions are animal products imported for own use from South Africa. Under special agreement, the following may be imported (per vehicle):
- 25 kg of raw meat (excluding pork)
- 10 kg biltong
- 25 kg processed meat (canned, cooked, bacon, polony, etc.)
- 10 kg or 10 litres of dairy products
- 2½ dozen eggs

Please note that conditions for the above products can change. Outbreaks of foot-and-mouth disease affect the importation of red meat and bird flu affects poultry. Check for the latest information with your nearest Namibian Tourist Board office, or be prepared to do lots of braaiing at the border post! Cats and dogs may be imported into Nam from SA if accompanied by an inter-territorial movement permit certified by a registered veterinarian.

COUNTING THE COST

Here are some average prices charged at supermarkets in the larger towns:

- Loaf white bread   N$5,60
- Mineral water (1 litre)   N$7,30
- Can of beer   N$5,50
- Can of Coke   N$5,40
- Milk (1 litre)   N$12,70
- Washing powder (1 kg)   N$21,50
- Lettuce   N$6
- Potatoes (1 kg)   N$9
- Onions (1 kg)   N$10
- Frozen chicken (1 kg)   N$28,80
- Boerewors (1 kg)   N$45
- Beef mince (1 kg)   N$53
- Eggs (1 doz)   N$15,70
- Bully beef (300 g)   N$12,40
- Cooking oil (750 ml)   N$9
- Tea (100 bags)   N$15
- Instant coffee (250 g)   N$22
- Sugar (1 kg)   N$8,20
- Rice (1 kg)   N$15,50

The Namibian dollar is equivalent to the South African rand.

GRUB'S UP!
You may want to consider taking some of the following cooking ingredients, but remember that all the items listed here can be bought in Namibia.

Durables
- Selection of canned meat, fish and vegetables (just a few for emergencies – they're heavy!)
- Selection of dehydrated food stuffs (also only for emergencies – some are disgusting)
- Breakfast cereal or muesli mix
- Sugar
- Powdered milk
- Tea and/or coffee
- Powdered isotonic drink
- Crisp bread or crackers
- Biscuits or rusks
- Salt, pepper, herbs and spices
- Stock cubes and garlic
- Dried fruit and nuts
- Rice and pasta
- Cooking and salad oil
- Honey or jam
- Peanut butter and/or Bovril
- Bottled water, cold drinks and beer

Semi-durables
- Bread
- Potatoes, onion, cabbage and carrots
- Apples and oranges
- Cheese and margarine
- Bacon and salami

Perishables
- Meat
- Eggs
- Salad
- Tomatoes
- Soft fruit

Health and safety 8

Namibia is one of the healthiest countries in Africa. Most of the country is dry and free of disease and there is a good network of doctors and hospitals, both public and private. It is also one of the safest, with little of the violent crime that plagues many other countries on the continent.

Nature (above) can be quite breathtaking in its beauty, but there are nevertheless dangers to consider. The dunes of the Namib (opposite) are bisected by many dry river courses.

Consult the professionals

You might say that being the healthiest and safest in Africa ain't saying much. Okay, so there was an outbreak of polio in 2006, and the crime rate in Windhoek has soared recently, but if you are coming from South Africa, you shouldn't have a problem. If you are planning to be out in the bush for a lengthy period, however, consult your doctor or travel clinic for advice and make sure you get your shots at least six weeks before you leave. You may need to have a dental check-up and organise a supply of any special medicines you require. Spectacles break and contact lenses are easy to lose in the wilds, so think of taking spares.

The medical profession in Namibia is well established and I have listed details of doctors and hospitals in most of the towns mentioned in this book. If in need, your hotel or lodge manager will also be able to recommend where to go for the best attention.

Immunisation

Although not necessary in Namibia, a yellow fever vaccination is good to have and is valid for 10 years. A tetanus shot is also recommended and while you're at your doctor's discuss with him cholera, hepatitis, typhoid, tuberculosis, polio, meningitis and rabies. The list may be scary and you probably won't encounter any of them, but let your doctor be your guide.

Medical insurance

You can never have too much insurance (that's what my broker says!), so make sure you have enough cover to pay for your evacuation in an emergency. Your existing medical aid might be enough but, if not, speak to one of the companies listed below.

Europ Assist
tel: +27-(0)11-991-8000,
fax: +27-(0)11-991-9000,
e-mail: info@europassistance.co.za,
website: www.europassistance.co.za

Netcare 911
tel: +27-(0)10-209-8911,
fax: +27-(0)10-209-8405,
e-mail: customer.care@netcare.co.za,
website: www.netcare.co.za

Along the way

Most municipalities in Namibia treat their tap water, rendering it safe to drink, but many tourists, especially those from Europe and America, still prefer to drink bottled water. This is

The dry south poses far fewer health risks than the wet north of the country.

cheap and plentiful, but a hassle to carry around. Whatever you drink, however, make sure you always have enough, as Namibia is a hot, dry country and it's easy to dehydrate. Unlike some countries further north in Africa, the food in Namibia's shops and restaurants is of a high hygienic standard and quite safe to eat.

If you do pick up a tummy bug, rest up, stop eating, and drink lots of clean fluids. If you think you are dehydrated as a result of diarrhoea or too much sun, you might need a rehydration

MEDICAL AND EMERGENCY NUMBERS
National emergency (cellphone): 112
National police: 1 0111

Windhoek (code 061)
- Police: 1 0111
- International SOS: 23 0505
- Emed 24: 299 9924
- Ambulance: 21 1111
- Medi-Clinic: 22 2687
- Roman Catholic Hospital: 270 2911
- Rhino Park Hospital: 37 5000
- Katutura State Hospital: 203 9111
- Traffic Department: 26 2901

Gobabis (code 062)
- Police: 1 0111
- Ambulance: 56 6200
- State Hospital: 56 6200

Katima Mulilo (code 066)
- Police: 1 0111
- Ambulance/hospital: 2 5140

Keetmanshoop (code 063)
- Police: 1 0111
- Ambulance/hospital: 22 3388

Otjiwarongo (code 067)
- Police: 1 0111
- Ambulance: 30 1014
- Medi-Clinic: 30 3734
- State Hospital: 30 0900

Rundu (code 066)
- Police: 1 0111
- Ambulance/hospital: 26 5500

Swakopmund (code 064)
- Police: 1 0111
- Ambulance: 410 6000
- International SOS: 40 0700
- Cottage Private Hospital: 41 2200
- State Hospital: 410 6000

Tsumeb Triangle, Etosha, Owamboland (code 067)
- Police: 1 0111
- Ambulance: 224 3000
- Private Hospital: 22 1001
- State Hospital: 224 3000

Walvis Bay (code 064)
- Police: 1 0111
- Ambulance: 20 9832
- International SOS: 08 1707
- Private Hospital: 21 8911
- State Hospital: 21 6300

fluid consisting of mainly salt, sugar and water. If you don't have an over-the-counter one, improvise with a Coke and salt, or Bovril, sugar and water (also see below for a simple recipe).

Malaria

Malaria is found mainly in the northern parts of Namibia. As it is spread by the female *Anopheles* mosquito, which first has to bite an infected person and then bite you to pass on the infection, it makes sense to avoid being bitten. Mozzies are most active between dusk and dawn, so avoid exposing arms and legs and use an insect repellent, and sleep under a net or an overhead fan (mozzies don't like wind). Speak to your doctor or a travel clinic for the latest prophylactic drugs, but the effective ones at present are Mefloquine, Malanul and Doxycycline.

If you experience any of the symptoms of malaria (which will include fever, sweating and shivering and sometimes headache, backache, diarrhoea, vomiting and/or malaise), get to a doctor or clinic fast. If these symptoms occur after you return home, don't rule out malaria and tell your doctor where you have been travelling. Go to www.malaria.com for the latest info.

HOMEMADE REHYDRATION SOLUTION
- ½ teaspoon salt
- ½ teaspoon baking soda
- 8 teaspoons sugar
- 1 litre clean water

PLAYING IT SAFE
Basic first-aid kit
- First-aid manual
- Malaria prophylactic tablets
- Aspirin or paracetamol (for fever and pain and also to gargle for a sore throat)
- Antiseptic for disinfecting cuts and abrasions
- Adhesive bandages (both strips and rolls)
- Gauze bandages and cotton wool
- Antihistamine for allergies and to ease the itch from bites and stings
- Thermometer (standard body temperature is 37°C)
- Insect repellent
- Analgesic eye drops
- Analgesic ear drops
- Scissors and tweezers
- Safety pins
- Water purification tablets (a few drops of iodine also work)
- Sealed and sterile syringes and needles
- Sunblock and burn gel
- Throat lozenges
- Flu remedy

Optional extras
- Malaria cure
- Antibiotics
- Vitamin tablets
- Diarrhoea tablets
- Rehydration mixture

Getting there and getting around 9

Whether your chosen mode of transport is by road, sea or air, Namibia is an easy country to access and travel around. You don't even need to drive your own vehicle, paddle your own boat or sprout wings – you can leave all the arrangements to one of the excellent companies that organise tours to this welcoming country.

Namibia's designated B and C roads are regularly graded and a pleasure to drive.

Getting there by road

From South Africa If travelling from the south or west of South Africa, your best route is up the N7 through Springbok to the border at Vioolsdrif/Noordoewer. This border post is open 24 hours a day and is fast and efficient (except at the start of South African school holidays when there can be long delays). The bridge across the Orange River joins the Namibian B1 highway, the main road that runs right up north, through Windhoek and all the way to the Angolan border. There are three other minor crossing points on the Orange: Alexander Bay/Oranjemund at the mouth of the river is open only to travellers with permission to enter Namibia's restricted diamond area, and the long-awaited ferry and border crossing at Sendelingsdrif is now operating daily from 08h00 to 16h15 (flood levels permitting, tel: +27-(0)27-831-1506 to check). Onseepkans/Veloorsdrif is east of Vioolsdrif and opens 08h00 to 17h00 daily.

The main route from the central and northern regions of South Africa is across from Upington on the N10 to the border at Nakop/Ariamsvlei. This post is open 24 hours a day and links up with Namibia's B3 to Grünau and the B1. North of Nakop are two smaller crossings in the sands of the Kalahari: Noenieput/Hohlweg and Rietfontein/Klein Menasse. The Mata Mata border gate on the western boundary of the Kgalagadi Transfrontier Park is now open for *bona fide* visitors who spend at least two nights in the park. It makes a great route for tourists wanting to enjoy this fine park before entering Namibia via the open spaces of the eastern desert.

From Botswana The border between Namibia and Botswana at Buitepos/Mamuno (open 07h00–24h00) is on the strategically important Trans-Kalahari Highway. This route links the west-coast harbour of Walvis Bay via Windhoek and Gobabis to the landlocked towns of Botswana, as well as creating a short cut to Johannesburg. North of Buitepos, the little-known border post at Dobe links the small dusty San settlement of Tsumkwe with the even smaller Gcangwa in Botswana. Deep in the sands of Bushmanland, this crossing

Not all Namibia's road signs are informative!

is strictly for 4x4s, but will reward the adventurous traveller with a chance of linking one of the wildest regions of Nam with off-the-beaten-track Drotsky's Caves and Tsodilo Hills in Botswana. Re-entry into Namibia could then be made through the Mohembo Gate (open 06h00–18h00) in Caprivi to view the Popa Falls on the Kavango river, and join the B8 to head west or east. The final border between Namibia and Botswana is at Ngoma Bridge across the Chobe River. This was always the preferred route to cross from the Caprivi to Zambia via the ferry at Kazangula, but now that the new bridge across the Zambezi at Sesheke has been opened, Ngoma Bridge is less popular. It is also the way through Botswana into Zimbabwe via Kasane.

From Zambia The only crossing point between Namibia and Zambia is the Wenela/Sesheke border post, just outside Katima Mulilo. Once across in Zambia you have the choice of staying on the western bank of the Zambezi and travelling north to Barotseland or crossing the new bridge and heading down to Livingstone and the Victoria Falls.

From Angola The long, stretched-out border between Namibia and Angola has at least five official crossing points, some of which are used only by the local population. Rundu is a popular shopping destination for deprived Angolans who cross the Kavango River by boat here, but there is no vehicular access. Travelling west along the river on the C45, and then the very minor D3405, will bring you to Katitwe, one of Nam's most isolated border posts. For some reason this remote spot is used by quite a lot of broken-down, overloaded transport trucks. Whether it is the only route into a hungry hinterland or a smuggler's paradise, I don't know. If you find out, please let me know.

The main crossing point between Namibia and Angola is at the extremely busy and chaotic Oshikango/St Clara border (open 08h00–18h00). Oshikango is at the far northern end of Nam's B1 and serves as a distribution point for the goods being transported up Angola's main artery through the southern provinces and even to Luanda. Two other posts are Omahenene, which crosses to the Calueque Dam, and Ruacana (open 08h00–18h00) at the falls of the same name on the Kunene River. The Ruacana border post is used by travellers wishing to visit the Parque Nacional do Iona and the mouth of the Kunene.

CROSSING INTO NAMIBIA
Border crossings are simple compared to some African countries, but you will need:

- A valid passport, which must be valid for longer than 6 months from the date of return from Namibia
- Visa (not for South African passport holders – see page 12 for a list of other exemptions)
- A nationality sticker for your vehicle (ZA for South Africa)
- Registration papers for the vehicle (or certified copies)
- Money to pay a cross-border charge (N$160 for a car/bakkie, and N$100 for a motorbike, caravan or trailer)

Getting there by bus

With a fine system of main roads in Namibia and most of its neighbouring countries, bus travel into Nam is easy. Three companies run international services to and from Namibia.

Intercape Sleepliner Based in Cape Town, Intercape runs luxury buses throughout southern Africa. Their routes that service Namibia are: Cape Town to Windhoek on Tuesdays, Thursdays, Fridays and Sundays, with return trips on Mondays, Wednesdays, Fridays and Sundays (cost N$680). The trips start at 10h00 at Cape Town Station and end 20 hours later in the centre of Windhoek opposite the Kalahari Sands Hotel; the return trip starts at 17h30. The Sleepliner is a modern coach with reclining seats, air-con and on-board toilets. The bus stops at towns along the way and links up with their services from Windhoek west to Swakopmund and Walvis Bay (N$190), and north to Grootfontein, the Caprivi, and Victoria Falls in Zimbabwe (N$460). A service also runs between Windhoek and Upington (N$450), where it links up with Intercape's extensive network to all points in South Africa. Their Windhoek depot is in Galilei Street (tel: 061-227-847).

For further information, tel: +27-(0)21-380-4400, fax: +27-(0)21-380-2076; e-mail: info@intercape.co.za, website: www.intercape.co.za.

Bailey's Reo Liner This is a local Windhoek company that operates from offices and a depot out of town, but uses the Wika Total service station in Mandume Ndemufayo Avenue as their city bus stop. They run services to and from Cape Town on Wednesdays, Fridays and Sundays (N$400).

For further information, tel: 061-262-522 or 061-263-758, fax: 061-262-650; or in Cape Town, tel: +27-(0)21-939-9777.

Trail bikers rest after a hard day's riding in the Brandberg region.

Ekonolux Ekonolux is a Namibian company that operates a service between Walvis Bay and Cape Town on Wednesdays, Fridays and Sundays both ways (N$695). Their offices in Walvis are in Theo-Ben Gurirab Street, in Windhoek at the Old Power Station Complex and in Cape Town at the main train station.

For further information, tel: 064-205-935 (Walvis Bay), 061-258-961 (Windhoek) and +27-(0)21-982-1000 (Cape Town), e-mail: ekonolux@iway.na, website: www.ekonolux.com.

Getting there by air

Hosea Kutako International, about 40 kilometres east of Windhoek, is Namibia's main international airport, with scheduled flights to the UK, Germany, Angola, Botswana, Zimbabwe and South Africa.

Namibia's international airlink, Air Namibia, has suspended its flights to Gatwick, London, but still flies five times a week to Frankfurt. Regionally, they also fly twice a day to Johannesburg and twice daily to Cape Town. Five times a week there is a flight to Victoria Falls in Zimbabwe, via Maun in Botswana, and five times a week they go to Luanda in Angola. Air Namibia's central booking office is in Windhoek, tel: 061-299-6333, e-mail: central.reservations@airnamibia.aero, website: www.airnamibia.com.na.

Regionally, South African Express and British Airways/Comair also fly regularly to Namibia.

South African Express,
tel: +27-(0)11-978-1111,
website: www.flysax.com

CROSSING BORDERS

The following are just a few personal suggestions on the protocol to follow when crossing the border.

- Approach the border slowly and sedately – make no commotion or disturbance.
- Park sensibly in the correct areas without blocking others.
- Dress properly – at least sandals, shorts and shirt – and don't wear a hat, cap or sunglasses.
- Wait your turn – unless it's a complete free-for-all.
- Greet and smile at all officials – act politely and never make snide, whispered comments, or laugh.
- Expect polite treatment, but don't make an international incident out of official rudeness – it is only you who will suffer.
- Have all your documents ready.
- Make sure you have been to both customs and immigration and have obtained all the stamps and documentation (including the Cross Border Charge certificate).
- Don't smuggle anything – you may be searched and will have to bear the consequences.
- Avoid all bribery – ignore any hints of it and never suggest it.
- Once the formalities have been completed, don't rush off, and be prepared to stop if asked.

British Airways/Comair,
tel: +27-(0)11-921-0111,
fax: +27-(0)11-973-3913,
website: www.comair.co.za

There are a number of air charter companies based in Namibia. The following operate locally and beyond the country's borders:

Wings Over Africa (strong connections with Angola), tel/fax: 061-255-001, e-mail: wrld@iafrica.com.na, website: www.flyinafrica.com

Comav (charters anywhere in southern Africa and medical evacuations), tel: 061-227-512, fax: 061-245-612, e-mail: enquiry@comav.com.na

Getting there by sea
Travelling by ship is such an adventure and approaching a foreign harbour by sea is so much more romantic than dropping in out of the sky or being hassled at crowded border posts. Fortunately, the royal mail ship *St Helena* calls into Walvis Bay en route between Cape Town and St Helena island, offering the opportunity of cruising up (or back) with your vehicle safely stowed aboard. RMS *St Helena* is a 7 000-tonne ship that can take 128 passengers. The trip from Cape Town to Walvis takes three days and fares start at N$2 750. To ship an average-sized 4x4 costs N$2 600, plus about another N$1 500 in harbour and clearing charges. To book on the *St Helena*, tel: +27-(0)21-425-1165, e-mail: sthelenaline@mweb.co.za, website: www.rms-st-helena.com.

Getting there by rail
The only cross-border rail link is the twice-weekly train between Windhoek and Upington in South Africa, via Keetmanshoop. The railways in Namibia are operated by TransNamib Holdings, who call their passenger service Starline. For further information, tel: 061-298-2032, fax: 061-298-2495, e-mail: paxservice@transnamib.com.na, website: www.transnamib.com.na.

Getting around by road
Namibia's road system is a pleasure to use. The well-established network of over 42 000 kilometres is uncrowded and well maintained. The main national roads are all tarred and designated with a B prefix followed by a number (the B1 runs from Noordoewer in the south to Oshikango in the north). A good proportion of the secondary roads (C-designated) are also tarred, and the rest (Ds) are all gravel but regularly graded.

Namibian drivers are careful and adhere to the rules of the road. Speed limits, however, are often ignored on the long stretches of excellent highway between towns, but with few traffic cops in the country, there is little danger of a fine. But don't speed on the gravel roads – the surfaces are so good it is tempting to go faster than you should, and sharp corners and blind rises can bite.

Animals on the road, both wild and domestic, are a real danger. Keep your eyes peeled and try not to travel at night.

Getting around on public transport
The international bus companies

It is not often that you will encounter water on Namibia's roads.

mentioned previously (see pages 54–55) are also useful for getting from town to town within Namibia. Minibus taxis operate non-scheduled inter-town services that pick up and drop off at big service stations or marketplaces on the outskirts of the towns.

Town Hoppers is a well-scheduled shuttle service between Swakopmund and Windhoek, which runs a daily return service. The Swakopmund stop is in the town centre on Tobias Hainyeka Street and the Windhoek stop is at the Tourism Information Office (opposite the Kalahari Sands Hotel). They charge N$220 and can be contacted on tel: 064-407-223, e-mail: townhoppers@iway.na, website: www.namibiashuttle.com.

The national passenger train network, Transnamib, operates a passenger service called Starline. It fans out from Windhoek to Walvis Bay, Tsumeb, Gobabis and Keetmanshoop, but this is not the preferred way to travel and is subject to changes in schedule, so be sure to check first. They also operate the stylish and luxurious Desert Express train between Windhoek and Swakopmund (see Windhoek section for details). Contact Central Reservations, tel: 061-298-2600, website: www.transnamib.com.na, e-mail: paxservice@transnamib.com.na.

Getting around by air

Because distances in Nam are so great, flying is a popular way of getting around. Most large towns have airports and many lodges even have their own landing strips.

The national airline, Air Namibia, operates from Windhoek's Hosea Kutako International or the smaller Eros airport and flies all over the country. Daily scheduled flights spread out to Katima Mulilo, Ondangwa, Walvis Bay, Lüderitz and Oranjemund. There are also a number of air charter operations. Other than those mentioned earlier in this chapter, there are also:

Sefofane
(from Windhoek),
tel/fax: 061-255-735,
e-mail: info@sefofane.com.na

Westair Wings
(from Windhoek), tel: 061-221-091,
e-mail: charters@westwing.com.na

Pleasure Flights and Safaris
(from Swakopmund),
tel/fax: 064-404-500,
e-mail: redbaron@iafrica.com.na,
website: www.pleasureflights.com.na

Atlantic Aviation
(from Swakopmund),
tel: 064-404-749,
fax: 064-405-832,
e-mail: info@flyinnamibia.com,
website: www.flyinnamibia.com

Guided tours

As with any country that is a popular tourist destination, Namibia offers a wide selection of options and prices when it comes to guided tours.

Wilderness Safaris offers the best of the best. Tailor-made or fixed itineraries, fly or drive, you will be accommodated in luxury in Namibia's most remote and beautiful spots. Contact them on tel: 061-274-500, fax: 061-239-455, e-mail: info@nts.com.na, website: www.wilderness-safaris.com.

Namibia Tracks and Trails is based in Swakopmund and can advise and book you anything, but specialise in desert tours. For information, tel: 064-416-820, e-mail: enquiries@namibia-tracks-and-trails.com, website: www.namibia-tracks-and-trails.com.

Chameleon Safaris operates out of Windhoek where they have a backpackers' lodge. They have a choice of camping, tailormade, fly-in, self-drive and horse riding safaris to all the highlights of Namibia. Contact them on tel: 061-247-668, e-mail: chamnam@mweb.com.na, website: www.chameleonsafaris.com.

Springbok Atlas is a professional, Cape Town-based operation that covers southern and East Africa and offers comfortable 4x4 overland truck safaris, as well as all the other types. Namibian trips can be linked with tours to other neighbouring countries. For information, tel: +27-(0)21-460-4700, fax: +27-(0)21-448-0003, e-mail: tours@springbokatlas.com, website: www.springbokatlas.com.

And now for something completely different!

Werner Schulz and Franco Picco are the team that make up **Africa Motion Tours** and they revel in taking adventurers into the wilds of Namibia on motorbikes. A visit to their website to view the list of available tours will make any off-road biker drool. Contact them on tel/fax: 061-237-258, website: www.africamotiontours.com.

Also, Dirk Trumer of **Trails of Namibia** will guide you on motorbikes through some of the little-known tracks and trails of the Namib. Where do I sign up? Contact Dirk on tel: 061-246-165 or 081-128-8620, e-mail: dirk@namibia-enduro-tours.com, website: www.namibia-enduro-tours.com.

Practical information 10

Wondering what to do once you get to Namibia? Where to hire a vehicle, how to use the phones or pay by credit card? Or do you need to find a foreign embassy, map or informative website? Where are the tourist bureaux, how reliable is the power and what are the customs regulations? Read on and all will be revealed …

A good map, guidebook and GPS will get you to most places in Namibia.

For easy reference, the following categories are listed alphabetically.

Activities

Angling If you're a fisherman who's already experienced Nam's piscatorial delights, then you may want to skip this section – you already know what thrills there are on offer. With not many rivers or dams in Namibia, most fishing is done in the sea, and rock and surf angling are the most popular, with the months between November and March the most rewarding. Kabeljou, galjoen, dassie and steenbras are most sought-after. The best spots are Paaltjies and Sandwich Harbour, south of Walvis Bay, and the West Coast National Recreation Area north of Swakopmund. Shark angling, for the coppershark or bronzy in particular, is practised on a tag-and-release basis and specimens of up to 190 kilograms of this strong fighter have been landed (Henties Bay is the centre for all this activity). Up north, the Kunene, Kavango and Zambezi rivers offer some exciting freshwater angling, with the tiger fish the real prize – most lodges up that way will probably be able to help you. Check out www.anglingnamibia.com, www.westcoastangling.com and www.seaace.com.na.

Birding With a large range of habitats ranging from dunes to savanna to wetlands, Namibia has a checklist of over 630 species. The coastal wetlands around Walvis Bay are some of the most important in Africa and nurture huge numbers of Palaearctic or intra-African migrants, while the riverine areas of eastern Caprivi are home to specials, such as the slaty egret and greater swamp warbler. The deserts are the preferred habitat of endemics such as Gray's lark and the rare dune lark.

A groundscraper thrush poses uncharacteristically.

Happy ticking! Contact the Namibian Bird Club at kori@iway.na and a good website for birding in Africa, country by country, is www.africanbirdclub.org.

Diving Namibia would not generally spring to mind as a diving destination, but in the highly technical field of cave or sinkhole diving, the country offers great challenges. Special skills are required to dive to depths of between 30 and 130 metres at an altitude of more than 1 450 metres above sea level, and the World Underwater Federation has classified Namibia's caves and sinkholes as type III. Lake temperatures are a moderate 17–23°C, but air temperatures vary significantly from –2° to 45°C (winter and summer). Most caves and sinkholes are on private land and special permission is required. Lake Otjikoto, a natural heritage site, is the best-known landmark (see page 154) and is best dived between April and October. To dive in some of the other lakes, such as Harasib, Guinas and Dragon's Breath, special qualifications and experience in abseiling techniques are required – to rig and de-rig these caves for diving takes at least a week of work by a team of six people. Contact the Windhoek Underwater Club, tel: 061-238-320, e-mail: theo@schoemans.com.na. Find them on www.divingnamibia.org.

Hiking With so much wilderness to explore, hiking is probably the best way to experience the best of it. The four-day Fish River Canyon hike is very popular, as is the selection of routes in the Namib-Naukluft Park. Guided walking trails are an option at most national parks and game lodges, and they also offer an exciting way to get up close and personal with the wild animals.

Hunting Love it or hate it, hunting plays an important role in Namibia. It constitutes a large slice of the tourist industry, makes a huge contribution to the economy and increases appreciation for, and the value of game. With such emphasis, importance and value being placed on wild animals by hunters and farmers (commercial and traditional), the protection of game is in everyone's best interest, not just some hard-pressed rangers.

The Ministry of Environment and Tourism is in favour of hunting within a strong regulatory framework. They realise that it provides an ideal way of deriving income for poor people in remote areas where other forms of tourism (such as game-viewing) are not feasible, and have encouraged the formation of conservancies on communal lands.

ON THE HUNT

Rules and regulations governing hunting are strictly enforced, and the local Namibian Professional Hunters Association (NAPHA) prides itself on high ethical standards. International sportsmen come for the great trophies that can be hunted in large, wild and unfenced areas. Try to lay your hands on a copy of *Huntinamibia* (www.huntnamibia.com.na), published by Venture Publications. For more info, contact NAPHA, tel: 061-234-455, website: www.natron.net/napha

Practical information

Off-road driving and quadbiking
Namibia is a paradise for off-road vehicles and quadbikes, but we all know how these activities can ruin the environment. Fortunately, much of the country's wilderness is criss-crossed by roads and trails that are rough enough not to necessitate going off-road. The sands of the Namib, Bushmanland and the Kalahari, the mountains and rocks of Kaokoland, and the swamps of eastern Caprivi are all challenge enough for the most intrepid adventurer. Private landowners also offer specialist trails and off-road routes.

Surfing The waves are not great in Namibia, but the wind does blow, so wind- and kite-surfing are big in places such as Walvis and Lüderitz. World Speed Week for these sports is held every September or October in Namibia, where numerous world records have been set. For more details on Speed Week go to www.speedworldcup.com.

Watersports Although Namibia is a dry country, the country's two main rivers are great adventure destinations. Down in the south four-day canoeing trips on the Orange River are relaxing, but up in the far north the action is a lot wilder as five-day whitewater rafting excursions are mounted on the Kunene River. Contact Felix Unite, tel: +27-(0)21-670-1300, fax: +27-(0)21-670-1419, e-mail: info@felixunite.com, website: www.felixunite.com.

Car hire

The Car Rental Association of Namibia (CARAN) represents the best car-hire firms in Namibia and enforces strict standards on its members (website: www.caran.org). All the large international firms have branches in the country and there are many more good local ones that specialise in 4x4 and camper hire. Check out the following:

Asco Car Hire, tel/fax: 061-377-200, e-mail: info@ascocarhire.com, website: www.ascocarhire.com

Camping Car Hire, tel: 061-237-756, fax: 061-237-757, e-mail: carhire@mweb.com.na, website: www.camping-carhire.com

---

ON CALL!
The country code for Namibia is 264, and the main area codes are:

◆ Windhoek and surrounds	061
◆ Gobabis and the east	062
◆ Mariental and the whole of the south	063
◆ Swakopmund, Walvis Bay and surrounds	064
◆ Opuwo and the northwest	065
◆ Rundu and the Caprivi	066
◆ Otjiwarongo and the central north	067
◆ MTC cellphone prefix	081

Tread softly with quadbikes and support only eco-sensitive operators.

Odyssey Car Hire, tel: 061-223-269, fax: 061-228-911, e-mail: odyssey@iway.na, website: www.odysseycarhire.com

Communications

Namibia's fixed-line telephone service is extensive and dependable. There are many public phone booths, most of which operate with a prepaid card.

The country's cellphone network is operated by MTC (all numbers have the 081 prefix) and has grown fast. It's coverage is good and it has roaming agreements with over 50 other countries. A better option than roaming is to buy a local Namibian SIM card when you arrive and purchase airtime as you need it. Cards, called Tango, are on sale at all Nampost or Telecom offices and cost only N$19, inclusive of N$10 airtime. Visit the MTC website: www.mtc.com.na.

Credit cards

Visa and MasterCard can be used as payment at most tourist hotels, restaurants and shops – Diner's Club and American Express cards are less popular. Do note, however, that credit cards cannot be used for buying petrol. For more information on currency and other money matters, see page 11.

Customs regulations

Visitors may import the following duty free:
* 400 cigarettes (or 50 cigars or 250g pipe tobacco)
* 2 litres wine
* 1 litre spirits

For more information on what may be considered 'imports', see also page 44.

Electricity

Electricity is rated at 220/240 volts,

Practical information | **63**

and power outlets are the 15-amp round three-pin type – all the same as South Africa.

Embassies

All embassies are based in Windhoek.

Angola: 3 Ausspann Street,
tel: 061-22-7535, fax: 061-27-1444

Botswana:
101 Nelson Mandela Avenue,
tel: 061-22-1941, fax: 061-23-6034

France: 1 Goethe Street,
tel: 061-27-6700, fax: 061-23-1436

Germany:
154 Independence Avenue,
tel: 061-27-3100, fax: 061-22-2981

Italy: PO Box 24065,
tel: 061-22-8602, fax: 061-22-9860

Netherlands: 2 Crohn Street,
tel: 061-22-3733, fax: 061-22-3732

South Africa:
Nelson Mandela Avenue,
tel: 061-205-7111, fax: 061-22-4140

Spain: 58 Bismarck Street,
tel: 061-22-3066, fax: 061-22-3046

UK: 116 Robert Mugabe Avenue,
tel: 061-27-4800, fax: 061-22-8895

USA: 14 Lossen Street,
tel: 061-22-1601, fax: 061-22-9792

Zambia: PO Box 22882,
tel: 061-23-7610, fax: 061-22-8162

Zimbabwe: Independence Avenue,
tel: 061-22-7738, fax: 061-22-6859

Maps

Sunbird has a new map of Namibia and all the main towns – available at South African bookstores or contact **Sunbird Publishers**, tel: +27-(0)11-622-2900. *The Namibia Map* (scale 1:2 000 000) of **Projects and Promotions**, PO Box 96003, Windhoek, tel: 061-25-5715, e-mail: proprom@iafrica.com.na is updated every year and available all over Nam and is endorsed by the Roads Authority.

For travel further afield, I like to use the *Road Atlas of Southern and East Africa* (scale 1:1 500 000) published by **Map Studio**, tel: +27-(0)11-807-2292, website: www.mapstudio.co.za.

In South Africa, the Chief Directorate of **Surveys and Mapping**, which falls under the Department of Land Affairs with its headquarters in Mowbray, Cape Town,

---

PUBLIC HOLIDAYS

1 January – New Year's Day
21 March – Independence Day
1 May – Workers' Day
4 May – Cassinga Day
25 May – Africa Day
26 August – Heroes' Day
10 December – Human Rights Day
25 December – Christmas Day
26 December – Family Day

Note: Namibia also observes the Christian holidays over Easter, which change from year to year.

issues a series of 14 maps (1:500 000) that cover Namibia. Although they are the aeronautical edition, they show all roads, tracks and topography. Contact them on tel: +27-(0)21-658-4300, fax: +27-(0)21-686-9884, e-mail: cdsm@.sli.wcape.gov.za, website: w3sli.wcape.gov.za

There are also some good off-road maps available in tourist shops locally in Namibia. Please note that the Namibian Roads Authority often upgrades and renumbers its roads, resulting in much motoring confusion. I have used the latest road numbers as shown on the Namibia Tour Planning Map, a 1:2 million scale publication of the Namibian Directorate of Survey and Mapping. This is endorsed by the Roads Authority of Namibia, and distributed free by the Namibia Tourism Board.

Tourist information

The Namibia Tourism Board offices – as well as their website www.namibiatourism.com.na – in Namibia and neighbouring countries tend to be very helpful, and are well able to offer sound advice and suggestions on where to go and what to see.

Namibia: 1st Floor, Channel Life Towers, 39 Post Street Mall, Windhoek,
tel: 061-290-600, fax: 061-254-848,
e-mail: info@namibiatourism.com.na

South Africa: Pinnacle Building, Burg Street, Cape Town, tel: +27-(0)21-422-3298, fax: +27-(0)21-422-5132, e-mail: namibia@saol.com; 1 Orchard Lane, Rivonia, Johannesburg, tel: +27(0)11-785-4626, fax: +27-(0)11-785-4601, e-mail: namibia@lloydorr.com

Germany: 42 Schiller Street, Frankfurt, tel: +49-69-133-7360, fax: +49-69-1337-3615,
e-mail: info@namibia-tourism.com

UK: Suite 200, Parkway House, Sheen Lane, London,
tel: +44-870-330-9333,
fax: +44-207-636-2969,
e-mail: info@namibiatourism.co.uk

Websites

Websites of individual establishments are listed within the body of this book. Other websites useful for general information include:

General tourism:
www.namibweb.com
www.namibiatourism.com.na
www.natron.net
www.holidaytravel.com.na
www.travelnews.com.na
www.tourbrief.com
Accommodation:
www.wheretostayonline.com
www.namibiagetaways.com
Tour and Safari Association:
www.tasa.na
Community-based Tourism:
www.nacobta.com.na
Hospitality Association of Namibia:
www.hannamibia.com
www.bed-breakfast-namibia.com
Namibia Wildlife Resorts:
www.nwr.com.na
Namibia Professional Hunting Association: www.natron.net/napha

Windhoek 11

Small, but quite cosmopolitan, Namibia's capital city is a balanced mix of low-rise city centre and leafy suburbs. Situated in the geographic centre of the country, Windhoek is also very much the nation's political, judicial, economic and cultural centre. Surrounded by the Eros mountains to the northeast, the Auas mountains in the southeast, and the rolling hills of the Khomas Hochland to the west, Windhoek lies at an easy altitude of 1 650 metres and has a pleasant, healthy climate.

The Namibian Transport Museum (above) is housed in the old Windhoek Station building. Windhoek's craft market (opposite) is a delight for both young and old.

Introducing Windhoek

Although many of the old German street names have been changed, Teutonic influences are still visible in the architecture and shop names. If you remember the 'old' Windhoek, you'll wonder where all the charm has gone. The little specialist shops that sold delicacies and the departmental stores that imported everything from Germany have made way for the latest wave of neo-colonialism – malls developed and stocked by South African super groups. Here and there you can still find an excellent bookshop or furrier that offers personal service by the owner and reminds you of how shopping used to be. Some of the old buildings' facades are still there, but will probably now house a casino or cash-loan business. But at least Windhoek is small and laid-back – no traffic jams and smog and no serious parking problems. There's also good accommodation, great restaurants and lots of fine coffee and beer.

On the down side, the crime rate is high. Beware of roaming gangs who will surround your car in broad daylight, pull open the doors and steal whatever they can grab. Keep your vehicle's doors locked, and park only in a garage or where there are security guards. Pickpockets are also a problem, so look after your bags and backpacks. Don't walk around at night, and to judge by the electric fences around every house in Windhoek, only stay at establishments with full security. Sad, but that's the reality.

Hot springs in the area had been attracting San and Nama for centuries before Jonker Afrikaner and his followers settled there in the 1840s and started calling the place Winterhoek. Soon a Rhenish mission station was established and the settlement flourished as a trading station. In the 1890s, under Curt von François, the Germans established a fort (the Alte Feste, which still stands today as a museum) to serve as headquarters of the *Schutztruppe*. A railway line was built to Swakopmund and the settlement officially became a municipality in 1909.

When South Africa took over the running of the country after the First World War, Windhoek jogged along quietly with little change until the Swapo uprising and eventual independence of Namibia. Since 1990 there has been modernisation and the steady, creeping influence of consumerism, which tends to average out all large cities into looking and feeling the same. But many Windhoekers still pride themselves on speaking German, while hunting and the outdoors influence many lives – so maybe Windhoek isn't so average after all. I'll let you be the judge!

Getting to Windhoek

Coming up from the south on the B1, you approach the first traffic circle (S22°37.119 E17°05.276). A left turn here would take you around Windhoek on the Western Bypass and on to Okahandja in the north, but rather carry on straight to reach the first traffic lights (S22°36.708 E17°05.186) where you can turn left into the campsites and bungalows of the Arebbusch Travel Resort. Continue down Auas Road to pass the Hotel Safari and Safari Court on your left (this is also where you would turn to reach Eros Airport for

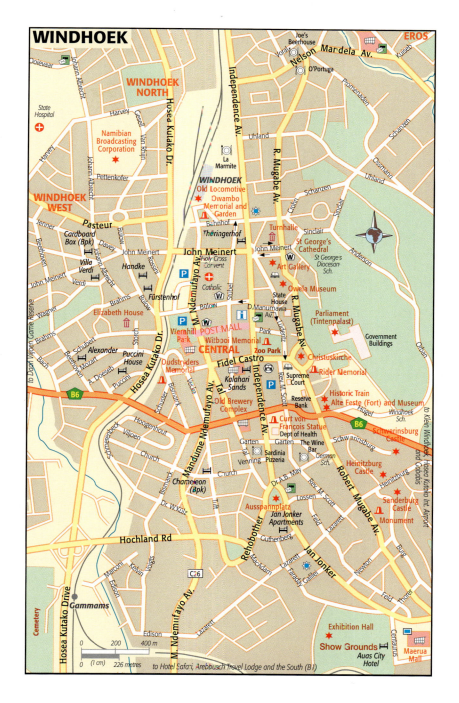

local flights). At the major intersection just past the hotel, turn right onto Mandume Ndemufayo Avenue to continue into town (a left would take you out onto the bypass). There is a large Shell service station on both sides of the road, with many motor agencies (VW, Mercedes, Renault and Daihatsu) and spares shops in the area. On the right, just past Shell, is Speedy (for tyres, batteries and silencers) and on the left is Trentyre. Drive on under the railway bridge and cross over the next traffic light (look out for Megabuild for gas refills and Pupkewitz Nissan). At the next traffic light turn right into Hochland Road, which swings up left past Ritters Toyota and becomes Rehobother Street to the Augustino Neto Gardens Circle, which is at the bottom end of Independence Avenue.

Windhoek centre is never too crowded and if you can ignore the cheeky hooting of the taxis, cruise slowly up the capital's main street. The popular Sardinia Restaurant is first on your left or, if you're in a hungry hurry, King Pie is across the street. The old-established departmental store of Woermann & Brock dominates the next left corner (Sam Nujoma Drive), and if you were to turn down here, you would find the old Brewery Building, now converted into coffee shops, galleries and the vibrant Warehouse Theatre. The right-hand side of Independence is taken up by City Hall, parking and a large curio market at the intersection of Fidel Castro Street.

Next up on the left is the Gustav Voigts Centre, above it the luxurious Kalahari Sands Hotel and behind and below it, a multistoreyed mall boasting branches of Nedbank, Checkers, CNA and Standard Bank, as well as a bottle store, bureau de change, pharmacy, and camera shop. After the intersection with Fidel Castro Street you pass two of the most attractive old buildings in Independence Avenue: Gathemann House (with a fine restaurant upstairs) and Erkrath Building. The offices of Namibia Wildlife Resorts are two building further down, next to Bushman Arts, and the Namibia Tourism Board is also in this area, on the first floor, Channel Life Towers, 39 Post Street Mall.

Next up, still on the left, are another bureau de change, pharmacy and First National Bank. Across the road is a telecentre of Telecom Namibia, where you can make international calls and access the internet. The Grand Canyon Spur Steakhouse and KFC are also along here. Back over on the left is a large Shoprite supermarket, a few fast-food outlets and the Medi-Pill Pharmacy, which is open 09h00–21h00 every day (tel: 061-232-083). Last, but not least, is the classy Thüringerhof Hotel and Famous Butcher's Grill.

Beyond this, Independence Avenue continues with service stations and used-car lots (of interest is the Land Rover agency and Pupkewitz Toyota). Towards the end of the street, on the right, is the inexpensive Motown Formula Inn accommodation.

Of course, not everyone arrives in their own vehicle. International flights arrive at the Hosea Kutako International Airport, which is 43 kilometres east of town on the Gobabis road. There are

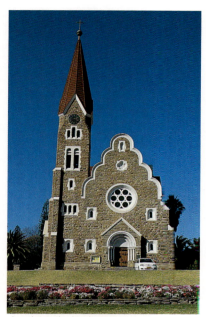

The Christuskirche dominates the Windhoek skyline.

many private shuttle services, but ask to see the driver's registration certificate and make sure he has an NTB registration disk on his windshield. Eros Airport is very central (just down the road from the Safari Hotel) and is used for local flights and charters. There is no public transport to or from this airport so you will have to use a taxi if your tour company has not organised transport for you.

Out and about in Windhoek

We will start our walking tour of Windhoek's sights in front of the very helpful information centre in the **Post Street Mall**. Over 30 meteorites that fell near Gibeon are on display as the mall's centrepiece. They fell to earth around 600 million years ago, part of the world's heaviest shower of meteorites.

Stroll up to the Clock Tower (a replica of the one that was originally on the Deutsche Afrikabank) and turn right into Independence Avenue. A little way down on the right are two interesting old buildings that have fortunately survived modernisation of Windhoek. **Erkraths Building** and **Gathemann House** were both designed by Willi Sander (responsible for many of Windhoek's old landmarks) and were erected in 1910 and 1913 respectively.

Cross the road for a better view and then stroll through the leafy Zoo Park into Fidel Castro Street. This takes you up the hill to Windhoek's most famous landmark building, the **Christuskirche**, an Evangelical Lutheran Church. Designed in the Art Nouveau and neo-Gothic styles by Gottlieb Redecker and built of local sandstone in 1910, it boasts stained-glass windows donated by Kaiser Wilhelm II.

Behind the church are the Namibian **Houses of Parliament**, housed in the old German colonial administrative offices. Still referred to as the Tintenpalast (Ink Palace) for the amount of ink used by the bureaucrats there, it has faithfully served successive governments. Tours are conducted on weekdays and can be booked through David Nahogandjo on 061-288-2583.

Turning south into Robert Mugabe Avenue we come to the **Alte Feste**, which rivals the Christuskirche for main landmark status. This is the original fort built by the *Schutztruppe* in 1890, and is now a national museum. It is open daily and admission is free.

At the bottom of Bahnhofstrasse, in the historical old Windhoek Station building, is the **Trans-Namib Museum**. Fascinating engines, carriages and other rolling stock are displayed outside, while inside the rooms are furnished and fitted out as station offices of yesteryear. The museum also features Namibian aeronautical and maritime history. For further information, tel: 061-298-2186.

The easiest way to see all Windhoek's sights is to take a half-day tour with **Gourmet Tours** (N$190 per person), tel: 061-231-281 or 081-128-0338. A visit to all the castles, churches, memorials and forts is topped off with a drive through Katatura Township and coffee at the Heinitzburg Castle.

Getting around Windhoek

Car hire There are many car-hire firms in Windhoek with a large selection of cars and light trucks. I will list just two of the larger companies that rent out the full range, from light run-about cars to station wagons and 4x4 double cabs with roof tents and camping gear. Vehicle and price options are complicated and best viewed and mulled over on the internet.

**Caprivi Car Hire,
135 Sam Nujoma Drive, Windhoek,
tel: 061-256-323, fax: 061-256-333,
e-mail: info@caprivicarhire-windhoek.com,
website: www.caprivicarhire-windhoek.com**

**Kea Campers,
286 Sam Nujoma Drive, Windhoek,
tel: 061-252-298, fax: 061-256-261,
e-mail: infoget@keacampers.co.za,
website: www.keacampers.co.za**

Taxis Fortunately, Windhoek is a relatively small city and easy to walk around in, because public transport is something of a problem. Dozens of small taxis buzz around the city, charging N$30 to N$50 a ride – but bargain hard as the locals pay a lot less. Jumping into just any taxi at night is not recommended; the safest option is to have the hotel or guesthouse at which you are staying call one for you.

Overnight in Windhoek

Although many travellers tend to just pass through the city on their way to the open spaces beyond, Windhoek has a good selection of accommodation for those who stop to savour the unique flavour of the capital city. Listed in order of price, from the most expensive hotel suite down to the cheapest backpackers' dorm, my selection is as follows:

Where would I stay if money were no object (wouldn't that be nice)? The four-star **Kalahari Sands Hotel**. Centrally situated at 129 Independence Avenue, it has comfortable rooms, a rooftop pool, wellness centre and smart bars and restaurants. Daily rates are the same for single or double occupancy and range from N$1 600 for a standard room to N$6 000 for the Presidential Suite (including breakfast). Contact the hotel on tel: 061-222-300, fax: 061-222-260, e-mail: ksands@sunint.co.za, website: www.suninternational.com.

Situated at the corner of Auas and Aviation roads on the southern outskirts of Windhoek is the largest accommodation complex in Namibia – **Hotel Safari** and **Safari Court Hotel**, with three- and four-star ratings respectively. There are about 400 rooms, a pool, small shop, bars and restaurants, all in a garden setting and a free, regular shuttle service into the city centre. Prices range from N$690 single to N$1 300 for a luxury double. For info tel: 061-296-8000, fax: 061-223-017, e-mail: marketing@safarihotel.com.na, website: www.safarihotelsnamibia.com.

The **Thüringerhof Hotel** is very central at the corner of Independence Avenue and Bahnhof Street. This classy hotel is a member of the Namib Sun Hotel Group and offers the best grills in town at their Famous Butcher's Grill. A single room is N$700 and a double is N$900. Contact them on tel: 061-213-231, fax: 661-246-661, e-mail: info@proteahotels.com, website: www.proteahotels.com.

The **Villa Verdi Guest House** at 4 Verdi Street is a boutique hotel that nestles in secluded gardens within walking distance of town. Like almost all accommodation establishments in Windhoek, it has safe off-street parking. Rooms range from N$980 for a single standard room to N$1 940 for a double luxury room. For more info, tel: 061-221-994, fax: 061-225-103, e-mail: villaverdi@leadinglodges.com, website: www.leadinglodges.com.

Klein Windhoek Guest House at 2 Hofmeyer Street, Klein Windhoek, is one of the nicest suburban accommodation establishments. A quiet, safe and secure haven where nothing is too much trouble for the owners, here are rooms with air-con, TV and telephone for N$460 single and N$590 double (including breakfast), or a self-catering flat for two at N$750 and a larger flat for four at N$850. For the lowdown, tel: 061-239-401, fax: 061-234-952, e-mail: kwgh@iway.na, website: www.kleinwindhoekguesthouse.com.

Jordani Bed & Breakfast is another equally pleasant place to stay in an up-market suburb of the capital. Situated at 55 Hamutenya Wanehepo Ndadi Street, Olympia, it offers a selection of well-furnished rooms with TV and fridge for N$450 single, N$580 double and N$820 family, including breakfast. Contact them on tel: 061-220-141, fax: 061-238-007, e-mail: jordani@iway.na, website: www.natron.net/jordani.

Good, clean, no-frills, in-and-out overnight accommodation can be found at **Auas City Hotel**, Centaurus Road, right behind the Maerua Mall on Robert Mugabe Avenue. The en-suite rooms offer air-con, TV and coffee/tea facilities, while the huge mall next door offers restaurants, shops and internet cafés. Double rooms cost N$590 and single N$460. To make reservations, tel: 061-239-768, fax: 061-239-826, e-mail: info@auas-city-hotel.com, website: www.auas-city-hotel.com.

The very central **Hotel Pension Handke** at 3 Rossini Street is kept neat as a pin under the helpful and friendly management of Amanda and Brigitte Kipka. Twelve rooms with all amenities, off-street parking, 24-hour security and walking distance to town make this a good Windhoek choice. Rates, inclusive of breakfast, are N$435 single, N$595 double and N$895 for a four-bed family room. Call the Kipkas on tel: 061-234-904, fax: 061-225-660, e-mail: pension-handke@iafrica.com.na, website: www.natron.net/handke.

The **Hotel Cela** is close to the centre of town at 82 Dr Frans Indongo Street. Recently sold and under new management, it has been upgraded. The motel-style accommodation is spacious and there is a TV, air-con and fridge in each room. Rooms cost N$435 single, N$595 double, and N$755 triple (breakfast included). For bookings, tel: 061-223-322, fax: 061-226-246, e-mail: info@hotelcela.com, website: www.hotelcela.com.

Another comfortable and affordable option is the **Jan Jonker Holiday Apartments** at 183 Jan Jonker Road, just off the Augustino Neto Circle at the southern end of Independence Avenue. Fully furnished flats, with well-equipped kitchens, contain all the comforts of home and cost N$595 for a standard double apartment, N$595 for a luxury single, and N$840 for a luxury double. For more info, tel: 061-221-236, fax: 061-228-218, e-mail: info@jan-jonker.com, website: www.jan-jonker.com.

Puccini House, at 4 Puccini Street, calls itself a budget guesthouse and offers accommodation ranging from a double room with shared bathroom at N$360, en-suite singles at N$385, and en-suite doubles at N$450. They also have triples, family rooms and a fully equipped self-catering kitchen for all to share. Tel: 061-236-355, fax: 061-245-332, e-mail: enquiry@puccini-namibia.com, website: www.puccini-namibia.com.

The old-established **Cardboard Box Backpackers** is still going strong at the corner of John Meinert and Johann Albrecht streets. It offers all the usual delights of a backpackers', plus pancakes and coffee for breakfast. Camping costs N$100, dorms N$120 and private singles or doubles N$270. For the lowdown, tel: 061-228-994, fax: 061-245-595, e-mail: cbbox@iway.na, website: www.namibweb.com/cbb.htm.

The new, improved **Chameleon Backpackers' Lodge** has moved to a very central but difficult-to-find location at 5 Voigts Street North. Almost too up-market to be labelled a mere backpackers', it boasts a pool, thatched entertainment area and some luxury accommodation, but still has all the basics that make a place like this a home for budget travellers. Dorm beds cost N$100, private singles N$200 and doubles N$260 (all sharing bathrooms). En-suite doubles cost from N$250 to N$390 (breakfast included in all accommodation). For details, tel: 061-244-347, fax: 061-220-885, e-mail: info@chameleonbackpackers.com, website: www.chameleonbackpackers.com.

I have left **Arebbusch Travel Lodge** for last only because it has such a wide range of accommodation, and if you don't want to be in the centre of town, it could be the ideal place for you. Just off the highway from the south as you enter Windhoek, Arebbusch is situated in natural surroundings on the banks of the usually dry Arebbusch River. A large complex of rooms, self-catering chalets, caravan sites, restaurant and swimming pool, it is protected by an electric fence and guard patrols.

Budget rooms (sharing ablutions with the campers) cost N$250 single and N$320 double. En-suite rooms have air-con, fridge, TV and telephone, and cost N$425 single and N$500 double. Self-catering chalets have all the above, plus a stove, crockery and braai facilities for N$480 single, N$600 double and N$680 for a family of up to five people. For bookings, tel: 061-252-255, fax: 061-251-670, e-mail: atl@mweb.com.na, website: www.arebbusch.com.

The Daan Viljoen Game Park is currently closed and under ownership review.

There is one last place I would like to mention. Although it's 15 kilometres north of Windhoek on the B1 to Otjiwarongo, it makes another good accommodation alternative to staying in the capital. **Elisenheim Guest Farm** nestles in the Eros mountains and offers nine comfortably furnished en-suite guest rooms (N$420 single, N$660 double) and grassy, shaded campsites (N$60 per person). Contact the farm on tel/fax: 061-264-429, e-mail: awerner@mweb.com.na, website: www.natron.net/tour/elisenheim.

Eating out in Windhoek

You can't stay in Windhoek without visiting **Joe's Beerhouse**. Like the Carnivore in Nairobi, the Dutch Milkhouse in Addis, or Bique's in Beira, it's famous among African overlanders and international travellers. And rightly so too – a phantasmagorical collection of memorabilia, displayed under a sprawling complex of thatched roofs that house pubs, restaurants, bomas, lapas, upstairs, downstairs, inside,

One of the best views over Windhoek is from the terrace of Hotel Heinitzburg.

outside and open fires. Vegetarians should stick to beer (there's a good wine list, too) as the menu leans heavily towards steaks and game dishes, with a little chicken and fish for the not-so-hungry. Find them at 160 Nelson Mandela Avenue, tel: 061-232-457, website: www.joesbeerhouse.com.

Also in Nelson Mandela Avenue, on the corner with Sam Nujoma Drive, is the German-sounding **Zum Wurzelsepp Restaurant** that serves African flavoured cuisine, tel: 061-232-796. Staying in Sam Nujoma Drive, there is the **O'Portuga Restaurant**, which serves authentic and tasty Portuguese and Angolan fare, washed down with a carafe of Vinhos Verdes, tel: 061-272-900.

Another African-experience restaurant is **La Marmite**, at the unfashionable northern end of Independence Avenue. Cameroon cuisine prevails, but there are dishes from all parts of Africa, authentically flavoured and served in wooden bowls (mopane worms served with garlic and black pepper is a speciality). To book, tel: 061-240-306. And yet another African-themed restaurant is the wonderfully positioned **Restaurant Africa** on the front veranda of the Alte Feste. With an imaginative and reasonably priced menu (Ethiopian Tibs caught my fancy), it makes a great place to watch the sunset over a beer and light supper. Another great sundowner spot is **The Wine Bar**, 3 Garten Street, tel: 061-226-514. High on a hill with views of the city lights, this indoor-outdoor venue has not only a snack menu but a great wine list, very knowledgeable waiters and smooth jazz music.

A popular Italian pizza/pasta restaurant is **Sardinia Pizzeria** at 47 Independence Avenue, tel: 061-225-600, but if you want a more exclusive (and expensive) meal that evokes the atmosphere of the Windhoek of yesteryear, drive north on Independence Avenue to Number 175 and head upstairs to **Gathemanns**. The menu is a fusion of Namibian and German cuisines and there is a good wine list – all served overlooking Independence Avenue. For details, tel: 061-223-853.

The Gourmet Restaurant, in the courtyard of the old Kaiserkrone in the Post Street Mall, is a good spot to relax in the centre of town with a meal or just coffee (tel: 061-232-360). Also in the middle of Windhoek's hustle and bustle is the leafy oasis of the **Café Zoo** in Zoo Park, opposite Gathemanns on Independence Avenue. The Grand Canyon Spur steakhouse is also on Independence – at Number 251.

Takeaways are available from KFC and King Pie shops in and around town, and the Maerua Mall is a good, safe place to go for restaurants and takeaways (there are also three cinemas).

Arts and entertainment

Namibia seems to encourage gambling – there are slot machines in most bars, bookmakers take bets on the South African horse races and casinos are popping up everywhere. Windhoek's classiest gambling joints are the Windhoek Country Club, Kalahari Sands Hotel and Hotel Safari.

The busiest and most interesting theatre in Windhoek is The Warehouse, situated in the Old Breweries Complex on the corner of Tal Street and Sam Nujoma Drive (just off Independence Avenue). Music, dance and theatre alternate on the bill and there is a lively bar too. One of Windhoek's favourite bars, El Cubano, is also in this complex. It has a wonderfully dark and dingy atmosphere with an eclectic décor, as well as a short Cuban menu and long Cuban cigars.

Nightlife

Nightlife is plentiful in Windhoek, but I'll be honest with you, I'm not the best judge. So I'll list, and you check it out. The long-running La-di-das (Ferry Street, Southern Industrial Area) gets going around midnight and dances till dawn. Funky Lab (/Ae//Gams Shopping

Centre, Sam Nujoma Drive) is the best, overcrowded party spot for fashionistas. Dylan's Bar (on the corner of Sam Nujoma and Stein) is for the older crowd who can't handle Funky's glitz. Some newer places are Pharaoh's Club at 22 Nelson Mandela Drive, The Palms at 12 Krupp Street and Zenso Lounge at Guthenberg Platz. I also near mention of Bump Entertainment (Kegler Street) and Kiepie's Dance Bar (Marconi Street), but who knows? Maybe the scene will have changed completely by the time you read this.

Shopping

The Shoprite, Checkers and Pick 'n Pay supermarkets are plentiful in Windhoek. They stock a wide variety of food and drinks that should allow you to stock up for your trip ahead. It is always a joy to find a well-stocked, helpful and knowledgeable bookshop, and Windhoek has at least two **The New Bookcellar** is on Fidel Castro Street, just down off Independence Avenue, tel: 061-231-615, fax: 061-236-164, e-mail: bookcellar@iway.na **The Book Den** is located in Wernhil Park, corner of Fidel Castro Street and Mandume Ndemufayo Avenue, tel: 061-239-976, fax: 061-234-248, e-mail elmarie@bookden.com.na.

There is an emergency pharmacy, **Mitzi's Medicine Depot**, situated at 43 Independence Avenue, tel: 061-238-247, which is open until 20h00 every day. And at the other end of Independence Avenue (at Number 347) is the **Medi-Pill Pharmacy**, tel: 061-232-083, which opens until 21h00.

For arts and crafts there is the curio market on the corner of Independence Avenue and Fidel Castro Street, or try the **Namibian Craft Centre** in the Old Breweries Complex.

For camping, fishing and hunting gear as well as 4x4 equipment and motor spares your one-stop shop is **Cymot**, 60 Mandume Ndemufayo Avenue, tel: 061-295-7000. And for the right outfit to go with all that gear, head for the Gustav Voigts Centre on Independence Avenue to visit **Safariland-Holtz**, tel: 061-235-941. If you want to hire camping equipment, **Camping Hire Namibia** has everything you can think of at individual daily hire rates. They also put together picnic and camping packs that contain all you need for the

Old and new buildings blend well in this pedestrian-friendly city.

outdoors. They are at 78 Malcolm Spence Street, Olympia, tel/fax: 061-252-995, e-mail: camping@iafrica.com.na, website: www.orusovu.com/camphire.

If you are a hunter, you will want to visit **A Rosenthal**, Namibia's oldest and leading gunsmith. They sell a full range of arms and ammunition, have rifles for rent and operate an on-site shooting range. They can be found at 26 Merensky Street, tel: 061-237-210, fax: 061-226-156, e-mail: arosenthal@iway.na.

Communications

Windhoek's main post office in the centre of town on Independence Avenue has a telecentre opposite the Clock Tower. Local and international calls can be made, as well as good internet connections (N$10 per 30 minutes). **Namibnet Internet Café** is around the corner in Daniel Munamavu and offers the same rates as well as printing at N$1 a page.

Festivals

Every April for the last 50 years the traditional German **Wika Carnival** has been held in Windhoek. It features a street parade, exciting cabaret evenings and an all-night masked ball. For details, tel: 061-244-244.

Oktoberfest is the big one! It is held every year at the Sport Klub Windhoek and features beer, sausage, band and dancing. What more do you want? For details, tel: 061-235-521.

Out and about in Windhoek

You may find the following useful.

Airline Offices

Air Namibia, Gustav Voigts Centre, Independence Avenue,
tel: 061-299-6000;
South African Airways, Carl List Building, Independence Avenue,
tel: 061-273-340;
TAAG (Angolan Airline), Sanlam Centre, Independence Avenue,
tel: 061-236-266

Birding
Dieter Ludwig,
tel: 061-223-986 or 081-127-0693

Breakdown services
Northern Breakdown Service,
tel: 061-230-823 or 081-124-2300

Motorcycling
Africa Motion Tours,
tel/fax: 061-237-258 or 081-129-1333, website: www.africamotiontours.com

Information
Windhoek Tourism Information Office, Post Street Mall,
tel: 061-290-2092, fax: 061-290-2203, e-mail: ghe@windhoekcc.org.na, website: www.windhoekcc.org.na

Laundry
Laundryland,
339 Sam Nujoma Drive,
Klein Windhoek,
tel: 061-302-330;
Baines Laundrette,
Baines Shopping Mall, Pionierspark

Medical emergencies
Windhoek Medi-Clinic,
Heliodoor Street,
Eros, tel: 061-222-687;
Central State Hospital,
Florence Nightingale Street,
tel: 061-203-9111

Resorts
Namibia Wildlife Resorts (NWR),
Gathemann Building,
Independence Avenue,
tel: 061-285-7200, fax: 061-22-4900,
e-mail: reservations@nwr.com.na,
website: www.nwr.com.na

Noordoewer to Windhoek 12

For many South Africans the area between Noordoewer and Windhoek is their introduction to Namibia. And what an introduction it is! The region has the extraordinary natural beauty of the Fish River Canyon, the mighty Orange River, the Ai-Ais hot springs and the lonely grandeur of the Namib Desert, while Lüderitz has history, grand old architecture and great seafood.

The veld around the Fish River Canyon explodes with colour after the rains.

Driving up from Cape Town, it is possible to reach Namibia on the first day, but if you are fortunate enough to have the time, take it slow through Namaqualand, especially if it is the flower season (from July to September). First buy oranges or naartjies from one of the farm stalls in the Citrusdal valley before enjoying a cup of coffee at the Cedar Inn, overlooking the Clanwilliam Dam (there's fuel, mechanical workshops and accommodation too). It's a lonely 258 kilometres, with few services between Vanrhynsdorp and Springbok, so refuel (also keep in mind that fuel is cheaper in Namibia) and have a bite to eat at one of the competing truck stops in Vanrhynsdorp before tackling the Knersvlakte.

If you want to overnight in Springbok but don't want to go into the town, pull into the **Kokerboom Motel** just south of the turn-off. They offer neat, basic, air-conditioned rooms at R500 per double or rather barren campsites at R60 per person. For details, tel: +27-(0)27-712-2685, fax +27-(0)27-712-2017, e-mail: jcb@mynet.co.za, website: www.namaqualandflowers.co.za. In town there's a lot of accommodation (often full during the flower season). **The Masonic Hotel** on Van Riebeeck Street, tel: +27-(0)27-712-1505, fax: +27-(0)27-712-1730, e-mail: jcb@mynet.co.za, is a comfortable three-star establishment. En-suite double rooms cost R578, while singles in the cheaper annex next door are R220. Breakfast is an extra R79. **Annie's Cottage** is representative of the many B&Bs in town. In a pretty garden setting at 4 King Street, the rooms boast some lovely antiques and cost R300 single and R500 double (including breakfast). Contact them on tel/fax: –27-(0)27-712-1451, e-mail: annie@springbokinfo.com, website: www.springbokinfo.com. Please note that all rates in Namaqualand increase during the flower season.

The last 126 kilometres of the N7 is covered quickly and you will soon reach the South African border post at Vioolsdrif (open 24 hours). Customs and immigration are usually handled quickly and efficiently, but be prepared for long queues and delays at the start of South Africa's June school holidays. Also remember to have your vehicle's registration papers and a letter of authority from the owner if you are not driving your own vehicle. Now cross the bridge that spans the Orange River to enter the Republic of Namibia.

The border formalities on the Namibian side are as straightforward as those in South Africa, except that there is a N$160 cross-border charge if you have a vehicle. This is a contribution towards the upkeep of the roads and is valid for one entry into the country – keep the receipt handy as proof of payment in case you are questioned by traffic officers. Very few countries' citizens require visas (see page 12).

Introducing Noordoewer

Noordoewer has always been a typical border town with just the bare necessities – fuel, accommodation and a general dealer – but the little town has recently benefited from the increase in river-running tourism and the growth of irrigation farming downstream. The first group of buildings you will encounter

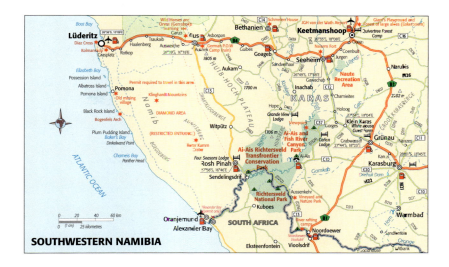

SOUTHWESTERN NAMIBIA

is a BP service station (fuel in Namibia is cheaper than in South Africa), a shop with an ATM and the **Orange River Lodge** and restaurant. The lodge is set in green gardens and offers comfortable, air-conditioned rooms with TV for N$290 single, N$400 double and N$515 for a family room. There is also a campsite a few kilometres down at the riverside at N$50 per person. Contact the lodge on tel/fax: 063-297-012, e-mail: orlodge@ iway.na, website: www.orlodge.iway.na.

Next up is the Engen service station. There is also a branch of Bank Windhoek and a Namibian post office (Nampost). The post office is a good place to buy a local starter pack and airtime for your cellphone. Having a Namibian SIM card in your phone is much cheaper and more convenient than international roaming on your home number. It also screens you from receiving unnecessary calls from your 'old life'. They should cost N$19, inclusive of N$10 worth of airtime, but if they have sold out, the shop next door takes advantage of the situation by charging more for the same item. Rather wait until the next Nampost office.

The **Camel Lodge** was closed at the time of updating the guide.

On to Grünau and Keetmanshoop

If you are in a hurry to get north, stay on the B1 and tackle the long 172-kilometre slog to Grünau. (After 156 kilometres you will reach the turn-off to Ai-Ais and the Fish River Canyon, but more about that on page 99.) The road is in good condition and uncrowded, but so boring that even reaching little Grünau is a welcome diversion. At the junction of the B3 from the eastern border of Ariamsvlei and Upington in South Africa (and another turn-off to the Fish River Canyon), you feel that this should be a larger, more important stop, but alas …

There is a roadside Shell service

station, shop and restaurant that offers overnight facilities in neat, self-contained chalets – N$220 single, N$380 double, N$420 triple plus N$50 per extra person. They also offer caravan sites with private ablutions at N$90 plus N$10 per person. Contact them on tel: 063-262-026, fax 063-262-017, e-mail: willa@iafrica.com.na, website: grunaunamibia.com. A more hospitable option, if you plan on overnighting, is to turn off into the village and stay at the old hotel that has now been refurbished as the **Grünau Country House**. With a bar and à la carte restaurant, satellite TV and pool table, and good security, they have single rooms at N$265 and doubles at N$425. For budget-conscious travellers, there are also bungalows (N$100 per person) and campsites (N$50) with shared ablutions. Contact the hotel on tel: 063-262-001, fax: 063-262-009, e-mail: grunauch@iway.na, website: www.grunauch.iway.na.

If you were travelling from Upington in South Africa, the border at Nakop/Ariamsvlei is as uncomplicated as the Vioolsdrif/Noordoewer post and the B3 to Grünau just as good as the B1. Along the way, the **Kalkfontein Hotel** in Karasburg has well-appointed rooms and safe parking for a reasonable N$250 single and N$400 double. For more details, tel: 063-270-172, fax: 063-270-457, e-mail: kalkfont@iway.na.

And on to Keetmanshoop

Another 156 kilometres of good, quiet road stretches into the distance as you leave Grünau. About 11 kilometres up the road is the signpost to the **White House Guest Farm** (S27°37.672 E18°24.219), the domain of Dolf and Kinna de Wet. Choose between huge en-suite farmhouse rooms with creaking floors and wonderful old furniture or newly built chalets, and order one of the delicious home-cooked meals – but make sure you're very hungry. Their rates are N$200 per person and dinner

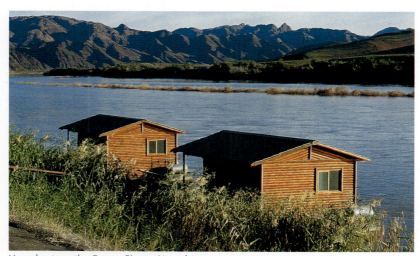

Houseboats on the Orange River at Norotshama.

is N$60. There is a rose-quartz mine on the farm and lovely stones, polished or unpolished, are sold at reasonable prices. Contact the De Wets on tel/fax: 063-262-061, e-mail: withuis@iway.na, website: www.withuis.iway.na.

Approaching Keetmanshoop (about 5 kilometres out), you will first encounter an Engen service station and the **Lafenis Lodge**. If you want to avoid turning off the B1 bypass and going into Keetmans, then pull in here to refuel and stay overnight. Accommodation is in bungalows that come equipped with air-con, TV and private braai facilities. The cost, including breakfast, is N$240 single and N$370 double. There are also shaded campsites with electric plugs for N$70 per site plus N$40 a person. For the lowdown, tel: 063-224-316, fax: 063-224-309, e-mail: lafenislodge@iway.na, website: www.lafenis-lodge.com.

You will pass a BP service station before you reach the intersection with the B4 to Lüderitz. Turn right to continue up the B1. If you decide to turn into town, you will find yourself travelling down Fifth Avenue into one of Nam's larger towns – Keetmanshoop the capital of the south. Originally a Nama settlement around a strong spring, it later became a staging post for early explorers, traders and hunters from the Cape Colony. It was the German missionary Johann Schröder who named the mission station Keetmanshoop after his main benefactor. Immigrants and soldiers arrived after the proclamation of Deutsch-Südwestafrika and the town's connection with Lüderitzbucht was strengthened when a railway line was built between the two towns in 1908. Farming, particularly with karakul sheep, was and still is the backbone of the region's economy.

On your left as you approach the town is a tyre sales and repair shop, and then a Caltex garage followed by an Engen. On the right is the Canyon Hotel and a couple of streets further, off to the right in Pastorie Street, is the Bird's Nest B&B. Continue on Fifth Avenue until you reach the traffic light at the intersection with Sam Nujoma Drive. The small park in front of you is the centre of town. Turn right here into Sam Nujoma to exit town and return to the B1, or turn left to reach the Toyota garage and the caravan park. Facing the park on the western side is the police station and the tourist information office, while on the opposite side is the post office. North of the park is the commercial side of town where you will find banks, supermarkets, an internet café, more accommodation and the medical centre.

Overnight in Keetmanshoop

The **Canyon Hotel** is the largest and easiest-to-find accommodation in Keetmanshoop. Prominently situated on the right as you enter town from the south, this three-star establishment has 70 rooms with air-con, TV and telephones, a beer garden and pool, and popular restaurant and bistro. Rates are N$330 single and N$500 double (including breakfast). For more info, tel: 063-223-361, fax: 063-223-714, e-mail: info@canyon-namibia.com, website: www.canyon-namibia.com.

Central Lodge is in the centre of town (where else?) on Fifth Avenue, just across from the park. With a splashing

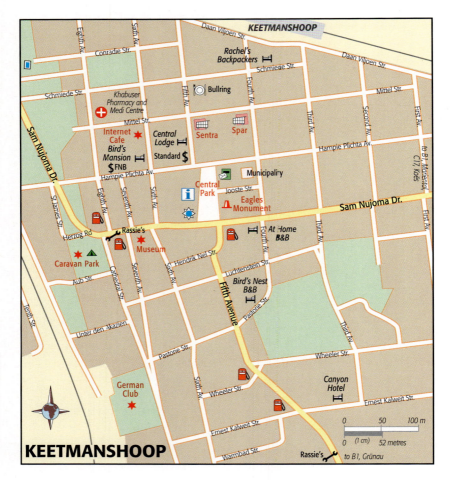

fountain in a shaded courtyard and the old-world ambiance of the stone-walled restaurant, the Central shows its heritage as the original Hansa Hotel of 1910. Comfortable, well-decorated rooms, secure parking, swimming pool and a good menu and wine list add to the reasons for staying here. Prices range from N$290 for a standard single to N$470 for a luxury double (breakfast included). Contact the Central on tel: 063-225-850, e-mail: clodge@iway.na,

website: www.central-lodge.com.

A third up-market option is the **Bird's Mansion Hotel,** one block west in Sixth Avenue. Similar to the Central, but more modern and without the history, it also has a shaded back patio, lapa and pool. Rooms with air-con and TV cost N$330 per single and N$500 a double. Contact them on tel: 063-221-711, fax: 063-221-730, e-mail: birdsmansions@iway.na, website: www.birdsaccommodation.com.

In the same stable as the Bird's Mansion

is the **Bird's Nest Bed and Breakfast** at 16 Pastorie Street. Very secure behind electric gates and fences, the rooms have telephones, TV and air-conditioning, and cost N$220 single, N$380 double and N$450 for a family room. Contact the B&B on tel: 063-222-906, fax: 063-222-261, e-mail: birdnest@iafrica.com.na, website: www.birdsaccommodation.com.

The oldest surviving German club in Namibia was recently privatised and refurbished as the quaint and comfortable **Schutzenhaus Guesthouse**. Situated in Cathedral Street, Schutzenhaus boasts 17 luxury en-suite and air-conned rooms as well as backpackers' accommodation. The bar has great atmosphere and the restaurant serves delicious German specialities. Rates are N$300 single, N$450 double and N$120 backpackers. Contact them on tel: 063-223-400, fax: 063-225-596, e-mail: schutzenhaus@iway.na.

Rachel's Backpackers is at 131 Schmiede Street. It looks a little dodgy, but is cheap at N$100 per person in an outside room and N$120 inside. You share a bathroom and get no breakfast, but do have the use of the kitchen. Call them on tel: 063-225-177.

The **Keetmanshoop Municipal Caravan Park** is to be found at the bottom end (west) of Sam Nujoma Drive. Sites are shaded, have electrical points, and cost N$23 a vehicle plus N$57 a person. There is someone on call 24 hours a day, but feel free to phone on tel: 063-221-265.

Out and about in Keetmanshoop

There are numerous takeaways in town (mostly at the service stations), but for a decent meal, I would suggest you

EMERGENCIES IN KEETMANS	
♦ Ambulance/ state hospital	063 22 3388
♦ Fire brigade	063 221 270
♦ Police	063 221 800

try the Canyon Hotel, Central Lodge or Bird's Mansion. For a little excitement and a chance to watch sport on a big-screen TV, head for the **Bullring Sportsbar** at the corner of Fifth Avenue and Schmiede Street.

The **Khabuser Medical Centre and Pharmacy** is on the corner of Eighth Avenue and Mittel Street and houses the doctors of Keetmanshoop. For more info, tel: 063-225-688 or 081-202-2313.

Aetos Services run public transport between Keetmans, Lüderitz and Windhoek, but have a flexible timetable, so contact them for details on tel: 063-222-291 or 081-261-4689. **The Horse and Bell Internet Café** is on Sixth Avenue, next to Bird's Mansion Hotel; the post office has a telecentre with public telephones and internet; and both large supermarkets are in the centre of town on Mittel Street. A number I hope you will never need is that of Wynand Erasmus, who runs **Rassie's Breakdown Service**. Rassie is kept busy towing in and fixing vehicles from the long sections of highway that stretch in all directions from Keetmans. Call Rassie on tel: 063-222-119 or 081-127-8582.

On to Mariental

The stretch of B1 between Keetmanshoop and Mariental is rather featureless, with no towns along the way. There is no fuel at Asab, although some maps indicate that there is. You may well find fuel by turning off to Gibeon, but rather push on through to Mariental. About 250 kilometres south of Windhoek, 220 north of Keetmanshoop and at 1 200 kilometres from Cape Town, it makes a good overnight stop for fast drivers. Approaching from the south, there is an Engen and Wimpy on the left, opposite the turn-off into town. There are other garages in town, including Southern Motor Mecca Nissan, Mariental Toyota, C&G Auto (for Ford and Mazda) and Trentyre. There is also a Standard Bank with ATM in the main street and a medical centre with doctors, a pharmacy and dentist in Mark Street. There was extensive flooding in the town in 2006 and a few businesses closed temporarily. The big Spar supermarket at the northern end of town has now reopened and Shoprite is in the old OK premises. For a 24-hour breakdown service, contact Marius Meyer at Highway Services, tel: 063-240-958 or 081-250-1774.

Overnight in Mariental

Accommodation is available at **Anandi Guesthouse**, just off the highway opposite the Engen garage. B&B services cost N$200 per person sharing in comfortable en-suite rooms and there is safe parking for vehicles. For more information, tel: 063-242-220, fax: 063-242-225, e-mail: anandi@iway.na, website: www.anandiguesthouse.com.

Just a kilometre further north along the highway is **River Chalets and Camping** (S24°37.489 E17°57.355). Their well-equipped and self-contained chalets boast air-con, stove and DStv for N$340 single, N$450 double and N$600 for four people. Camping costs N$60 a person on sites that have their own individual private ablutions. For bookings, tel: 063-240-515, fax: 063-242-601, e-mail: garbers@iway.na, website: www.riverchalets.com.

If you were to turn down at the Engen station, you would reach the neat-as-a-pin **La Vida Inn**, a guesthouse on the banks of a small river with good bird life. Spacious en-suite rooms with air-con and DStv cost N$315 single and N$490 double (B&B), but there are self-catering units available for N$355 per unit. Call La Vida on tel: 063-242-121, fax: 063-241-600, e-mail: lavidainn@iway.na.

The only other accommodation option in town is the **Mariental Hotel** – a traditional small-town hotel, somewhat ruled by its bar and slot machines. Rates are N$330 single and N$450 double. Contact the hotel on tel: 063-242-466, fax: 063-240-738, e-mail: mrlhotel@iafrica.com.na, website: www.marientalhotel.com.

Beyond Mariental

About 15 kilometres north of Mariental is the turn-off (S24°29.791 E17°55.635) to the **Hardap Dam Recreation Resort and Game Park**. With a surface area of 25 square kilometres, Hardap is Namibia's largest dam and supplies water for a fertile irrigation scheme as well as the town of Mariental. It is a favourite spot for angling and birdwatching, and the area has been stocked with antelope and black rhino. The resort offers an impressive modernist restaurant and solid spacious bungalows, all overlooking the dam. B&B chalets for four people cost N$1 600,

B&B bungalows for two cost N$600 and camping is N$50 per site plus N$50 per person. Contact Namibia Wildlife Resorts for more details and bookings (see page 42).

Continuing north on the B1, you first reach Kalkrand, a small settlement with a police station, Shell garage, shop and bar. About 100 kilometres on is Rehoboth. The petrol station closest to the highway has a shop and takeaway, and accommodation is available at the Reho Spa, a rather run-down hot-spring resort, popular with local Namibians over long weekends. A far better accommodation option is the **Lake Oanob Resort and Game Reserve**, 7 kilometres west of Rehoboth. Overlooking a large dam, the resort offers watersports, birding and game-watching. The main building, which houses the bar and restaurant, is an attractive wood-and-thatch creation with great views over the lake. Accommodation is in lodges dotted around the lakeshore and the camp spots are also attractively sited. Self-catering chalets cost N$1 080 per night double and en-suite rooms cost N$830 double. Camping is N$60 per person. For details, tel: 062-522-370, fax: 062-524-112, e-mail: reservations@oanob.com.na, website: www.oanob.com.na.

The final 85 kilometres of the B1 takes you through the foothills of the Auas mountains to the capital city, Windhoek.

But let's retrace our steps to Mariental to swing west towards the desert and the sea. From Mariental the C19 branches off the B1 westward toward the Namib-Naukluft Park, passing through Maltahöhe. Here you will find a Standard Bank, police station, general dealer and service station. Accommodation is available at the **Maltahöhe Hotel** for N$560 double B&B, tel: 063-293-013, fax 063-293-133, e-mail: info@maltahoehe hotel.com, website: www.maltahoehe hotel.com, and out on the western edge of town is a little travellers' oasis called **The Pappot**. The friendly pair of Henriette and Mannetjie run this secure little complex of shop, restaurant, B&B and campsite. From the kitchen come fresh pies and bread, the shop stocks everything, and the accommodation is quiet, shaded and comfortable. B&B costs N$220 per person in en-suite rooms, and camping is N$50 per person. For further information, tel: 063-293-397, e-mail: pappot@mweb.com.na.

Spring flowers on the drive north through Namaqualand in South Africa.

The B4 to Lüderitz 13

Head south out of Keetmanshoop to pick up the B4, which will take you west to the coast to Lüderitz – another 335 kilometres of good, quiet tarred highway. After the first 43 kilometres you will reach Seeheim and the turn-off onto the C12, which will take you south past the Fish River Canyon and on to the Ai-Ais hot springs (more about that on page 99).

The impressive Felsenkirche (above) overlooks a quiet corner of Lüderitz lagoon. Goerke House (opposite), now a museum, is one of Lüderitz's grandest 'diamond palaces'.

Seeheim was once a station on the old, disused railway line between Lüderitz and Keetmanshoop. Its only point of interest now is the original **Seeheim Hotel**, which nestles in a little gully behind the station and still offers succour to weary travellers. Down a cold beer in the old-world atmosphere of the bar, enjoy a light lunch under the thatched lapa next to the pool, or stay the night in one of the beautifully furnished old rooms. B&B rates are en-suite single N$660, double N$960. Contact them at tel: 063-250-503, fax: 063-250-531, e-mail: seeheim@iway.na, website: www.seeheim.co.za.

On to Aus and beyond

After another 63 kilometres you pass the turn-off north to Bethanien, Helmeringhausen and on to Duwisib Castle and Sossusvlei (see page 105). After 105 kilometres you'll reach Aus. Aus is enjoying a slight revival as the operation at the Skorpion Zinc Mine and refinery at Rosh Pinah grows. The railway line from here to Lüderitz is being rebuilt, and the local hotel has been refurbished.

Aus gained notoriety as the South African prisoner-of-war camp that held the German colonial troops after their surrender in 1915 during the First World War. Weathered ruins and a commemorative plaque are all that remain now – drive through town on the way out towards Rosh Pinah to find the site.

Centrally situated in Aus is the recently restored **Bahnhof Hotel**. The 13 rooms have been redecorated and the restaurant offers local and international cuisine. Rates are N$565 single and N$990 double (inclusive of breakfast). Tel: 064-461-677, fax: 064-461-488, e-mail: kaikoro@iway.na, website: www.hotel-aus.com. Also centrally situated is the **Namib Garage**, which has fuel, a tow-in service, shop and restaurant. They also operate a rustic guesthouse (N$150 a person with shared ablutions) and a campsite (N$45 a

The wild horses of the Namib congregate at Garub Pan.

person). For details, tel/fax: 063-258-029, e-mail: namibaus@mweb.com.na.

About 2 kilometres beyond the turn-off to Aus is the turn-off to the **Klein Aus Vista** resort. Snug up against the hills, this is a restful spot with large en-suite rooms in the main house, cottages with views over the desert, and a lovely campsite up an isolated valley. There are hiking, horse and mountain bike trails too. Accommodation in the Eagle's Nest Lodge is from N$795 per person, at the Desert Horse Inn from N$555, in a hikers' cabin N$150, while camping costs N$80 per person. For the lowdown, tel: 063-258-116, fax: 063-258-021, e-mail:

ausvista@namibhorses.com, website: www.namibhorses.com.

Continuing on the B4 towards Lüderitz, look for a turn-off (S26°35.693 E16°04.533) to the right, about 20 kilometres out of Aus. This is the short, 1-kilometre detour to **Garub Pan** where you are most likely to see the Namib's wild horses. Descendants of horses that escaped from troops and farmers, they have learnt to survive in the desert. A wooden hide overlooks a waterhole and you might spot up to 100 of these feral horses.

Back on the B4 you are faced with 115 kilometres of **Sperrgebiet**, where you may not even leave the road – in case you're tempted to pluck diamonds from the sand. But the driving is fast and easy and soon you pass the deserted mining town of **Kolmanskop**. About 10 kilometres further, you enter Lüderitz, a sleepy, laid-back town with quaint, old German colonial buildings and a history to match.

Introducing Lüderitz

Bartholomeu Diaz was the first European to set eyes on this coast when, on Christmas Day, 1487, he took refuge from a storm in Lüderitz Bay. It took nearly another 400 years for foreign powers to discover the rich guano deposits on the offshore islands and start exploiting the whales that visited the area. The trader Adolf Lüderitz concluded a treaty with the Namas in 1883 to acquire the land around the bay, and a year later Germany assumed protection of the area. At the start of the 20th century the harbour town became the base and supply station for the *Schutztruppe*, who were now chasing the Namas away. But the real excitement came in 1908 when diamonds were discovered just outside town at Kolmanskop. Lüderitzbucht boomed until mining moved south to Oranjemund and the town fell back to harvesting the bounty of the sea again – fishing and rock lobster.

Art nouveau cottages in Berg Street, Lüderitz.

Because of its isolation, many of Lüderitz's old buildings have survived and the way of life for many of its inhabitants has not changed much.

On entering Lüderitz there's a Total service station on your right and a Trentyre workshop just beyond. On the left is a signposted turn-off to Diaz Point followed by the Obelix Village accommodation. Continuing on down Bay Road you will find the Bogenfels Restaurant on the corner of Lessing Street, with the better-known Legends Pub behind it – across the road is the police station.

Further down Bay Road, on the left, is Kapps Hotel, also home to Rumours Bar and Restaurant, and across the road are the town council buildings with beautiful tiled murals commemorating the landing of Diaz. The road then swings right into Bismarck Street, with the post office on the left and old railway station on the right. Bismarck is the main street and travelling down it you will find the Diamond Reef Casino on the left, followed by the extremely knowledgeable and helpful Lüderitz Safaris and Tours, then the Standard Bank with ATM. On the right-hand side is the attractive old Deutsche Bank building (now a Nedbank with an ATM), then a Link Pharmacy and First National Bank (also with ATM and bureau de change).

Out and about in Lüderitz

The architecture of the fine old German buildings in Lüderitz dates from the 10-year boom period between 1905 and 1915 and can best be appreciated on a leisurely walk around this compact little town. Start from the bottom end of Bismarck and take note of the Deutsche Afrikabank (now Nedbank) on your left, followed by the old Station Building. Swing left into Bay Road to look in at the old Kegelbahn next door to Kapps Hotel. The men of the town still regularly play a game of skittles here over a drink or two. Higher up, also on the right, is the Kapps Konzert- en Ballsaal – now housing an electrical business. The old stage and balcony are still to be seen, and one can imagine the high times that were had here in the past. Cut across town and climb the hill up to Goerke House in Diamantberg Street. Finely furnished in period style, it's open during the week 14h00–16h00 and on weekends 16h00–17h00. A little higher up the hill, in Kirchweg, is the impressive Felsenkirche. This church has beautiful stained-glass windows – the altar window was donated by Kaiser Wilhelm II – which are best photographed in the late afternoon. Open daily 16h00–17h00. On your walk back down into town, stroll past Kreplin House and the row of quaint, restored cottages in Berg Street. The Lüderitz Museum is situated in Diaz Street at the intersection with Nachtigall. Interesting old photographs and artefacts depict the history and flora of the region. Open 15h30–17h00 Monday–Friday. Entrance is N$10.

An interesting excursion, if you have the time and the vehicle, is a drive around the peninsula west of Lüderitz. The gravel road is signposted to Diaz Point (22 kilometres) and heads south out of town, past the oyster farm to the southern tip of the lagoon (good birdwatching). The tracks across the peninsula are a little confusing, but you can't really get lost. First swing north to Sturmvogelbucht, where the rusty remains of storage tanks remind us of the old whaling station based here. The folks from the Bay View Hotel in Lüderitz have opened a coffee shop (also selling oysters and wine!), self-catering bungalows and a campsite here. Another couple of kilometres west brings you to rocky and exposed Diaz Point. A replica of the original cross that Bartholomeu Diaz planted in 1487 has been erected here. Heading down the coast you should spot colonies of seals, African (jackass) penguins and cormorants. The Sperrgebiet starts at Grosse Bucht, so here the road turns inland again and takes you back past the lagoon to Lüderitz town. You will need a couple of hours to do this excursion and probably need warm clothes too, as it can get very cold and windy out on the peninsula.

A closer alternative is a drive out to Agate Beach, north of town. Follow the signs from the intersection of Hafen and Industry roads, which will take you out past the sewerage works. There are braai areas and toilets for day-trippers.

Kolmanskop and beyond

You can't stop at Lüderitz without visiting the ghost town of **Kolmanskop**, situated about 10 kilometres inland from Lüderitz on the B4, don't miss out! Very interesting and informative guided tours in English and German are conducted around this old diamond-mining town Mondays–Saturdays at 09h30 and 11h00 and Sundays at 10h00. Purchase tickets (N$45 per person) beforehand at Lüderitz Safaris and Tours in Bismarck Street.

When diamonds were first discovered here in 1908 they could be scooped up off the ground, so rich was the area. Fabulous fortunes were made and Kolmanskop developed into one of the most modern and comfortable towns in southern Africa. The miners enjoyed the grandest houses, delicious fresh food and drink, sporting facilities and exotic entertainment.

Elizabeth Bay is another ghost town 40 kilometres south of Lüderitz and can be visited on a half-day tour that also includes Kolmanskop (N$400 a person). To really experience the harsh environment and desolation of this coast, take the full day tour to **Pomona** and **Bogenfels**. Starting at 09h00, you travel 100 kilometres south, passing old mining operations along the way. The famous Bogenfels Arch is visited and lunch is taken at the quaint old town of Pomona (tour cost N$950). Bookings for both these tours can be made through Lüderitz Safaris and Tours.

The Coastway Trail is an exciting new route between Lüderitz and Walvis Bay. This guided six-day trail follows the coastline of the Namib-Naukluft Park through the high dunes of the old Sperrgebiet – a tough 4x4 challenge in the tracks of the old diamond diggers and other fortune hunters. Contact Lewis Druker of Coastway Tours on tel: 063-202-002, fax: 063-202-003, e-mail: lewiscwt@iway.na, website: www.coastways.com.na.

Overnight in Lüderitz

In Lüderitz you are spoilt for choice. The posh address is **The Lüderitz Nest Hotel** at Ostend beach (to get there follow the signs out left past the old power station). This is a beautifully positioned hotel on the rocks overlooking the bay, with a pool and 70 en-suite rooms with air-con, TV, phone and balconies with stunning sea views. Their Penguin Restaurant is also the best place to enjoy fresh oysters and the other seafood this coast has to offer. Hotel rates are N$630 a person sharing. For bookings, tel: 063-204-000, fax 063-204-001, e-mail: reservations@nesthotel.com, website: www.nesthotel.com.

Another smart option is the **Seaview Hotel Zum Sperrgebiet**. More centrally situated at the corner of Woermann and Stettiner streets, it too has a pool, good views of the bay and well-appointed rooms at N$704 single and N$1 123 double (B&B). Tel: 063-203-411, fax: 063-203-414, e-mail: info@proteahotels.com, website: www.proteahotels.com.

There are two other hotels in the lower price bracket, but both are still clean and comfortable. **The Bay View Hotel**, centrally located on Diaz Street, doesn't look like much from the outside, but has neat rooms around a central courtyard and pool. Singles cost N$440 and doubles N$740, including breakfast. For details, tel: 063-202-288, fax: 063-202-402, e-mail: bayview@namibnet.com, website: www.luderitzhotels.com; the other is **Kapps Hotel** in Bay Road. An old historic establishment that has been renovated, the restaurant and bar can be a little noisy, but is good value at N$350 single and N$570 double. For more info, tel: 063-202-345, fax: 063-203-555, e-mail: pmk@mweb.com.na.

But, Lüderitz also has some very good guesthouses and B&Bs. **Hansa Haus** must have the best views from the top floor of this old German-styled residence at the end of Mabel Street. There are four rooms, a lounge with TV and a communal kitchen. Rates are N$200 single and N$375 double. For further information, tel: 063-203-581, fax: 063-283-071, e-mail: badgers@iafrica.com.na.

The place that caught my fancy – for its impeccable old-world charm, original art

The old mining town of Kolmanskop has been reclaimed by the desert.

on the walls and Bauhaus furniture – was **Krabbenhoeft und Lampe**. Upstairs, over a furniture store in upper Bismarck Street, there is a huge three-bedroomed flat, a smaller one-bedroomed flat and single rooms. All accommodation is equipped for self-catering and costs N$145 for the single rooms, N$300 single and N$400 double in a flat, and N$832 for six people in the largest flat. Contact the manager on tel: 063-202-674, fax: 063-202-549, e-mail: info@klguesthouse.com, website: www.klguesthouse.com.

Another very comfortable guesthouse is the beautifully decorated and maintained **Haus Sandrose** at 15 Bismarck. Situated around a secluded garden courtyard behind the Sandrose gift shop, these self-contained flatlets are well equipped and good value at N$470 single and N$670 double. For details, tel: 063-202-630, fax: 063-202-365, e-mail: sandrose@ldz.namib.com.

The **Backpackers' Lodge** is at 7 Schinz Street and has all the amenities that a good backpackers' should have. Dorm beds cost N$145, double rooms N$365 and large rooms that sleep five people N$495. For more info, tel/fax: 063-202-000. Camping is out across the causeway on **Shark Island** (N$50 per site plus N$50 per person). With sites nestled between the rocky outcrops and views of the bay and harbour, it can be an idyllic spot, but if the wind blows, you'll be flattened! Book through Namibia Wildlife Resorts (NWR) – tel: 061-285-7200, fax: 061-224-900, e-mail: reservations@nwr.com.na, website: www.nwr.com.na – or, if it's out of season, arrive and pay at the gate. The old lighthouse on the island is an interesting accommodation option. It has four beds in two rooms and costs N$1 800 for the whole lighthouse for a night (just don't turn out the light!). It and three other bungalows on the island are available through NWR. If you really want to stay away from it all, head out to Diaz Point to the campsite and bungalows there. Camping costs N$75 per stand plus N$35 per person and bungalows are N$175 per person. Book and pay through the folks at the Bay View Hotel, in town. Website: www.diazpoint.com.

Eating out in Lüderitz

The **Penguin Restaurant** and bar at the Lüderitz Nest Hotel have wonderful seafood and other local dishes. **The Bogenfels Restaurant** in Bay Road is popular. There is a pool table and large-screen TV, while the menu offers oysters, lobster and steak. The sports bar in **Kapps Hotel** has a fancy, loud music system and is popular with a younger crowd – at least the grill room is separate – but for the best music, sometimes live, head for **Barrels** in Berg Street where the menu is short and simple but tasty and the atmosphere cosy. **Ritzi's** is down at the new Waterfront development and serves good seafood and steaks. For the best coffee and cake in town, as well as hearty lunches, you can't beat the **Diaz Coffee Shop** at the intersection of Bismarck and Nachtigall. It's also a good spot for gifts and curios. There is also a coffee shop out at Diaz Point that sells coffee, cake, beer, oysters and wine – well worth the drive. For fish and chips and late-night shopping head to **Beira Mar** general dealer at the intersection of Tal and Industry streets.

Shopping and useful services

The much-vaunted Waterfront development, down at the harbour, is a bit of a disappointment, but worth visiting to eat at Ritzi's. Also in the complex is the members-only Yacht Club.

Across the road in the new shopping mall, is OK Grocers, which stocks everything – food, booze, bakery and butchery. Behind OK's is the CDC Coin Laundry, which offers washing, tumble drying and ironing. The new railway station behind OK's will hopefully one day ferry visitors out to Kolmanskop. (The line is being rebuilt all the way through to Aus, to carry supplies to and zinc from the Skorpion Mine at Rosh Pinah.)

Around the corner in Bahnhof Street is a FedEx agency, Caltex garage, the large Spar supermarket and a bottle store. There is another laundry, Flowers, in Moltke Street.

For mechanical repairs, I would try **Schwab Motors**, tel: 063 203-659, in Lessing Street (behind Bogenfels Restaurant), or **M&Z Commercial Vehicles**, tel: 061-203-965, in Bahnhof Street. For tyres, there is **Trentyre**, tel: 063-202-137, in Bay Road, and with **Cymot**, tel: 063-203-855, at 4 Nachtigall Street in town, you will always be able to get motor spares and accessories, but be aware that this branch does not stock much camping gear.

Gas cylinders can be refilled at **Pupkewitz Megabuild** at the bottom of Bismarck Street, tel: 063-202-036. Car-hire companies in Lüderitz include **Avis**, tel: 063-203-968; **Budget**, tel: 063-202-777; and Imperial, tel: 063-202-728.

An internet service is available at Extreme Communications at the Waterfront, as well as the Teleshop at the post office, which also offers a courier service. Other courier services include **FedEx**, tel: 063-207-000, on Hafen Street, and **DHL**, tel: 063-203-241, on Insel Street.

Small, run-down taxis cruise the streets, but play it safe by getting your hotel to organise one. For daily public transport to Keetmanshoop, contact **Extreme Liner**, tel: 063-204-256, at Extreme Communications at the Waterfront. **Lüderitz Safaris and Tours**, in Bismarck Street, are the best people to contact for tours and a wide variety of tourist information – Marion has been in Lüderitz all her life and is friendly and helpful. She handles bookings for the Intercape bus lines and all desert tours, helps to find you accommodation and also has a shop with a wide selection of books on Namibia and related subjects, curios, clothing, maps and photographic film. Contact her on tel: 063-202-719, fax: 063-202-863, e-mail: ludsaf@africaonline.com.na, website: africa-adventure.org/l/luderitz.com.

Namibia Wildlife Resorts has an office in Schinz Street and can be contacted on tel: 063-202-752 to make bookings for the Shark Island campsite or any other of their camps and resorts around Namibia. The hospital and ambulance service, tel: 063-202-446, is in Tal Street, and there is a private doctor's surgery next to the old power station in Diaz Street. Finally, kitesurfing is very popular in Walvis with annual competitions and world records claimed. Contact Jeff Marting at jeff@kw-africa.com. And if you're in town over the Easter weekend, enjoy the Crayfish Festival!

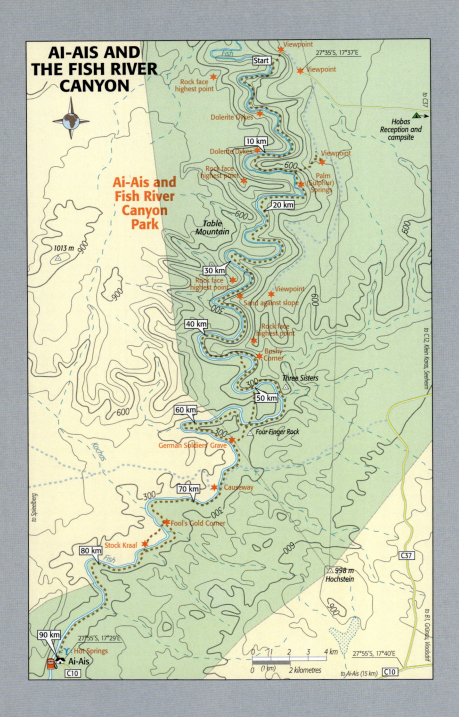

Ai-Ais and the Fish River Canyon 14

The Ai-Ais and Fish River Canyon conservation area forms an interesting combined tourist destination, and if you are driving up from the south, it will probably be your introduction to Namibia. Linked now with South Africa's Richtersveld to form the 6 000-square-kilometre Ai-Ais Richtersveld Transfrontier Park, the area offers stunning views, canoeing, hiking or just lazing around the hot springs.

The C10 winds down to the hot springs at A-A.s.

The Fish River Canyon is an impressive sight at any time of the day.

A further 10 kilometres brings you to the canyon edge and one of the most spectacular sights you'll see in your life. Early-morning photography is best and there are braai spots and toilets, so this is a good place to absorb the grandeur of Africa's second largest canyon.

Out and about

The **Cañon Mountain Lodge** is the luxury option in this area. On the C37, 7 kilometres south of the road down to Hobas Camp and the viewpoint, is the turn-off (S27°40.033 E17°45.728) to Cañon Mountain Lodge. The thatched chalets are built of local stone and blend in so well that they seem part of the rocky hills. The old farmhouse has been tastefully restored and extended and, whether you are spending a few days here or have just dropped in for lunch and a cold beer, you feel right at home. The lodge makes its own cheese, cures its own meats and grows fresh salads, so the food is excellent. Late-afternoon game drives show off the natural beauty of the farm and a stop to watch the sunset while sipping an ice-cold G&T will have you enquiring about property prices in the area. Accommodation in the chalets – on a B&B basis – costs N$1 120 single, N$1 790 double and dinner is N$225.

A cheaper, but still very pleasant option is the **Cañon Roadhouse** (a member of the Gondwana Collection with Cañon Lodge). About 16 kilometres north of Hobas on the C37, this compact roadside lodge oozes character and has nine rooms centred around a cool courtyard. The bar must be one of the best decorated in Nam, overflowing with old car memorabilia. Rooms cost N$695 per single and N$1 110 double (including breakfast), and camping is available at N$85 a person. They also serve lunches and, most importantly, sell fuel (petrol and diesel). For bookings, tel: 061-230-066, fax: 061-251-863, e-mail: info@gondwana-desert-collection.com, website: www.gondwana-desert-collection.com.

The Namib-Nakluft 15

The region covered in this chapter is one of the most popular in the whole of Namibia – easily accessible, a good infrastructure and lots of interesting things to see and do. From the abundance of the cold, nutrient-rich Atlantic Ocean, across red dunes of the Namib and up steep passes of the Khomas Hochland onto the central plateau, these are the layers that make Namibia such a fascinating country.

The Namib is a pure, still wilderness

Bordered as it is by the Atlantic Ocean in the west, the B2 highway in the north, B1 in the east and B4 down south, almost all the roads in this section of the country are gravel. But they are better than the tarred roads of many other countries, as this is where the art of road grading was perfected. Make sure you have an up-to-date map, especially as many of the roads' numbers were changed a few years ago.

En route to the Namib-Naukluft

If you are continuing a trip that started in the south and took in Ai-Ais, Fish River and Lüderitz, you will probably find yourself on the C13 heading north from Aus. A welcome stop along this road of open spaces is Helmeringhausen. There is an Engen fuel station and one of those cavernous village general dealers that sells everything. From hot pies, ice cream, bread and booze to hardware, spares and fertiliser, they stock it. Across the road are the pretty gardens and coffee shop of the **Helmeringhausen Hotel**, tel/fax: 063-283-307, where you can enjoy light meals of bratwurst and apple pie. Bed and breakfast will cost you N$500 per person (single) and N$380 per person (double), and camping is N$160 for a site. Keep an eye open for the collection of interesting old farm implements, tel/fax: 063-283-307, e-mail: info@helmeringhausen.com, website: www.helmeringhausen.com.

From here you have the choice of taking the C27 west towards Sesriem (turn left about 4 kilometres before Helmeringhausen) or straight ahead on the C14. The C14 takes you north for 59 kilometres to the turn-off left (S25°23.832 E16°47.631) to **Duwisib Castle**. Follow the signposts along the D831 to reach the unlikely sight of this fortress in the veld. Built by ex-*Schutztruppe* captain Von Wolf and his rich American wife in 1909, no expense was spared. Italian stonemasons and German carpenters created a solid, but comfortable, home for the couple's fine furniture and lifestyle. But, the First World War intervened and the captain was killed on the battlefields of Europe and his wife returned to the United States, never to set foot in Africa again. The castle is now state property and is maintained as a museum (entrance fee N$50 pp) but also offers great campsites (N$100 per site plus N$50 per person). Booking is through Namibia Wildlife Resorts. From Duwisib, keep heading west until you meet the C27, which will carry you through to Sesriem.

West of Maltahöhe, the road forks right via the C14 to the Naukluft mountains and Solitaire, or left via the C19 to Sesriem and Sossusvlei. This entire area is worth exploring, and I suggest we first head for Sesriem (S24°29.204 E15°48.068).

Sesriem

The office at Sesriem sells permits to visit Sossusvlei and **Sesriem Canyon** and accepts payment for the campsites. There is also a service station for fuel and tyres, as well as a small, poorly stocked shop. Pay your entrance fees (N$60 per person plus N$10 a car) and head first for the nearby Sesriem Canyon. Hike down the gully to find yourself in a deep, narrow gorge with birds nesting in the cliffs overhead. Named for the six leather thongs that had to be tied together to reach down into this canyon, Sesriem was always a dependable source of water in this dry country.

Sossusvlei

Back at the office, head through the gates (open from sunrise to sunset) into the park and enter the red-dune landscape of Sossusvlei. A tarred road follows the dry bed of the Tsauchab River for 60 kilometres to the first parking area. Park here if you are not driving a 4x4 – another 5 kilometres of deep, soft sand lies ahead. You have three options: hike, hitch a ride with a passing 4x4 driver, or pay N$100 per person to the driver of a waiting Land Rover taxi to take you to the vlei.

The next parking area is for Dead Vlei, the photographers' favourite. Park and follow the signs over the dunes to this flat white pan dotted with the skeletons of dessicated trees. A kilometre further brings you to **Sossusvlei**. This is where the Tsauchab River gives up trying to

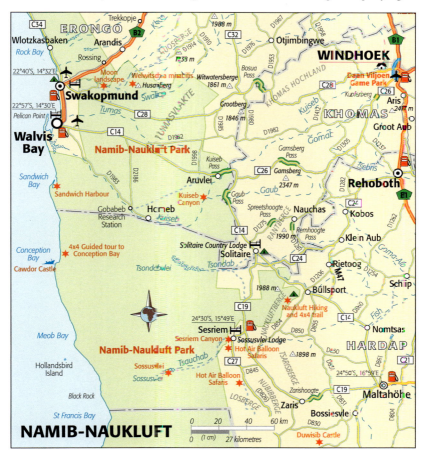

make it to the coast. Huge dunes block its path to form a pan, usually white and dry. A lucky few have seen the vlei filled with water after scarce rain, when it becomes a haven for water birds and buck, at the same time the usually barren, red dunes are covered with grass waving in the breeze.

On the way back, you might still have the energy and inclination to climb some of the high dunes. Dune 45 (about 45 kilometres from the gate) is one of the highest, and Elim Dune (close to the gate) is most photographed, as the sunset can be caught before making it back to camp before dark.

The only accommodation in the area around the park office is camping. Well-shaded sites look inviting, but there is no grass and it can be unpleasant if the wind blows. If the campsites are all full (and they often are), there is an overflow area that is rundown and miserable. Booking is through NWR and costs N$300 per site plus N$150 per person.

Overnight in the Sesriem/Sossusvlei area

Just outside the gate is one of the best and most up-market lodges in the area, **Sossusvlei Lodge**. Built in Bedouin style, with canvas shade cloth and adobe plaster walls, it creates a feeling of camping in the desert, but with five-star luxury back-up. The lodge's adventure centre can organise guided tours to both Sesriem and Sossusvlei, nature drives, scenic flights and awesome balloon flights over the dunes. Accommodation comprises 45 separate en-suite bedrooms under canvas and costs N$1 532 single and N$2 040 double, with dinner an additional N$250. They also have a new self-catering camp situated 4 kilometres away, where singles cost N$585 and doubles N$720. Contact the lodge on tel: 063-693-223, fax: 063-693-231, e-mail: adventure@sossusvleilodge.com, website: www.sossusvleilodge.com.

Heading north on the C19 you will come across **Solitaire Guest Farm,** best known for its nature walks, sunset drives,

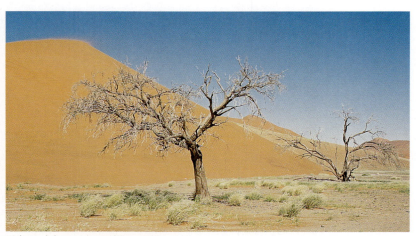

High sand dunes surround Sossusvlei.

a swimming pool and farm cooking in the spectacular Namib Desert. Bed and breakfast in en-suite rooms costs N$430 per person and camping N$70. For more information, tel: 062-682-033, fax: 062-682-034, e-mail solgf@solitaireguestfarm.com, website: www.solitaireguestfarm.com.

The nearby **Weltevrede Guest Farm** is similar in character and has en-suite bungalows for N$490 per person (DB&B) and camping for N$60. For details, tel: 063-683-073, fax: 063-683-074 e-mail: aswarts@mweb.com.na, website: www.weltevredeguestfarm.com.

Solitaire

At the junction of the C19 and the C14 is Solitaire. Not quite a village, it boasts a service station for fuel and minor repairs, a general dealership offering light meals, a campsite, and a 25-roomed lodge. There is a Wild West feel to the place, but it is a welcome oasis – your car gulps the fuel, your passengers gobble up Moose's famous apple pie, the campsites are shady and the **Solitaire Country Lodge** is a comfortable stopover for a couple of days. Camping costs N$65 per person, dinner N$160 and the spacious en-suite rooms are N$460 single and N$640 double B&B. Part of the Namibia Country Lodges collection, they can be contacted on tel: 061-347-750, fax 061-256-598, e-mail: solitaire@nc.com.na, website: www.namibialodges.com.

The annual **Desert Festival** takes place here (check dates with Solitaire Country Lodge) when about 2 000 people jam into little Solitaire for a drink-up with Dozi and a bunch of other live bands. An area is set aside for stalls selling all things Namibian and the campsite spills out into the desert. The hills are alive with the sound of quadbikes and the 4x4 trails are churned to a pulp by hundreds of *manne*. Not for the faint-hearted!

Be careful when exiting Solitaire – make sure you get onto the road you want. An immediate right takes you south on the C19 past Sesriem, but to get onto the C14, first turn left and then travel a couple of hundred metres to reach this junction. Left takes you north to Walvis Bay and right will take you south to Maltahöhe, via the beautiful Naukluft mountains. This road (C14) runs up a valley towards the stony crags and peaks of this rugged massif, refuge of Hartmann's mountain zebra, smaller antelope, leopard and a wide variety of birds. About 55 kilometres from Solitaire, you will reach the well-established **Büllsport Guest Farm**. Comfortable en-suite accommodation and wholesome cuisine make this the preferred option when visiting the Naukluft region. They offer horse riding and hiking and easy access to the park. Dinner, bed and breakfast cost N$800 a person. Contact them on tel: 063-693-371, fax: 063-693-372, e-mail: info@buellsport.com, website: www.buellsport.com.

On to the Namib-Naukluft

Turn off the C14 opposite Büllsport onto the D854 (S24°09.213 E16°21.895) and drive 9 kilometres to the Naukluft Park gate (S24°13.565 E16°20.248). Wind up through the hills for another 12 kilometres to the office, where you can book and pay for camping and hiking in this Shangri-la wilderness. Further up the valley you will pass the Hikers' Haven house, the start and end of the Naukluft Hiking Trail. Across a stream at the end of the track is one of the best-situated camps in Namibia (N$100 per site plus N$50 per person). Wedged into a narrow kloof of folded mountains, terraced sites line the gurgling stream. There is a simple stone ablution block, shade trees, but no electricity and no caravans – just good old-fashioned fellow campers who hike during the day and sit around a fire at night. Bliss!

Some of the most exciting and challenging hiking can be done here. The **Olive Trail** is a 10-kilometre, four-hour hike that involves a fairly steep climb up onto the plateau and back, while the **Waterkloof Trail** is longer (seven hours) and follows a gorge with rock pools to an impressive viewing site and back via the Naukluft River. Both trails start and end at the campsite. The main **Naukluft Hiking Trail** is 120 kilometres long and best completed in eight days. Overnight accommodation is in stone shelters, where water is provided, but no fires are permitted, so you will need a camp stove. This is a very tough trail and must be hiked in groups of between three and 12 people. Due to the extreme heat in summer, it is only open from March to October. The trail costs a mere N$100 per person to hike. For more details and bookings, contact Namibia Wildlife Resorts (see page 42).

Other accommodation in the area includes the **Tsauchab River Camp** situated at the point where the D850 turns off the D854. It offers camping at private, isolated sites along the dry riverbed at N$100 per site plus N$70 per adult, and rustic chalets on a B&B basis for N$530 per person sharing. There are also hiking trails, 4x4 routes and a very impressive bird list. You can contact the camp, tel/fax: 063-683-256, e-mail: tsauchab@iafrica.com.na, website: www.natron.net/tsauchab/.

A very attractive laid-back option in this area of strenuous hiking and horse-riding, is to stay at the **Neuras Wine Estate** (yes, wine in this desert!). About 10 kilometres down the D850 from the D854 are the compact vineyards of Allan and Silvia Walkden-Davis. With less than one hectare under vines, they produce fewer than 1 000 bottles of Shiraz and Merlot. A little stone cellar and a couple of self-catering cottages nestle snugly under palm and thorn trees where rosy-faced lovebirds play. Rates are reasonable at N$288 for a single and N$495 a double. Contact Allan and Silvia on tel/fax: 063-293-417, e-mail: neuras@mweb.com.na.

> **Basie from Solitaire says** that the corners on Remhoogte Pass are so sharp that if you look in your rear-view mirror, *'jy kan jou eie briekligte sien'* (you can see your own brake lights)!

If you want to complete an interesting circular drive around the main sights of this area, continue on down the D854 to where it meets the C19, turn right and you will pass Sesriem and Sossusvlei on your way back to Solitaire. But before we continue our journey to Walvis Bay and Swakopmund, I'd like to introduce you to an interesting excursion that includes a couple of exciting mountain passes and can be done in a day.

Turn off the C14 onto the C24 about 14 kilometres south of Solitaire to struggle up the short and sharp Remhoogte Pass. After 42 kilometres, turn left onto the D1261 (S23°51.306 E16°22.646) to cut across to Spreetshoogte (the C24 carries on to Rehoboth to join the main B1 highway to Windhoek). We are now up on the central plateau and the empty plains of the Namib have given way to rocky koppies covered with thorn trees.

The bird life is prolific along here and at **Guisis Farm** (16 kilometres from the intersection at S23°45.165 E16°17.660) I spotted 35 species in about 90 minutes. Guisis is also a hunting farm and offers camping and picnic sites alongside a large dam. For details, contact Mr van der Merwe on tel: 063-572-001.

Nauchas lies 29 kilometres from the C24 – turn left here to join the D1275, which takes you down the spectacular Spreetshoogte Pass (a right turn here would put you on the road to Windhoek). There is a police station at Nauchas, but the café and bungalows that were there are now closed. Between Nauchas and the top of the pass is the very comfortable, attractive and well-run **Namibgrens Guest Farm**. It has been in the Rabie family for generations and they offer an eco-experience of hiking, camping, 4x4 trails, as well as en-suite accommodation and bar and restaurant in the main farmhouse. B&B costs N$450 per person sharing. Contact Namibgrens on tel/fax: 061-222-893, e-mail: rabie@namibnet.com, website: www.namibgrens.com.

The precipitous **Spreetshoogte Pass**

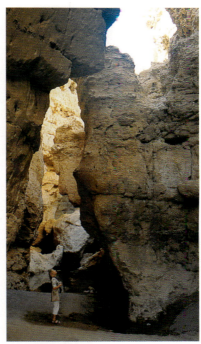

It's cool and dark in the narrow Sesriem Canyon.

follows a rugged gravel road that is paved on the tight, steep corners, but is definitely not for caravans or trailers. Viewpoints at the top offer the opportunity to stop for a picnic while drinking in the beauty and atmosphere of one of Africa's great mountain routes. Halfway down (at S23°39.544 E16°09.882) is a new campsite, which takes full advantage of the views. It is operated by the **Spreetshoogte Guestfarm** at the bottom of the pass, which also offers basic en-suite rooms in the farmhouse. Rates are N$90 per person for camping, and N$460 for dinner, bed and breakfast. For further information, tel/fax: 062-572-010, e-mail: spreetshoogte@iway.na, website: www.natron.net/tour/spreetshoogte.

The sun sets over the Namib from the Rostock Ritz.

Back to Windhoek

The D1275 reaches the C14 about 9 kilometres north of Solitaire to continue our trip to Walvis Bay. Now we are back among the dunes of the Namib, and 30 kilometres from Solitaire we reach the turn-off to the **Rostock Ritz**. Set up on a ridge away from the road, this lodge has unique stone-built luxury accommodation that blends in with the rocky hilltops. The cool, cavern-like interior of the main building offers the comfort of an up-market bar and restaurant, while the deck outside is the place to be for 180° sunset views. During full moon (and most other times) mountain zebra can be observed as they graze on the vast plains below. Rates start from N$975 per person (B&B). For details, tel: 061-257-467, fax: 061-257-469, e-mail: info@rostock-ritz-desert-lodge.com, website: www.rostock-ritz-desert-lodge.com.

The last place of interest before we reach Walvis is the Kuiseb River, which is crossed after descending the Kuiseb Pass. There is a picnic spot at the bridge and camping is permitted (if you have a permit from NWR – see page 42 or contact the offices in Swakopmund).

For an interesting alternative to driving on the C14, take the third turn-off to the left (S23°18.680 E15°34.428) after the bridge signposted to Zebra Pan, Homeb, Mirabib and Gobabeb. Although a permit is required, it is unlikely that you will even see anyone, let alone be asked for a permit – this is a very isolated road. After 11 kilometres, keep left to make your way to Zebra Pan and Homeb and around Zebra Pan you might see some ostrich, gemsbok and springbok. After another 63 kilometres the road forks (at S23°36.534 E15°10.996) – take the left again down to Homeb, a settlement of Topnaar Namas in the dry riverbed of the Kuiseb. There is also an unserviced campsite, but the area is very sandy and 4x4 is recommended. Permits are available from and payments made through NWR. Retrace the 4 kilometres back up to the fork and swing west towards Gobabeb. Keep left at the next fork to reach the river at the government research station at Gobabeb. With the river on your left, keep heading northwest. You are now on the D1983, which runs parallel to the Kuiseb, until you reach a T-junction, signposted right to Walvis. This brings you back to the C14 just before the town of Walvis Bay.

Walvis Bay 16

The history of Walvis Bay is an interesting mix of colonial squabbles. Bartholomeu Diaz first dropped anchor in 1437, but despite the wonderful protection that the bay afforded the ships in his fleet, there was no fresh water. Although the Portuguese showed no further interest in this coast, they did tell others of the abundant fish, seals and whales spotted in the area. This information brought British and American fishing fleets, but no attempt was made to establish a permanent settlement until 1793, when the Dutch showed an interest and dispatched a ship from the Cape to annex the land around Walvis Bay. Two years later the British occupied the Cape and so inherited Walvis.

A corner of Sandwich Harbour to the south of Walvis Bay.

Traders and missionaries slowly moved in and in 1878 Britain formally annexed a 750-square-kilometre enclave around the bay – the hinterland was deemed to be of little value. But the Germans had already colonised the interior and were developing nearby Swakopmund as their main harbour, which left Walvis out in the cold – that is, until the start of the First World War, when South Africa occupied German South West Africa and concentrated on the better, safer harbour of Walvis. South Africa continued to rule South West Africa until Namibia's independence in 1990, but only handed over Walvis Bay four years later.

Introducing Walvis Bay

Walvis has traditionally been the poor, working-class cousin of Swakopmund, but has recently blossomed into the preferred adventure tourism destination along this part of the coast. Windsurfing, kayaking, fishing, 4x4-ing, quadbiking, birding and seal-watching – the tourists come for all these exciting activities. Accommodation has been increased and upgraded, and the commercial fortunes of the town have also been boosted by the establishment of an Export Processing Zone, as well as the building of the Trans-Kalahari and Trans-Caprivi highways, which link the port with Nam's neighbours to the east.

Whether you arrive from the east via Kuiseb Canyon, or the north via Swakopmund, you will enter Walvis Bay at Diaz Circle. Leaving the circle west down 18th Road will bring you into the town centre and the harbour beyond. South down Union Street bypasses the town and ends at the lagoon. The town is laid out on a grid with numbered streets (many now renamed after the current crop of politicians) and roads (west to east), so it should be easy to find your way around.

Walvis Bay has none of the quaint old houses and shops that Swakopmund has, but it does have the lagoon and Sandwich Harbour. The **Walvis Bay Lagoon** is on the southern outskirts of town and is a Unesco Ramsar site, protected for its marine and bird life. All the best homes and guesthouses are out this way, and it's also where the windsurfing, kitesurfing and kayaking take place. There's obviously enough room for everybody as the flamingoes and pelicans still flock there in their thousands.

Sandwich Harbour is more difficult to reach and you will definitely need a 4x4. Even if you have your own, it is better to go with a tour operator as it is easy to get stuck or lost along the way. To reach **Sandwich Harbour**, first buy permits at the MET in Heinrich Baumann Street, also available at some local service stations, before driving south down the Esplanade along the lagoon to the salt works. Turn left here and follow the tracks through the dunes until you reach a small freshwater lagoon between the high dunes and the rough surf. The main part of the lagoon, where ships could enter before it silted up, lies another 6 kilometres further on, but it is off limits in the Sperrgebiet.

Another interesting excursion down this way, especially if you are a keen birder or fisherman, is to **Paaltjies**. Turn right at the salt works and wind your way between the pans to the seashore,

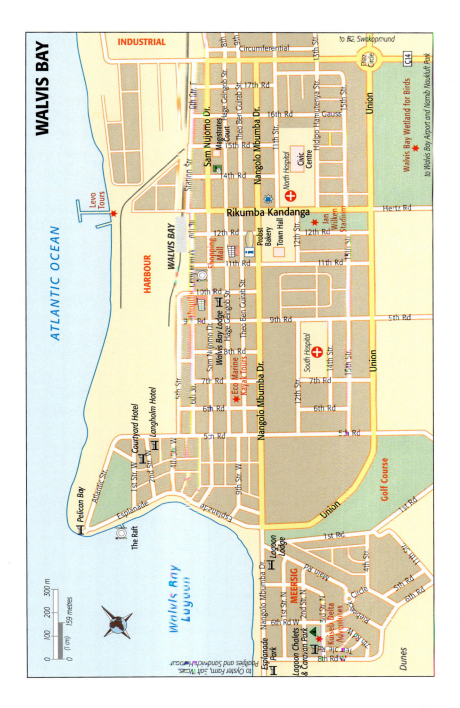

observing a good variety of aquatic birds along the way. The Paaltjies are fishing spots along the beach and are numbered one, two, three and four (poles planted in the sand). Cormorants can be seen in their hundreds, as well as other marine birds. A 4x4 is essential for any driving beyond the salt works and a thorough wash is recommended afterwards to get rid of the sand and salt.

For more birdwatching, visit the town's sewerage works. Turn east into 13th Road off Union Street, pass the dairy and riding stables on your right, and explore the reeds and ponds on the left. The tracks are sandy, so beware of getting stuck.

A wind- and kitesurfing competition is held at the lagoon every year around October. World records are established, when speeds of up to 80 kph are maintained over one nautical mile. Contact Jeff Marting at jeff@kw-africa.com or speak to the folks at Walvis Bay Kite and Windsurfing Centre, situated on the Esplanade. They are very knowledgable, hire out equipment and give lessons.

Overnight in Walvis

The grandest address in Walvis is the new **Pelican Bay Hotel** at the point of the entrance to the lagoon, where the old yacht club used to be. The well-equipped en-suite rooms all have beautiful sea views from their private balconies, and the hotel boasts one of the smartest restaurants and bars in Walvis. B&B rates are N$860 single and N$1 045 double. For reservations, tel: 061-213-231, fax: 061-246-660, e-mail: info@proteahotels.com, website: www.proteahotels.com.

The friendly, family-run **Langholm Hotel** is popular with all travellers, business or pleasure. Set in quiet gardens near the lagoon at Number 24, 2nd Street West, the accommodation is very comfortable and the parking secure. There are internet facilities and a cosy bar. B&B rates are from N$380 per person sharing. For details, tel: 064-209-230, fax: 064-209-430, e-mail: desk@langholmhotel.com, website: www.langholmhotel.com.

Lagoon Lodge faces the lagoon in the Esplanade. A tastefully converted luxury home, it offers eight uniquely decorated rooms with lagoon views, and meals prepared (on request) by the French owners. B&B rates are N$804 single and N$1 180 double. Contact the lodge on tel: 064-200-850, fax: 064-200-851, e-mail: french@lagoonlodge.com.na, website: www.lagoonlodge.com.na.

Free Air Guest House is situated on the northern edge of the lagoon at 56 Esplanade. Most rooms have great views and range in price from N$550 single to N$765 double, tel: 064-202-247, fax: 064-203-412, e-mail: res3@namibiawalvisbay-guesthouse.com, website: www.namibia-walvisbay-guesthouse.com.

Also in the lagoon area is the **Courtyard Hotel** at the corner of 2nd Street West and 3rd Road. A secure complex of rooms and suites (some self-catering), they charge N$490 single and N$540 double. Contact the hotel on tel: 064-213-600, fax: 064-213-620, e-mail: courtyrd@iafrica.com.na, website: www.thecourtyardhotel.com.

The most central accommodation in Walvis is the **Protea Hotel,** on the corner of Sam Nujoma Avenue and 10th Road. Each standard en-suite room is well equipped with air-con, DStv and free internet access. A single room costs N$730, a double N$860. For res, tel: 064-213-700, fax: 064-213-702, e-mail: info@proteahotels.com, website: www.proteahotels.com.

There are two chalet complexes in Walvis, each offering economic self-catering. At the southern end of the Esplanade, overlooking the lagoon, is **Esplanade Park**. Laid out like a small village, it offers 27 cottages, some with one bedroom and sleeping three (N$326 per unit), others sleeping five or two bedrooms (N$466). A spacious lounge/kitchen area comes fully equipped with stove, fridge, cutlery and crockery and there is also a braai, TV and lock-up garage. For bookings, tel: 064-206-145, fax: 064-215-510, e-mail: bfernandez@walvisbaycc.com.na, website: www.walvisbaycc.com.na.

Lagoon Chalets and Caravan Park also offers chalets and the only campsite in Walvis. Signposted off the southern end of the Esplanade, they can be found in 8th Road West. Offering similar accommodation to Esplanade Park, plus 24 caravan stands all within a secure compound, they charge N$300 for a double bungalow, N$400 for a four-sleeper and N$100 per site plus N$50 per person camping. For the lowdown, tel: 064-217-900, fax: 064-207-159, e-mail: lagchres@mweb.com.na.

Eating out in Walvis

The Raft has the most spectacular position for a restaurant – perched on pilings at the end of a jetty at the northern end of the lagoon. Watch the birds, enjoy the sunset, savour the delicious fish and meat dishes and linger for a night-cap in the bar – it's the sort of place you don't want to leave. For further details, tel: 064-204-877.

Crazy Mama's is an Italian pizza/pasta trattoria that also serves good steak (this is Namibia, remember!). Centrally situated in town on the corner of Sam Nujoma and 11th Road, they're popular, with limited seating, so book ahead by calling tel: 064-207-364. The best daytime venue for breakfast, coffee or lunch is the **Probst Bakery** on the corner of 9th Street and 12th Road. The service is pleasant and the food, with a German flavour, good. For further information and reservations, tel: 064-202-744.

There are a couple of pubs and restaurants in 6th Street between 10th and 11th roads. Lothar's Steak House serves a good eisbein, and next door is Champs Pub for a late-night session. A few blocks away, at 140 Theo-Ben Gurirab Street (9th Street), you will find the Hickory Creek Spur Steak Ranch serving up their good-value/good-food menu of steaks and salads. A new restaurant, Anchors, has opened in a picturesque spot at the waterfront, where the marine tour boats leave from.

Adventures in Walvis

For an exciting and fascinating four-hour quadbike tour into the dunes of the Kuiseb Delta, contact Fanie du Preez of Kuiseb Delta Adventures. He will personally guide you through the spectacular landscape of the Namib, explain the origins of the region and point out the flora and fauna, ancient Topnaar middens and petrified human and animal tracks. Fanie offers the same trip in a comfortable 4x4 vehicle, or can combine it with a trip down to Sandwich Harbour. Contact him on tel: 081-128-2580, tel/fax: 064-202-550, e-mail: fanie@kuisebonline.com, website: www.kuisebonline.com.

Levo Tours offers trips out into the bay, which are informative and very entertaining. Huge bull seals slip nimbly up onto the boat to be fed and photographed while cormorants and pelicans surround you. A visit is made to the seal colonies and lighthouse, and you might also see whales and turtles. The trip ends with a delicious spread of snacks, oysters and champagne – all-round good fun for the entire family. Contact Cathy at tel: 064-207-555, fax: 064-200-709, e-mail: bookings@levo-tours.com, website: www.levotours.com.

To view the abundant bird life on Walvis lagoon, contact Jeanne at Eco Marine Kayak Tours at 63 Theo-Ben Gurirab Street. She is very knowledgeable and has safe, seaworthy kayaks equipped with all the safety gear. Contact Jeanne on tel: 064-203-144, e-mail: jeannem@iafrica.com.na. And for birdwatching in the wetlands around Walvis and down to Sandwich Harbour by 4x4 contact Sandwich Harbour 4x4, tel: 064-207-663, fax: 064-207-593, e-mail: info@sandwich-harbour.com, website: www.sandwich-harbour.com.

I have mentioned the popularity of wind- and kitesurfing on the lagoon, which culminates in the International Speed Week around October. This event draws surfers from around the world, and is supported by the guys at Walvis Bay Kite and Windsurfing Centre, who also rent out equipment and give lessons. Find them on the Esplanade, opposite The Raft restaurant. Contact Andreas Hubner, tel: 081-373-9284, e-mail: jibemann. namibia@gmx.de.

Out and about in Walvis

Below is a list of the facilities that will make a stay enjoyable and hassle-free.

Banks All the major banks and ATMs are situated in Sam Nujoma Avenue.

Car hire Avis, Walvis Bay Airport, tel: 064-207-527;
Budget, Protea Hotel, tel: 064-204-128;
Imperial, 124 Sam Nujoma Avenue, tel: 064-207-391

Car washes A1 Car Wash, corner 10th Road and 6th Street, tel: 064-209-296

Couriers DHL, 132 6th Street, tel: 064-209-243;
Fedex, Schoemans Building, 12th Road, tel: 064-201-2021

Laundromats Washing Well, 122 Sam Nujoma Avenue, tel: 064-209-697

Motor repairs Novel Motor Co. (Ford, Land Rover, Mazda and Mitsubishi), 78 Circumferential Road, tel: 064-203-411;
M&Z Motors (Mercedes and Jeep), 130 6th Street East, tel: 064-203-792;
Pupkewitz Motors (Nissan), corner 18th Avenue and 11th Street, tel: 064-206-152; Indongo Motors (Toyota), 18th Road, tel: 064-203-561

Motor spares and outdoor gear
Cymot/Greensport, 136 Hage Geingob Street, tel: 064-202-241

Pharmacies Walvis Bay Pharmacy, 120 Sam Nujoma Avenue, tel: 064-202-117

Public transport Ekonolux, Theo-Ben Gurirab Street, tel: 064-205-935

Shopping Shoprite, corner Sam Nujoma and 10th Road; Pick 'n Pay and Woolworths, Seagulls Shopping Mall, Hage Geingob Street

Swakopmund 17

About 10 kilometres out of Walvis Bay on the B2 to Swakopmund is a parking area overlooking a wooden guano platform built in the sea beyond the breakers. Cormorants and pelicans can be observed there, especially at dusk, when they return from the feeding grounds to roost for the night. The stretch of coastline between Walvis Bay and Swakopmund is fast developing into an up-market residential and resort area.

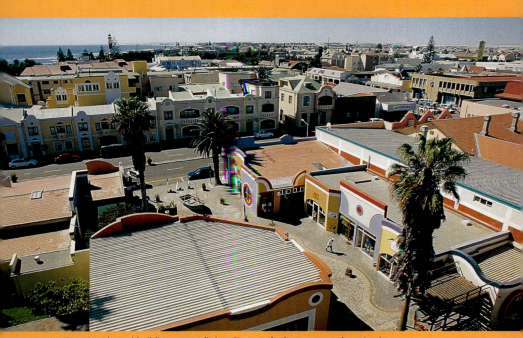

Vibrantly coloured buildings are a distinct feature of urban areas such as Swakop.

Long Beach lies midway between Walvis and Swakop and offers a couple of welcoming guesthouses as well as a caravan and chalet park. **Longbeach Lodge** is very smart and situated right on the beach. Their rates of N$650 single and N$800 double include breakfast and a sea view. Contact the lodge on tel: 064-218-820, fax: 064-218-855, e-mail: info@proteahotels.com.

The **Burning Shore** is the ocean-side lodge chosen by Brad Pitt and Angelina Jolie as home when they had their baby in 2006. Whether that's good or bad depends on how you like their movies, I suppose, but it is nevertheless very exclusive and offers personalised service for N$894 (single) in standard accommodation and N$2 430 (double) in luxury. For details, tel: 064-207-568, fax: 064-209-836, e-mail: info@proteahotels.com, website: www.proteahotels.com.

The **Dolphin Park Chalets** (just south of Long Beach) are part of a resort that offers swimming pools, lawns and a play park. Popular for family holidays, functions and day-trippers, the costs are N$303 for a double chalet and N$430 for a four-bedded chalet. For more information, tel: 064-204-343, fax: 064-215-510, e-mail: bfernandez@walvisbaycc.com.na, website: www.walvisbaycc.com.na.

The nearby **Long Beach Leisure Park** is similar, but also has 120 campsites with electricity points and windbreaks (but no shade). Sites cost N$94 plus N$28 per person, and the contact details are the same as for Dolphin Park. Closer to Swakop is the sprawling quadbike operation of **Dare Devil Adventures**, where you can arrange for sandboarding or quadbiking excursions into the dunes. For the lowdown, tel: 064-400-858, e-mail: daredev@iway.na.

Introducing Swakopmund

Swakopmund is the best-preserved German colonial town you are likely to see anywhere in the world and almost all the old architecture dates back to a short 25-year period before the First World War. After Germany proclaimed this southwest African territory a protectorate in 1884, they were forced to develop the port of Swakopmund as the English had already annexed Walvis Bay. Trading houses were established, banks followed and many fine residences were built for the prospering colonists. But all this changed when South Africa took over the running of South West Africa as a League of Nations-mandated territory after the First World War and Swakop languished as a local holiday resort. No one tore down the fine buildings to modernise the town – thank goodness!

You can approach Swakopmund from three directions: via Walvis Bay in the south on the B2, from Okahandja and Windhoek in the east (also on the B2), or from Henties Bay in the north via the C34 – all roads lead to Sam Nujoma Avenue, the main street of Swakop.

Out and about in Swakopmund

A good way to get to know Swakopmund (or any other town) is by taking a walking tour. Start by parking your car at the old iron jetty that juts out into the

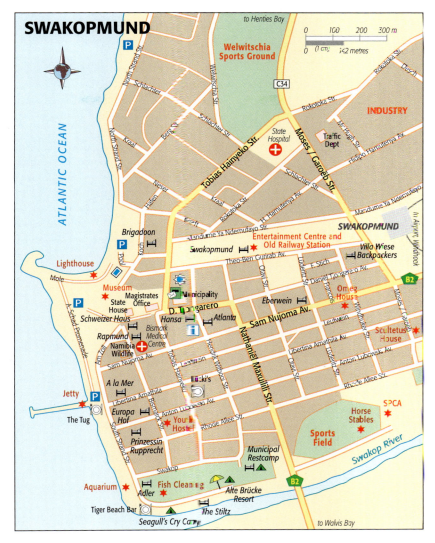

sea from the beach opposite Libertina Amathila Street. The jetty has a bit of a chequered history – planned for offloading cargo ships but incomplete at the outbreak of the First World War, it was made obsolete when Walvis Bay was subsequently used as the main harbour for South West Africa. It was then used as a public promenade and popular fishing spot until declared unsafe in 1985. Following some recent repairs the jetty is once again open to the public.

The **Tug Bar and Restaurant** situated at the jetty is a brilliant concept. The entire superstructure of a tugboat was

The Hohenzollern Building in Swakop is a grand and imposing structure.

transported from Walvis and plonked down on the beach to make the most perfect spot for wining, dining and watching the sunset. After the walking tour, you'll be thirsty, so you need to have something to aim for.

Cross the road (Strand Street) and head right to turn up Anton Lubowski Avenue. The first intersection, with Bismarck Street, is an interesting one. On the southwest corner is the historic **Hotel Prinzessin Rupprecht**. Built in 1902 as a military hospital, it became a guesthouse in 1914, but also served as a maternity ward, school hostel and old-age home. Quiet, discreet, inexpensive and set in pleasant gardens, it is Swakop's undiscovered accommodation gem. Across the road is another classier, more expensive, but equally Germanic place to stay, the **Hotel Europa Hof**.

It is difficult to tear yourself away from this intersection – on the southeast corner is the old **Kaserne**. Built in 1906 as a fort, it still has its tower and turrets, but is now used as a youth hostel. On the final corner of this Bismarck/Anton Lubowski intersection is the **Bacchus Taverne**. This pleasant little pub is a step back in time and culture and a much better place to enjoy a drink and snack with the locals than some of the more popular tourist traps in town.

Let's stay in Bismarck Street and head north across Libertina Amathila Avenue to reach the imposing **Woermannhaus**. Built in 1905 for the Damara & Namqua Trading Company, it was bought in 1909 by the still-going-strong Woermann Brock Co. In later years it was used as a hostel and, almost inconceivably, nearly demolished in the 1970s. Fortunately, this imposing old historic building was renovated and now houses the local library and art gallery, while the tower used to serve as lookout for ships arriving by sea and ox wagons arriving from the desert.

Bismarck now meets Sam Nujoma (wouldn't that be interesting!) Avenue. On the northwest corner are the offices of the **Namibia Wildlife Resorts**, where you can make bookings for all resorts on the ground floor and obtain MET permits for the Namib-Naukluft Park on the first floor. The important **Bismarck Medical Centre** is across on the other corner and houses doctors, a dentist, pharmacy and specialists, as well as a private hospital. They will be moving soon to a new complex adjacent to the Medicity Cottage Hospital on the road to Henties Bay.)

Heading east up Sam Nujoma, we pass the **Woermann Arcade** on the right, cross Tobias Hainyeko, and find the **Swakopmunder Buchhandlung** on the left. This well-stocked and well-staffed bookshop would put others in much larger cities to shame and is well worth a visit. Just past the bookshop is the entrance to the **Brauhaus Arcade**, followed by Nedbank. Then there is the **Swakopmunder Apotheke** and the **Namib i,** Swakop's information centre.

Turn left into Hendrik Witbooi Street and pass the Atlanta Hotel on your right and the top-class Hansa Hotel on your left before turning left again into Daniel Tjongarero Avenue. The left-hand side of this street is lined with smart jewellery, art, and clothing stores while the municipality and post office is on the right. Now cross Tobias Hainyeko and head for the lighthouse. Built in its present form in 1910, it stands 21 metres high and, on a clear night, can be seen from 30 kilometres out to sea. Don't stray too close to the nearby State House – the guards get jumpy when the president is in residence.

Below the lighthouse stands the **Swakopmund Museum**, which houses a series of rooms furnished in period style to recreate the days of the German colony. Open daily 10h00–13h00 and 14h00–17h00, the entrance fee is N$25 for adults and N$5 for children. Nearby is the town's heated Olympic-sized indoor swimming pool – a good place to head for if the dreaded coastal fog is chilling you to the bone.

Protruding out into the sea is the Mole. Completed in 1903 to form a protected harbour for Swakop, it was never a success. By 1906 it had silted up, prompting the building of the iron jetty, but it did give the town its best beach and a safe launching ramp for pleasure boats. All that remains of our walk now is a stroll down the palm-shaded Arnold Schad Promenade to enjoy that well-earned drink at the Tug.

Overnight in Swakopmund

Regularly voted 'Best Hotel in Namibia', the **Hansa Hotel**, at 3 Hendrik Witbooi Street, is an elegant four-star classic. Smoothly run with discreet, personalised service and excellent cuisine, its architectural beauty and central position make it the favoured address for well-heeled travellers. Rates start at N$1 250 a single and N$1 800 a double but increase during high season. For further details, tel: 064-414-200, fax: 064-414-299, e-mail: reservations@hansahotel.com.na, website: www.hansahotel.com.na.

Also four-star but definitely the new kid on the block, the **Swakopmund Hotel and Entertainment Centre**, 2 Theo-Ben Gurirab Street, uses the tastefully restored façade of Swakopmund's old railway station to hide behind. This comfortable, modern, resort offers 90 luxurious rooms, restaurants, casino, swimming pool, gym and conference centre at N$1 200 single and N$1 600 double. For details, tel: 064-410-5200, fax: 064-410-5360, e-mail: swakopmund@

legacyhotels.co.za, website: www.legacyhotels.co.za.

The Stiltz occupies another stunning site, on the banks of the Swakop River. Built on wooden pilings above the reeds at the river mouth, these luxury bungalows offer views of desert, lagoon and ocean from the comfort of your private deck. Rates start from N$970 single and N$1 300 double. For more info, tel: 064-400-771, fax: 064-400-711, e-mail: info@thestiltz.in.na, website: www.thestiltz.in.na.

You could be excused for thinking you'd taken a wrong turn and ended up somewhere in the Bavarian Alps when staying at the **Hotel Europa Hof** at 39 Bismarck Street. The timber frames and flower boxes set the scene for the traditional German restaurant. Comfortable rooms with good security cost N$610 single and N$915 double (including breakfast). For bookings, tel: 064-405-061, fax: 064-402-391, e-mail: nicole@europahof.com.na, website: www.europahof.com.

Brigadoon Cottages are like a breath of Scottish Highland air in Swakop. Just north of the museum at 16 Ludwig Koch Street, this well-run B&B offers one of the best breakfasts in Namibia, served on your own little terrace. Rates are N$650 single and N$860 double. They also have an exclusive, up-market two-bedroomed apartment in the **An der Welle** complex across the road. Overlooking the beach, and boasting the latest and most luxurious fittings, this is self-catering at its best (N$1 500 double and N$2 100 for 4 persons). For both establishments, tel: 064-406-064, fax: 064-464-195, e-mail: brigadoon@iway.na, website: www.brigadoonswakopmund.com.

One of Swakop's best-kept secrets is the **Secret Garden Guesthouse** at 36 Bismarck Street. Situated in the heart of the historic part of town, its unassuming exterior opens into an oasis of a garden courtyard, onto which eight double en-suite rooms and two very well-equipped self-catering suites face. Rates start from N$300 per person sharing. For information, tel/fax: 064-404-037, e-mail: sgg@iway.na, website: www.natron.net/tour/secretgarden.

Another centrally situated establishment under good personal supervision is the **Hotel Pension D'Avignon** at 25 Libertina Amathila Street. Secure parking in spacious gardens and a swimming pool for the hot summers make this a good, affordable option. Singles cost N$290, doubles N$470 and quads N$690. For details, tel: 064-405-821, fax: 064-405-542, e-mail: hotel.davignon@iafrica.com.na, website: www.natron.net/tour/davignon.

You can really feel history walking the corridors of the **Hotel Prinzessin Rupprecht**. Since 1902, this gracious old building at 15 Anton Lubowski Street has been a refuge and boasts spacious rooms furnished in period furniture that add to the illusion. En-suite singles cost N$360 and doubles N$700 – less if you share a bathroom. For the lowdown, tel: 064-412-540, fax: 064-412-541, e-mail: info@prinzrupp.com.na.

The **Hotel Pension à la Mer**, 4 Libertina Amathila Avenue, is the closest accommodation to the jetty and Tug restaurant – any closer, and you'd have sand on your feet! Comfortable and imaginatively decorated rooms with off-street parking and 24-hour security make this a favourite with travellers. Rates are N$400 single and N$620 double, including breakfast. For details, tel: 064-404-130, fax: 064-404-170, e-mail: alamer@iway.na, website: www.pension-a-la-mer.com.

Self-catering accommodation

The **Alte Brücke Resort** is just what the camper and self-caterer is looking for. Situated at the southern end of Strand Street, just up from the Swakop River mouth, Alte Brücke is a busy, well-run complex of neat chalets and grassy campsites. The chalets sleep one to six people and cost N$585 single, N$760 double and N$1 380 for four people. Each site has its own private ablution block and costs N$280 each, with double occupancy, thereafter N$80 per person extra. Contact the resort on tel: 064-404-918, fax: 064-400-153, e-mail: info@altebrucke.com, website: www.altebrucke.com.

The **Swakopmund Municipal Restcamp** started life decades ago as a basic camp with small fishermen's cottages

This impressive structure is now the summer residence of the president.

and has grown with the addition of the popular A-frame chalets and VIP bungalows. All units are fully equipped for self-catering and are well maintained and serviced daily, but do note that there is no camping allowed. Rates are a very reasonable at N$200 per day for a two-bed self-catering bungalow, N$380 for four beds and N$550 per day for a fully equipped A-frame house that sleeps six. This is good, solid, value-for-money accommodation and very popular, so try to book ahead on tel: 064-410-4333, fax: 064-410-4212, e-mail: info@swakopmund-restcamp.com, website: info@swakopmund restcamp.com.

Backpackers and overland trucks are also catered for in Swakopmund. Their first option is **Villa Wiese Backpackers' Lodge** at the eastern end of Bahnhof Street. This rambling old house and its outbuildings offer the backpacker a choice of the busy buzz of sports on the TV in the bar, or chilling with a book in a quiet corner. There is good security, assistance with information, and bookings for activities. Dorm beds cost N$110, a triple room N$480, en-suite double N$385 and singles N$330. The **Dunedin Star Guest House** is a block away at 50 Daniel Tjongarero Street and is operated by the folks at Villa Wiese. Newer and quieter, they offer similar accommodation and at the same rates. Contact details for both are tel/fax: 064-407-105, e-mail: enquiry@villawiese.com, website: www.villawiese.com.

The **Dunes Backpackers**, 12 Anton Lubowski Avenue, is more central and closer to the beach. It has a large indoor pool with bar and pool table and offers laundry and internet services. Rates are N$145 for a dorm bed, N$345 for a single en-suite room, N$440 for a double and N$585 for triple. For more info, tel/fax: 064-463-139, e-mail: info@dunes.com.na, website: www.dunes.com.na.

If you drive to the southern end of Strand Street and then down to the mouth of the Swakop River, you will run straight into the **Seagull's Cry Camping**. The camp is new and still trying to establish grass for its sites, some of which have electrical points, and the ablutions are a little basic but you can't beat the scenic position. Stands are N$100 a night, plus N$30 per person. For details, tel/fax: 064-402-395 or 081-214-6854.

Last but not least is the youth hostel situated in the **Alte Kaserne,** on the corner of Lubowski and Bismarck. This old fort was built in 1906 and still has its original tower and turrets. It caters mainly for youth groups, but is negotiable for individual travellers. For further information, tel: 064-404-164, fax: 064-405-373.

Very last – and very least – please don't be tempted to book a site at any of the 'Mile' camps up the coast north of Swakop. They are desolate, dreary, isolated and only for fanatical fishermen who care more for rods and reels than for rest and recreation. If you must, then book through NWR.

Eating out in Swakopmund

Swakopmund is a resort town – the many good restaurants and pubs attest to that. From traditional German cuisine to the best steaks and seafood, you would have to go out every night for two weeks to enjoy the best of them. I have not attempted to list them in any particular order, so choose what you like and enjoy.

The Grapevine Restaurant, at 42 Libertina Amathila Avenue, tel: 064-404-770, offers a delightful dining experience. The service is discreet and professional, the menu imaginative and tasty, and the wine list sensational. You are encouraged to taste a selection of wines from the extensive cellar before making your choice, and all wines are available by the glass.

The **Bacchus Taverne**, on the other hand, is an entirely different can of sauerkraut. Small and intimate and catering mainly for the German-speaking locals, you will find it in traditional Bismarck Street on the corner with Anton Lubowski Avenue. Typical German pub food and a barman who knows how to draw a draft with a proper head of foam add to the charm of this old pub.

Similar in origin, but different in size and patronage, is the **Swakopmund Brauhaus**. Big and brash and popular with the tourists, it serves great eisbein and other traditional dishes with a good selection of local and imported draft beers. It is centrally positioned in the smart Brauhaus Arcade off Sam Nujoma Avenue, so you can pop in anytime. For reservations, tel: 064-402-214.

Kücki's Pub, 20 Tobias Hainyeko Street, tel: 064-402-407, is now more of a restaurant than a pub, but still popular with the tourists, so book ahead. **The Tug**, on the beach opposite the jetty, also started out as a good place for a sundowner and more, but has now become respectable and encourages diners only. But it's still a great place with a great view. Call for bookings on tel: 064-402-356.

If you're feeling like a beach bum and want to chill out under the stars with the sound of crashing surf around you, head on down to the **Tiger Reef Beach Bar** at the end of Strand Street. The breeze blows through the tamarisks and on a cold evening they light fires on the beach to keep the customers warm. Light meals are also available, some without sand. At the other end of Strand Street, in the building that houses the indoor swimming pool, you will find the **Lighthouse Pub and Restaurant** – a popular place with backpackers and overlanders.

Most of Swakop's hotels offer good dining. The **Hansa Hotel** is very posh, and the **Europa Hof** serves good buffets at reasonable prices. The smart Swakop Hotel and Entertainment Centre in Theo-Ben Gurirab Avenue offers fine food in the **Station Grill** and **Platform One** restaurants, as well as an international casino.

Café Anton in the foyer of the Schweizerhaus Hotel, near the lighthouse, bakes a decadent selection of cakes and pastries, and the brew served at the **Coffee Bar** in Woermann & Brock supermarket is some of the best in town. The best ice cream is available at **Raith Gourmet and Gelatoria** in Tobias Hainyeko Street – it's also a good delicatessen. And for value-for-money seafood, try the **Ocean Basket** on the corner of Hendrik Witbooi and Libertina Amathila streets.

For takeaways try KFC at 14 Hendrik

Quadbiking over giant sand dunes is fun, but take care of yourself and the environment.

Witbooi Street or **Napolitan Pizzeria**, one block up in Nathaniël Maxuilili Street. Finally, the ever-changing club scene was favouring **The Siding**, which is in the dodgy area out beyond the Entertainment Centre on Mandume Ya Ndemufayo Street. Rather try the disco/bar at the Swakop Lodge, previously known as the Gruener Kranz.

Activities and tours

Fishing Walvis Bay to the south and Henties Bay to the north are favoured by fishermen. See those chapters for details.

Golf The Rossmund Golf Course is a beautiful all-grass, 18-hole, desert course set among palm trees with springbok grazing the fairways. A well-equipped pro-shop has clubs and carts for hire, and there is a fine clubhouse with a bar and restaurant. For more information, tel/fax: 064-404-664, e-mail: rossmund@iafrica.com.na, website: www.swakopresorts.com/golf.htm.

Horse-riding Okakambe Trails offers half-day, full-day or longer guided trails on horseback from their stables about 11 kilometres east of Swakop off the B2. For details, tel: 064-402-799, fax: 064-405-258.

Quadbiking and sandboarding The best quadbiking is done in the Kuiseb Delta (see Walvis Bay listings), but for simple dune-bashing head south for 10 kilometres towards Walvis on the B2 to the Dare Devil Adventures operation, tel: 064-400-858, fax: 064-401-188, e-mail: daredev@iway.na. Alter Action specialises in sandboarding and can be contacted on tel: 064-

> **NAMIB i**
>
> Namib i is centrally situated on the corner of Sam Nujoma Avenue and Hendrik Witbooi Street and offers information on everything pertaining to Swakopmund and the surrounding area. Here you can also make reservations for all accommodation and tours. For further details, contact the information office on tel: 064-403-129, fax: 064-404-827, e-mail: namibi@iway.na, website: www.natron.net/tour/swakop/infoe.htm

402-737, e-mail: alteraxn@iafrica.com.na, website: www.alter-action.info.

Skydiving and scenic flights Pleasure Flights and Safaris offers exactly what its name implies and can be contacted on tel/fax: 064-404-500, e-mail: redbaron@iafrica.com.na, website: www.pleasureflights.com.na; Desert Skydiving Adventures is based at the Swakop airport, tel: 064-401-055, as is the Skydiving Club, tel: 064-405-671.

Tour operators Charly's Desert Tours, Sam Nujoma Avenue, tel: 064-404-341, fax: 064-404-821, e-mail: charlydt@mweb.com.na, website: www.charlysdeserttours.com.

Out and about in Swakop

Below is a brief list of the facilities and institutions that will make a stay in Swakop enjoyable and hassle-free.

Banks All the major banks and ATMs are clustered around the intersection of Sam Nujoma Avenue and Tobias Hainyeko Street.

Bicycle rentals Cycle Clinic, 10 Hendrik Witbooi Street, tel: 064-402-530

Breakdown services Auto Perfect (24 hours a day), tel: 081-127-5434; also off the Henties Bay Road, at the old prison, is Hidipo Hamutenya Avenue in the industrial area.

Head here for anything mechanical or hardware.

Car hire Avis, Entertainment Centre, Bahnhof Street, tel: 064-402-527; Budget, 14 Kraal Street, tel: 064-463-380

Car washes Magic Car Wash, Theo-Ben Gurirab Avenue, tel: 081-286-8824

Couriers DHL, Brauhaus Arcade, tel: 064-405-300

Internet Compucare, 12 Hendrik Witbooi Street, tel: 064-463-775, e-mail: comp@mweb.com.na – open 7 days a week, have a fast satellite connection, and offer software support and computer repairs; i Café, Woermann & Brock Mall

Laundromats The oldest and best established is Swakopmund Laundry, just outside the Swakopmund Municipal Restcamp, 15 Swakop Street, tel: 064-405-238

Motor repairs Land Rover Parts Centre, Nathaniël Maxuilili Street, tel: 064-403-713; Pupkewitz Mega Motors (most makes of vehicles), 54 Sam Nujoma Avenue, tel: 064-405-900; RW Motors (Mercedes and Mitsubishi), 14 Libertina Amathila Ave, tel: 064-402-741; Steckels Toyota, 77 Sam

Nujoma Avenue, tel: 064-402-719
Motor spares, accessories and camping gear Cymot, corner Otavi and Sam Nujoma, tel: 064-400-318
Postal facilities The Post Office, north on Tobias Hainyeko Street, also has an international call centre.
Public transport and taxis Taxi Kraus, tel: 081-298-886; Taxi Services, tel: 064-462-793; Town Hoppers (daily bus service between Swakop and Windhoek, costing N$220 one-way), tel: 064-407-223, e-mail: townhoppers@iway.na, website: www.namibiashuttle.com; Ekonolux (buses through Swakopmund to and from Walvis) (see page 116)
Tyres Continental Tyres and Dunlop are both on the left of the Henties Bay Road as you leave Swakop.

Festivals in Swakop

There are a number of regular festivals in Swakopmund. A traditional German carnival the **Küska Karneval** is held every August. For more information contact Johan Klein, tel: 064-402-611, e-mail: skv@webmail.co.za.

A very important annual cultural event is the **Swakopmunder Musikwoche**, a week at the beginning of December during which more than 200 amateur musicians from Namibia, South Africa and even Europe come to hone their skills under expert guidance and present a wonderful final concert. Contact Günther F. Kesselmann, tel: 064-404-140, e-mail: ag@kesselmann.net.

Shopping in Swakop

Entering Swakopmund down Sam Nujoma Avenue from the east, you will see the big Shoprite Centre on your right. Other than the Shoprite supermarket, this mall has the usual mix of South African stores selling furniture, clothing, jewellery, cellphones and booze.

Pick 'n Pay supermarket is on the Hendrik Witbooi corner of Sam Nujoma Avenue, with Woolworths in the same block. The Woermann Arcade is one block down on the Tobias Hainyeko corner and houses a supermarket with good deli, bakery and coffee shop, an internet café, travel agent and photo kiosk for passport photos.

For African arts, crafts and jewellery try the Brauhaus Arcade behind Nedbank in Sam Nujoma Avenue, where you can also shop for safari clothing and furs.

And finally, a moment's silence for the Hansa Brewery that closed down in Swakop – they ran a good brewery tour. The historic ties were strong, but they could make their beer cheaper elsewhere. Shame on you, Namibian Breweries!

EMERGENCIES IN SWAKOP

◆ Ambulance	064-410-6000
◆ Bismarck Private Medical Centre	064-405-000
◆ Fire Brigade	064-410-4111
◆ Fire Brigade (24 hours)	081-128-5613
◆ Hospital	064-410-6000
◆ Police	10111
◆ Sea Rescue	064-404-213

Henties Bay and the Skeleton Coast 18

Henties Bay is just 72 kilometres north of Swakopmund on the C34. But, be careful – it is a salt road that can be potholed and rough in parts and slippery when wet. Mile 14 is one of a few basic campsites along this coast that fills up during the summer season, but is empty and forlorn at other times of the year. Wlotzkasbaken is the next little fishing spot that, at least, has a few houses and shacks, and then there's Jakkalsputz, 10 kilometres before Henties. A lichen field, signposted next to the road at S22°21.011 E14°26.011, is worth a stop, but tread softly.

Don't drive the beaches of the Skeleton Coast unless you are brave, extremely knowledgeable and have a permit.

Out and about in Henties

Take the turn-off into town and head down Jakkalsputz Road until you reach the Total service station and the **Eagle Shopping Centre**, which includes a bar, restaurant, bottle store, shop and accommodation. The centre also offers cottages of different capacities, which average N$160 a person. For details, tel: 064-500-032, fax: 064-500-299, e-mail: eaglesc@iafrica.com.na, website: www.eagleholiday.com.

> **HEALTH MATTERS IN HENTIES**
> The new Benguela Medical Centre, cnr Benguela and Seemeeu streets, houses the Henties Bay Pharmacy (064-500-599), Sister Joey's consulting rooms (081-244-9149), a doctor and a small emergency clinic (064-500-423).

Turning inland from Eagles will bring you to an unusual establishment that could only be found in fish-crazy Henties. **The Skubbe Bar** (S22°06.877 E14°17.150) is centred around fish-cleaning and gutting tables and includes a car wash. Thirsty fishermen can down a cold Windhoek or Klippies and Coke, while staff clean and prepare their catch for tonight's fish braai. Other helping hands wash the sand and salt from the double-cab. Life is tough in Henties! Turn down past the police station (opposite Skubbe) to reach **Bucks Camping Lodge**. The lodge offers exposed campsites, each with its own private ablution block, at N$200. For more information, tel: 064-501-039, e-mail: buckscamp@mweb.na.

Just north of Eagles is another short row of shops and an Engen service station. There is a Standard Bank, a pharmacy, OK grocer, takeaway, laundromat, car wash and the Spitzkoppe bar and restaurant. **Henties Motors** (tel: 064-500-752) across the road will do mechanical repairs. Continue to the dip of the dry Omaruru River in which a nine-hole golf course has been laid out with grassed tees and greens. The main beach is situated at the mouth of the riverbed and perched on a high dune – and overlooking all of this is the **Hotel de Duine**. There is a feel of seaside holidays here – but hopefully not the type of place where Dad fishes all day while Mom plays with the kids on the beach and at night Dad hangs out in the bar while Mom does bath duty with the kids. Happy holidays! This hotel was recently acquired by the Protea Hotel group and will be upgraded before announcing new accommodation rates. E-mail: info@proteahotels.com, website: www.proteahotels.com.

There are a couple of guesthouses, the best of which is the three-star **Byseewah Guest House** on Auas Street. Quality accommodation, personal service and assistance in organising fishing trips makes this a comfortable home from home. For details, tel: 064-501-111, fax: 064-501-177, e-mail: info@fishermanslodge.com.na, website: byseewahguesthouse.com.

A more economical establishment, but also with good, friendly attention, is the **Namib Shore B&B**. They have a couple of rooms attached to the house and safe parking in the yard. Rates are N$300 per single and N$500 per double. Contact the B&B on tel/fax: 064-500-182, e-mail:

namshore@iway.na, website: www.namshore.iway.na.

But fishing is what most people come here for and what better time to come than over the last weekend in August when the annual **Henties Bay Fishing Festival** is held. An angling competition, street festival and live evening entertainment draws thousands to the town. Contact Estelle of the Henties Bay Tourist Information office for assistance and all the town's info. They are situated at the Total Service Station on Jakkalsputz Road, tel: 064-501-143, e-mail: info@hentiesbaytourism.com, website www.hentiesbaytourism.com.

On to the Skeleton Coast

The C34 road continues north of Henties past more fishing spots in the sand to Cape Cross, home of the largest breeding colony of Cape fur seals on the southern African coast. Open every day for visitors, the **Cape Cross Seal Reserve** is best visited during the breeding season in November and December, when as many as 200 000 seals can be seen. The entrance fee is N$30 per person and N$10 per car. This smelly, noisy place is also the spot where Portuguese navigator Diego Cão planted his first stone cross in 1486. Luxury accommodation is available at the nearby **Cape Cross Lodge**. It offers ocean-view rooms, daily desert excursions, fishing trips and a restaurant for day visitors. The rates for sea-facing rooms are N$1 315 for a single and N$2 000 for a double. For more details, tel: 064-694-012, fax: 064-694-015, e-mail: bookings@capecross.org, website: www.capecross.org.

It is another 180 kilometres north to **Torra Bay**. Along the way you will pass into the **Skeleton Coast Park** and have to pay fees of N$60 per person and N$10 for the car. Stretching up to and beyond the Kunene River, the desolation and lack of any sustenance combined with the rough seas and thick fog, were the reasons this stretch of coast was given the S name. Many a seaman and the odd airman perished here after being wrecked in this inhospitable place. Still rather inhospitable, the coast has only two accommodation options. Torra Bay has a basic campsite that is open only during December and January (N$100 per site, plus N$50 per person), and Terrace Bay has bungalows that are available on a bed-and-breakfast basis (N$800 per person). Prebook through Namibia Wildlife Resorts.

It is probably best to visit this wild coast through a specialist tour operator – and there aren't many. The best and most luxurious is **Wilderness Safaris**, which offers fly-in, tented-camp packages that can also be combined with other wilderness areas. For particulars, tel: 061-274-500, fax: 061-239-455, e-mail: info@nts.com.na, website: www.wilderness-safaris.com.

The other option is old-established **Skeleton Coast Safaris** run by the Schoeman family who know the area well. Contact the Schoemans on tel: 061-224-248, fax: 061-225-713, e-mail: info@skeletoncoastsafaris.com, website www.skeletoncoastsafaris.com.

On to Windhoek

The easiest route from Swakopmund to Windhoek is via the Trans-Kalahari Highway (B2) through Usakos and Karibib to Okahandja and down the B1 into the capital. The turn-off north to Spitzkoppe and other important sites is approximately 120 kilometres from Swakopmund and about 24 kilometres short of Usakos. These important sites and the route north are described in Chapter 28.

The **Namib Wüste Farmstall** is on the western approaches to Usakos. It offers light meals, as well as some of the best biltong around, and also does light meals with beer on tap. Camping is at a very reasonable N$60 per site, plus N$20 per person, and there's also clean, comfortable, but cramped backpackers' accommodation in an old railway carriage on the premises for N$150 B&B. For details, tel: 064-530-283.

The town of Usakos looks as if it has been abandoned, in spite of there being good through traffic and some attractive old colonial buildings. The only other accommodation is at the **Bahnhof Hotel** in the main street. Rates are from N$280 for a standard single room to N$510 B&B for a luxury double. For the lowdown, tel: 064-530-444, e-mail: websmith@iway.na, website: erongo.50megs.com/usakos-accommodation/. There is also a take-away in town, and the **Khan Service Station**, tel: 064-530-475, offers a tow-in service.

Karibib is another drive-through town with all the basic amenities but nothing much to make you stop. If you do decide to stop, pop in at the **Henckert Tourist Centre** in the middle of town. They have a huge gem and curio shop, coffee bar, internet café and an in-house weaving mill where local wool is carded, spun and woven on looms to create very attractive carpets and wall-hangings. For more information, tel: 064-550-700, e-mail: tourist@henckert.com, website: www.henckert.com.

Accommodation is available at **Irmi's Lodge** at the eastern entrance to town. All rooms have a shower, toilet and ceiling fan and there is a braai area and swimming pool. Bed and breakfast rates are N$320 single and N$500 double. Contact Irmi on tel/fax: 064-550-081, e-mail: imstrobl@iway.na.

About 3 kilometres east of Karibib is the turn-off to Omaruru and on to the exciting northern region of the country. Don't pass through Omaruru without visiting Michael Weder's **Kristall Kellerei** where Colombar and Ruby Cabernet wines are made. Michael also makes a selection of schnapps and offers food and accommodation. Contact him on tel: 064-570-083, fax: 064-570-593.

If you stay on the B2 you will reach **Okahandja** (see page 140) where your choice is north to Etosha or south to Windhoek. An alternative scenic route from Swakopmund to Windhoek is the gravel-surfaced C28 through the Khomas Hochland. Leave Swakop on the B2 and, just past the airport turn-off, turn right (S22°39.909 E14°34.642) onto the C28, sign-posted to the Namib-Naukluft Park. It's a good gravel road, but the landscape is at first very bleak across the plains of the Namib. **The Bosua Pass** is reached at about the halfway mark. Similar to the Spreetshoogte Pass in that the very steep corners are paved, it is also not suitable for either caravans or trailers. The road becomes tarred 30 kilometres out of Windhoek and a couple of kilometres further you pass the turn-off into the Daan Viljoen Game Park (temporarily closed) before rolling into the capital.

Gobabis and south to the Kalahari 19

The southeastern quarter of Namibia offers a gateway to Botswana and access to the Kgalagadi Transfrontier Park via the gate at Mata Mata. But even if you are just curious to see what Gochas, Aranos and Koës look like, this land of dunes and dry riverbeds will bind you under its spell.

A Kalahari game drive is best enjoyed as the sun sets over the sand.

Take the B6 east out of Windhoek and after 20 kilometres you will reach the **Trans-Kalahari Inn**. Although they offer comfortable accommodation, vehicle storage is their main game. Being so close to Windhoek's international airport, it's convenient for travellers from all over the world to leave their vehicles in the care of Hartwig and Burghardt Grimm. They also have nine comfortable rooms, which cost N$300 for a single and N$525 for a double, with campsites at N$40 per day plus N$40 per person. There is a small restaurant and bar, and pick-ups from the airport can be arranged at N$175. Vehicle storage costs N$320 per month under roof. For further details, tel/fax: 061-222-877, e-mail: grimm@transkalahari.com, website: www.transkalahari.com.

Hosea Kutako Airport is 45 kilometres out of Windhoek and the good tarred road carries on – straight, empty and quiet, but not boring: there are warthogs and baboons, antelope graze the verges, and there are good sightings of southern yellowbilled hornbills, Burchell's glossy starlings, lilac-breasted rollers and hovering raptors.

Halfway to Gobabis, where the D1808 turns south (S22°21.471 E18°04.586), there is the **Kalahari Farm Stall**, which sells good biltong as well as coffee and tea and fresh meat. They also offer a free picnic and overnight campsite with clean toilets (but no shower) as long as you buy something from them – almost too good a deal to pass by. Contact them on tel/fax: 062-560-283. **Witvlei** is the only other spot worth mentioning along this stretch of highway. There is a Shell service station and **Die Broeihuis B&B**, a newish establishment that charges N$225 per single, N$350 double and N$550 for a four-bed family room. Contact Die Broeihuis on tel: 062-570-079, fax: 062-570-063, e-mail: diebroeihuis@yahoo.com.

Gobabis

Gobabis has always been the centre of a vast cattle-ranching region and was a lonely outpost on the rough road to Ganzi and the Okavango swamps until the construction of the Trans-Kalahari Highway. This wide, new road through the sands of Botswana has brought new visitors to the town and, although one can hardly talk of a tourist boom, there is now new life in Gobabis.

As you approach the town from Windhoek, you will first notice a dam on your right (hopefully it will have water in it). Located here is the **Transkalahari End Resort** – Die Dam. A smart restaurant overlooks the water, and solid face-brick and thatch bungalows and grassy, shaded campsites line the shore. Bungalows cost N$500 double and camping costs N$55 per person. For more information, contact the resort on tel: 062-565-656 or 081-241-8811, e-mail: gobabisdam@mweb.com.na, website: www.transkalahariendresort.com. The alternative in Gobabis is the **Big Five Central Hotel** (turn right into Heroes' Lane as you enter town). With a big bar and pool tables, it's popular with bikers who do the 200-kilometre stretch from Windhoek as a breakfast

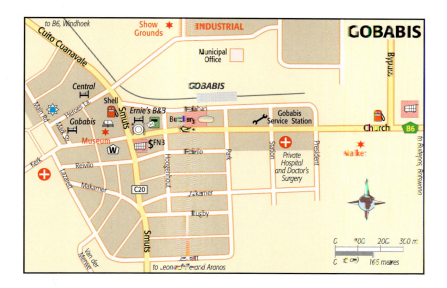

run! Rooms range from N$250 single to N$570 triple, and for bikers who prefer to spend their money on women and booze, camping is only N$50 a night. For details, tel: 062-562-364, fax: 062-564-902, e-mail: big5gb@iway.na, website: www.big5namibia.com.

Gobabis Toyota and the Standard Bank are also in Heroes' Lane, and continuing into town along Cuito Cuanavale Street will take you past a motor-spares shop and **Ernie's B&B and Pub** on the left, with the Shell Nissan garage and a pharmacy on the right. Ernie's is a motel-style operation with rooms in a shaded backyard for N$250 single and N$400 double with TV and kettle, and the pub/restaurant spills out onto a cool patio. Contact the B&B on tel: 062-565-222, fax: 062-565-221.

The Shoprite supermarket dominates the central crossroads in town. Continue straight across to get to the C20, Leonardville and Aranos, or turn left to stay on the B6 to Botswana. The way out to Botswana (Church Street) takes you past the post office, First National Bank, Isuzu garage, butchery, bakery, tyre workshop, and a private hospital and surgery (tel: 062-563-983 or 062-562-084). It is another 95 kilometres to the Buitepos/Mamuno border with Botswana.

Into the Kalahari

The C20, which heads south out of town, follows the usually dry riverbed of the Nossob into the heart of the Kalahari. A good gravel road runs down for 130 kilometres to the small village of **Leonardville**, where there is fuel and gas available at the farmers' co-op. There is also a police station and a motor workshop there's no fuel, but they can do repairs.

If you have no business in **Aranos** and want to shortcut to Stampriet, turn right onto the M42 about 38 kilometres south of Leonardville at S23°48.639 E18°52.530. This brings you back onto the C20 at Stampriet. Continuing on down the C20 brings you to Aranos, which is rather a tatty spot, but does boast both Standard and First National banks with ATMs, a Spar supermarket, Total garage, a farmers' co-op and the **Aranos Hotel** – a typical frontier-type establishment that makes far more out of selling booze to people who shouldn't be drinking than from their rooms, which cost N$420 single and N$615 double. For particulars, tel: 063-272-031, fax: 063-272-300.

Head west now on the C20 to **Stampriet**, where you will be surprised to find a fine Afrikaans private school that holds the trophy for best schools rugby in Namibia. The little village also has fuel and a kiosk, as well as the comfortable **Stampriet Historical Guesthouse**, where air-conditioned rooms cost N$440 single and N$800 double. A cosy bar and restaurant complete the picture. For information, tel: 063-260-013, fax: 063-260-215, e-mail: stampriet@iway.na, website: www.stampriet.iway.na.

If you've developed a taste for Kalahari driving and want to head on down to Gochas and Koës to join the B1 at Keetmanshoop, take the C15 (C23 on some maps) out of Stampriet at S24°20.687 E18°24.820. Roads in this part of the world run either parallel or at right angles to each other. This is because they have to run between the dunes (often along dry riverbeds) or directly over them – dunes can't be tackled at any other angle. So be ready for a roller-coaster ride of stomach lurches!

Gochas (pronounced *koggas*) is reached after 72 kilometres, but not

The Kalahari dunes and sandy landscape around Auob Lodge, Gochas.

before reaching the luxury **Auob Lodge** (S24°40.214 E18°46.414), just short of town. Auob Lodge is another fine establishment in the extensive portfolio of Namibia Country Lodges and offers comfortable accommodation, fine dining, a pool and sundowner game drives. There is a good gravel airstrip, too, in case you are flying and not driving. Rates are N$635 single, N$900 double and N$160 for dinner. Camping is N$65 per person. Contact Central reservations on tel: 061-374-750, fax: 061-256-598, e-mail: auob@ncl.com.na, website: www.namibialodges.com.

Gochas town is down at the crossroads with the C18, and across the bridge on the eastern side of the Auob River. It offers an Engen garage, a bottle store (of course) and a fairly well-stocked OK Grocer. The only place of historic interest is the cemetery in the centre of town (S24°51.643 E18°48.554), which contains German graves dating back to the Nama resistance around 1904 to 1908.

Not surprisingly, there are two other accommodation options in Gochas, as more travellers use the Mata Mata border gate of the Kgalagadi Transfrontier Park. This makes the route through Gochas an interesting shortcut from the heart of South Africa into the heart of Namibia.

Stony's Hotel has been extensively renovated, and now offers en-suite, air-conditioned rooms at N$400 single and N$600 double (breakfast included). Camping is offered for rooftop tents and caravans in a secure and shaded area with private light, tap, plug and braai for N$75 per person, tel: 063-250-237, fax: 063-250-236, e-mail: gochashotel@mweb.com.na.

The Kamelruhe Guest House is smaller, but boasts a good view from its prominent position in the centre of town. A converted house with six air-conditioned rooms, a bar/dining room and pool, they charge N$512 for single and N$720 double, including breakfast. Camping is N$65 per person. For details, tel: 063-250-224, fax: 063-250-225, e-mail: kamelruh@iway.na.

> If you need public transport, the Starline Passenger Service runs regularly between Keetmanshoop and Mariental, via Koës, Gochas and Stampriet.

Staying on the C15, at 35 kilometres south of Gochas, you will reach the **Tranendal Farm** and **Red Dune** campsite. The friendly couple Pieter and Marieta Liebenberg offer shady, grassed campsites around the farmhouse, with hot showers, flush toilets, braai spots, firewood and electricity for N$75 per person. The farm boasts an interesting succulent garden with lots of birds and also offers phone, fax and e-mail facilities. Rooms in the farmhouse are N$350 pp sharing, B&B. But, to really get away from it all and experience the red-dune world of the Kalahari, drive out and stay in quiet isolation at their Red Dune campsite. Covered wooden decks are kitted out with mattresses, bedding and mozzie nets, while the boma comes equipped with table, chairs, bar, hot shower and flush toilet. B&B rate is N$1 380 per person sharing. Contact the Liebenbergs on tel/fax: 063-250-164 or e-mail: mariet@iway.na.

The good, gravelled C15 continues south down the Auob River until, at 95 kilometres from Gochas, it forks (S25°29.735 E19°18.164). Left takes you to the (hopefully) soon-to-be-opened border gate into South Africa via the old Kalahari Gemsbok Park, and right takes you to Keetmanshoop via Koës (pronounced *kwees*). Stay on the Keetmans road for another 20 kilometres down the dune valleys to where the road takes a sharp right turn to go up and over, up and over the dunes (keep to the left-hand side of the road when cresting the blind rises). The little settlement of **Koës** is 47 kilometres down this road, but don't blink – you just might miss it.

There is a post office, Total service station and Agra Co-op, and further down on the opposite side of the road is the dumpy **Koës Hotel**, where farmers (or ex-farmers) drink Klippies-'n-Coke at nine in the morning! The hotel also offers B&B at N$280 a person and dinner for N$90. The hotel may be reached on tel: 063-252-716.

The nearby **Koës Pan** comes alive every July as the centre of the Namibian off-road universe, when a weekend rally is organised. For the brave there is a 150-kilometre off-road rally and high-speed sprints on the pan. And for the foolish there is dune-charging and ramping! If you make it through the day's mayhem, there's a dance each night in the Boerevereniging Saal, with lots to eat and drink. It sounds like a wonderful *jol* – if anyone survives it, please let me know more. Contact the hotel for more info.

About 40 kilometres short of Keetmanshoop you will come across the **Mesosaurus Fossil Site** and **Quiver Tree Park** (not to be confused with the original Quiver Tree Forest, closer to Keetmans). The Mesosaurus was an ancient crocodile-like creature that helps prove the continental drift theory (the same remains are found in Brazil). Found in the rocky badlands of this farm, you can also view 5 000 quiver trees. Camping costs N$75 per person, or stay in a rustic little stone-and-thatch cottage for N$220. For bookings, tel: 063-222-990, e-mail: info@mesosaurus.com, website: www.mesosaur.com.

About 16 kilometres outside Keetmanshoop are the **Quiver Tree Forest Rest Camp** and **Giants' Playground**, easily accessible from the B1 and a popular stopover on the road north. They have more quiver trees than the Cape Flats has Port Jackson bush and the Giants' Playground is a fantastic area of dolorite rocks, piled into precariously balanced formations. Rooms with private shower and toilets are N$440 single and N$680 double, while accommodation in self-catering bungalows costs N$330 single and N$465 double. Camping is N$80 per person, and if you just want to visit for the day the charge is N$25 plus N$20 per car. For the lowdown, tel/fax: 063-222-835, e-mail: quiver@iafrica.com.na, website: www.quivertreeforest.com.

North to Etosha 20

Heading north out of Windhoek on the B1 does not immediately evoke feelings of tackling exciting, wild new horizons. Okahandja, at only 65 kilometres, has become almost a suburb of the capital, so the road is busy. Biltong stalls and farmstays beckon along the way until you cross the Okahandja Bridge.

The Hoba meteorite, largest in the world, fell to earth near Grootfontein.

The road junction across the Okahandja Bridge offers the option of turning right into town or left to the King's Highway Rest Camp – a comfortable, convenient, safe and cheap overnight spot and a good alternative to stopping in Windhoek. There are no frills here, but small rondavels that sleep two and share ablutions with the campers cost only N$220. A VIP Bungalow with en-suite shower and toilet, fridge, kettle and microwave costs N$480 double, and camping is N$80 per person, plus N$25 for your vehicle. The sites are shaded, but stay as far from the main road as possible, as it can be noisy. Contact the camp on tel: 062-504-086.

Okahandja

Most travellers will hurry on past Okahandja to reach their destinations at the coast or further north but, as I said, if it's just fuel, food or accommodation you need, the town's a good alternative to stopping in Windhoek. Turn right just across the bridge to refuel at the Shell garage, which also has a restaurant, takeaway and shop. Across the road from the garage is one of the largest curio markets in Namibia, with handicrafts from all over southern Africa – a great place to spend some money on your way home. Carry on down Martin Neib Avenue into the centre of town. At Kolbe Street, you can turn right to get to the old Rhenish Mission and the Friedenskirche, near which are the graves of three influential Namibian leaders: the 19th-century Oorlam leader Jonker Afrikaner, Herero Chief Hosea Kutako (leader of resistance against South African rule in Namibia), and Chief Clemens Kapuuo (former Democratic Turnhalle Alliance president who was assassinated in 1978).

Further down the main street, on the left, is Bäckerei Decker, which serves great coffee and fresh rolls, bread and confectionary. A Total garage and Nissan agent (tel: 062-501-311) is on the right at the next intersection, with a large, well-stocked Spar supermarket just beyond it. Here the road forks, but keep right to stay in the main street and pass the old fort on your left. Erected in 1894, for many years it served as the police station. This part of town contains the banks, the post office, pharmacy and takeaway joints, but is rather rundown.

Keeping left at the fork takes you into Voortrekker Street and past the attractive old railway station. Across the road is a military museum glorifying fighting and war, but nextdoor is the far more interesting Closwa Biltong Factory. Further up on the right are Shoprite and Pick 'n Pay supermarkets, an Engen garage and Continental tyre repairs. Carry on out of town on Voortrekker Street, past the **Caltex/Toyota** garage (tel: 062-501-722) if you are heading north on the B1 to Otjiwarongo, or turn left and across the railway line for the B2 and Swakopmund.

Across the railway line you can also follow the signs down Hoogenhout Street to two suburban guesthouses in the area. The first is **Villa Nina** (at the corner of Conradie Street), which offers rooms at N$300 single and N$400 double. For details, tel: 062-502-497, fax: 062-503-350, e-mail: villa-nina@okahandja.com, website: www.windhoek.de.

The nearby **Sylvanette Guesthouse** (at 311 Hoogenhout Street) is set in pretty gardens with a pool and lapa, and offers nine en-suite rooms at N$390 single and N$600 double, breakfast included. Like Villa Nina, Sylvanette has good security and off-street parking. For further information, tel: 062-505-550, fax: 062-505-560, e-mail: sylvanette@iway.na, website: www.sylvanette.com.

On the way north out of town you will pass the Reit Club, originally the 1909 home of the town's mayor and now a pleasant bar and restaurant. The grounds also serve as the headquarters and stables of the local equestrian club. Just before the road joins the B1 you will find the smart, up-market **Okahandja Lodge**. It boasts 22 comfortably furnished en-suite rooms arranged in a horseshoe shape around extensive lawns with a natural water feature, large trees and good bird life. The impressive thatched main building contains a spacious restaurant, cosy bar and outside patio. A little way from the main building is a rustic campsite with basic reed-hut ablutions attractively situated on the banks of the dry Okahandja River. Singles cost N$345 and doubles N$570 (all inclusive of breakfast). Camping is N$80 per person. For more, tel: 062-504-299, fax: 062-502-551, e-mail: okalodge@africaonline.com.na, website: www.okahandjalodge.com.

On leaving or passing through Okahandja, make sure you are on the right road to your destination – the road system is confusing and it's easy to take a wrong turn.

Waterberg Plateau Park

The 170-kilometre stretch of good tarred road north to Otjiwarongo is punctuated by comfortable, shaded lay-bys and the turn-off, 28 kilometres south of that town, to the Waterberg Plateau Park. To reach this striking sandstone barrier take the C22 off the B1 for 42 kilometres to turn left onto the D2512. After another 17 kilometres of this gravel road the turn-off left into the park is at S20°31.537 E17°14.993. The escarpment looms above you like castle ramparts as you approach the offices and shop. The nearby campsite is attractively located, with grass, shade and good ablutions, while the pool, bar and restaurant (all closed when I was there) are halfway up the slopes with good views. Higher up, and just under the sandstone cliffs, are the comfortable and solidly built bungalows. But keep them locked – the resident pack of baboons can open any door or window and will steal anything that is not nailed down!

Easy, attractive walks have been laid out to enable you to get up close and personal with the unique flora and fauna of the plateau, and a couple of pleasant days can be spent just relaxing and recharging life's batteries. Standard two-bed rooms cost N$500 pp, two-bed bungalows, fully equipped for self-catering, are N$650 pp, and a luxury four-bed bungalow is N$750 pp. A campsite is N$100 plus N$100 pp, and everyone pays N$100 a day and N$10 per car. Book through Namibia Wildlife Resorts in Windhoek or take a chance if out of season.

Introducing Otjiwarongo

Approaching Otjiwarongo from the south, you will pass the golf course on your left before you see the long white walls of the Out of Africa Town Lodge

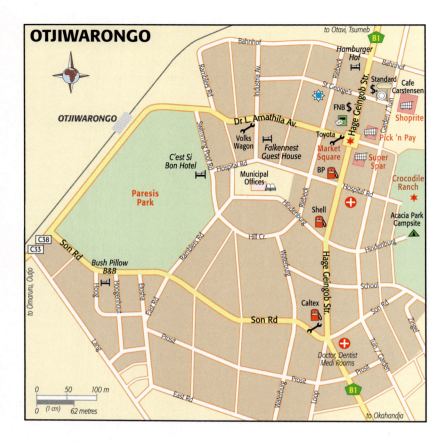

on your right as you enter town. The first four-way stop on Hage Geingob Street has a Caltex garage and Trentyre workshop, the next intersection a Shell garage (with car wash) and a cosy, thatch-roofed restaurant called Kari's. The next four-way stop (this is slow-going!) offers a BP garage and Spar supermarket as well as the **Engen/Toyota** agent (tel: 067-303-867).

The next intersection boasts a traffic light – turn left here to take the C38 up via Outjo to the Okaukuejo Camp in Etosha. Continuing on Hage Geingob, you will reach the centre of town, which has a post office, chemist, banks and small shops. Passing through to follow the B1 to Otavi and Tsumeb, you will see Dunlop Tyres and more garages, including **Jan Gey Auto** (tel: 067-303-031) – agents for Ford, Mazda, Mitsubishi and Nissan – on the corner of Second Street, and **Namibia Motors** (tel: 067-302-037) – agents for GM, Opel and Isuzu – in Bahnhof Street.

Back in the centre of town, a right turn into St George's Street will take you past Café Carstensen, a bakery that also serves coffee and light meals, to the large Shoprite shopping centre. The Pick 'n Pay supermarket is right down at the traffic lights. For the best (and only) tourist information in town, visit **Omaue Namibia** (tel: 067-303-830) at 5 St George's Street. This marvellous shop sells a fine selection of semiprecious stones, minerals and crystals as well as quality handicrafts and curios. There's just enough room in this crowded little Aladdin's Cave for a display of tourist brochures, and the owners are always happy to assist with advice on the region.

Overnight in Otjiwarongo

Your best accommodation option in Otjiwarongo seems to be the two-star **C'est Si Bon Hotel** in Swimming Pool Road. An extravaganza of polished wood, stout poles and acres of thatch around a sparkling pool, it is pretty standard for Namibia, but this one has a personal touch, is in a quiet area and is popular with the local businessmen and farmers – always a good sign. Rooms have air-con and satellite TV (you will appreciate this if you've watched Namibian Broadcasting's efforts), and cost N$699 single, N$885 double and N$1 160 triple, all B&B. For further details, tel: 067-301-240, fax: 067-303-208, e-mail: info@namibweb.com, website: www.namibweb.com/sibon.htm.

The **Out of Africa Guesthouse** in Tuin Street has comfortable rooms in a pleasant suburban setting for N$170 single, N$250 double, and a family room (for four) at N$400. They also run the new **Out of Africa Town Lodge** at the southern end of town, where they charge N$270 for a standard single room, and N$350 for a double. Contact Out of Africa on tel: 067-302-230, fax 067-302-236, e-mail: oatlodge@iway.na, website www.out-of-afrika.com.

Two smaller but very charming guesthouses grace the suburbs of Otjiwarongo. The **Bush Pillow** is an art-filled B&B at the sports-grounds end of Son Street. Bright and cheerful and tastefully furnished, the B&B rate is N$400 for a single and N$470 a double. For further information, tel: 067-303-885, fax: 067-301-264, e-mail: info@bushpillow.hypermart.net, website: www.bushpillow.hypermart.net.

Falkennest is west on Libertina Amathila Avenue, behind an extensive succulent garden. Good security, under-roof parking, braai areas, a pool and communal kitchen make this good value at N$190 single and N$330 double (including breakfast). For details, tel/fax: 067-302-616, e-mail otjbb@iafrica.com.na, website: www.natron.net/tour/falkennest.

The **Acacia Park Campsite** is east down Hindenburg Street, where they charge N$65 per person or N$480 for four in an on-site mobile home. There are standing tents for two at N$180 per night, double rooms with shared ablutions for N$280, and self-catering double en-suite chalets for N$380 per night. Tel: 067-303-100, e-mail: caciapa@mweb.com.na. Next door is the run-down and forlorn Crocodile Farm where you might rustle up a guided tour for N$25, or even a crocodile steak in their restaurant. Phone first on 067-302-121.

Outjo and beyond

Let's head out on the C38 to Outjo,

where we can decide whether we want to strike out north into Etosha, northwest towards the wilds of Kaokoland, or west to Khorixas and Twyfelfontein.

The countryside becomes more wooded as we travel north and just outside Outjo we come across the green oasis of the **Ombinda Country Lodge** (S20°07.197 E16°09.305). One kilometre south of town, Ombinda consists of 15 cosy, thatched cottages arranged around a sparkling pool and bird-filled garden. The central bar and restaurant is a warm and friendly place and the food on the à la carte menu is excellently prepared by a master chef. Add to this a grassed and shaded campsite with neat ablutions, tennis courts and even a nine-hole golf course and you might never want to leave – well worth a couple of days recuperating from the rigours of the road. Singles are N$430, doubles N$700 (all B&B) and camping N$80 per person. For more information, tel: 067-313-181, fax: 067-313-478, e-mail: ombinda@namibnet.com.

Entering Outjo on the C38 from the south, you will find yourself on Sam Nujoma Drive. Pass the OK Grocers on your right and then turn down Krupp Street to reach the old-world charm of the **Etosha Garten Hotel**. Set in a well-established garden, this hotel also has all the attractions of a comfortable, well-run establishment. A pool, spacious bar, excellent home-grown and home-baked food and good security make accommodation a difficult choice in Outjo. Single rooms cost N$390 and doubles N$660, including breakfast. For details, tel: 067-313-130, fax: 067-313-419, e-mail: info@etosha-garten-hotel.com, website: www.etosha-garten-hotel.com.

Continuing up Sam Nujoma Drive takes you past the bank and police station. Turn left into Hage Geingob Avenue at the top for a pharmacy, post office, more banks, and the centrally situated Outjo Bäckerei – the best place in town for coffee, cake and a light meal. Across the road is the museum-like SWA Gemstones Shop, with a huge selection of Namibian stones for sale and also very helpful tourist information. Also in Hage Geingob is **Weimanns Garage** (tel: 067-313-111), the place to call if you have a breakdown. The two doctors in town, Drs Kesslau and Burger, share consulting rooms at 60 Etosha Road (tel: 067-313-020). Now carry on through town, filling up at the Total garage before you leave, and hit the C38 to Etosha.

But just 5 kilometres out of town is one final accommodation option – **Buschveld Park Lodge**. Just off the road and nestled against a hillside, five spacious bungalows – solid and cool – offer great views over the Ugab valley. Each unit has a bedroom, lounge, bathroom and separate toilet, and comes equipped with a fridge and kettle. The restaurant overlooks a swimming

---

EMERGENCIES OTJIWARONGO

- Otjiwarongo Medi Clinic,
  Son Street,   067-303-734
- Pro Health Medical Centre,
  Son Street
  (doctor)   067-302-122
  (dentist)   067-302-677
- State Hospital,
  Hospitaal Street   067-300-900

pool and the camping is on grassed sites with a light and electric point. Single B&B rates are N$280, doubles N$460 and camping N$50 per person. For more details, tel/fax: 067-313-665, e-mail: bfeld@mweb.com.na.

On to Etosha

About 9 kilometres out of Outjo the C40 branches off to Kamanjab and on to Kaokoland, but we stay on the wide, tarred C38 and head for Okaukuejo in the Etosha National Park. The effects of poor management, much-needed maintenance and an unfair booking system in most of Namibia's national parks has led to the opening up of many camps and lodges just outside the borders of these parks. So it is with Etosha and there are a couple of private lodges outside both the southern Andersson Gate and the eastern Von Lindequist Gate.

The first one we encounter is the **Etosha Gateway Lodge**, 25 kilometres south of Andersson Gate, opposite the D2695 turn-off. The 16 spacious en-suite bungalows perch on a rocky ridge under mopane and white syringa trees. A sparkling pool, bar and restaurant perk you up after a long dusty day and there is a campsite too. Doubles cost N$900, including breakfast, and camping is N$85 per person. Contact the lodge on tel: 067-333-440, fax: 067-333-444, e-mail: toshari@iway.na, website: www.etoshagateway-toshari.com.

Another great alternative to rushing straight into the park is to spend a few days at **Tandala Ridge** with Tim and Laurel Osborne. Animal fundis and birding experts, this friendly couple runs

Roan antelope were introduced to Etosha in 1970.

a small B&B and are actively involved in bird and mammal research. They have two new, comfortable bungalows that offer views down the ridge to Etosha in the distance, as well as a campsite. To reach them, take the D2695 to their gate (S19°22.277 E15°29.377), turn in right and it's another three fairly rough kilometres to the bungalows. It costs N$700 per person in the bungalows, which includes all meals, drives and walks and N$100 per vehicle in the campsite. Contact the Osbornes on tel: 067-333-408, e-mail: kori@iway.na, website: www.tandalaridge.com.

The closest private camp to the national park is **Etosha Safari Camp** (S19°24.672 E15°55.504), only 10 kilometres from Andersson Gate. Perched on a hill of the Onduncuzonanadanana (try saying that after a few Tafels!) mountain range, it offers canvas-sided bungalows at N$570 single and N$910 double (B&B), and camping on level, shaded sites with a good ablution block for N$85 per person. For reservations, tel: 061-230-066; fax: 061-251-863, e-mail: info@gondwana-collection.com, website, www.gondwana-collection.com.

Etosha National Park 21

Etosha is the real deal. It is Namibia's flagship game park and one of Africa's best. Forget everything you've come to expect from more commercial ventures – Etosha is where animals have always been and, hopefully, always will be. Sit quietly in your vehicle, watching the game drink at a waterhole, or rush around frantically trying to see as much as you can. The choice is yours, and if you hear jackals and hyenas prowling inside the 'gameproof' camps at night while you stoke the braai coals, you are enjoying what money can't buy – real Africa. Although camps can, admittedly, be overcrowded and noisy, this too is part of the real Africa, for you know that the real dangers lurk all around.

Black-faced impala (above) gather at a waterhole in Etosha National Park. Etosha (opposite) means 'Great White Place' or 'Place of Emptiness'.

Etosha National Park is dominated by a huge, 130-by-70-kilometre pan. Sometimes under a few centimetres of water, usually dry, but always alkaline, it attracts a vast number and variety of game. The first Europeans to explore and write about the area were Charles Andersson of Sweden and Francis Galton from England who came to hunt and trade here in 1851. It remained a wild and mostly unvisited place until the 1890s when the German administration built two small forts in the area, Okaukuejo and Namutoni, to control the spread of the livestock disease *rinderpest*. These forts were also used as police posts to help control the Owambos to the north, but in 1904 Namutoni Fort was attacked by King Nehale and several hundred Ndonga warriors and burnt to the ground. Rebuilt two years later, it became an outpost in the reserve proclaimed a year later by Governor Von Lindequist to protect the already dwindling numbers of game.

This far-sighted proclamation originally included the whole of Kaokoland right up to the Kunene River and was nearly 100 000 square kilometres when the land between the Ugab and Hoanib rivers was incorporated. An apartheid homeland for the Damaras in 1970 was one of the reasons it has shrunk to its present size of 'only' 23 000 square kilometres.

Introducing Etosha

For all its size, visitors have access only to the southeastern sector and most of the roads are between the three camps, Okaukuejo, Halali and Namutoni. There are three gateways into Etosha: Andersson Gate near Okaukuejo, Von Lindequist Gate near Namutoni, and the newly opened King Nehale Gate in the northeast.

There is a vast variety of wildlife in Etosha – 110 reptile, 114 mammal and more than 340 bird species have been identified. A system of good gravel roads (no 4x4 needed) links many of the waterholes, and fuel is available in each camp. All visitors must be in camp from sunset to sunrise, so the best times to get out to view the game are just after sunrise and in the late afternoon before sunset. Each camp has a waterhole at the boundary fence, which is floodlit at night and a pleasant hour or two can be spent waiting and watching with a cup of warm coffee or a cold beer, depending on the time of day.

Each camp also has rooms, bungalows and a campsite. There are shops selling most of what you will need, as well as a bar, restaurant and swimming pool for your comfort. In spite of many moans and groans, the camps are reasonably maintained and run, but don't bother asking the rangers about the animals or ecology of the park – there seems to be a general lack of interest in what goes on outside the camp gates (in fairness, though, the staff are generally friendly and pleasant).

Etosha's famed for its zebra.

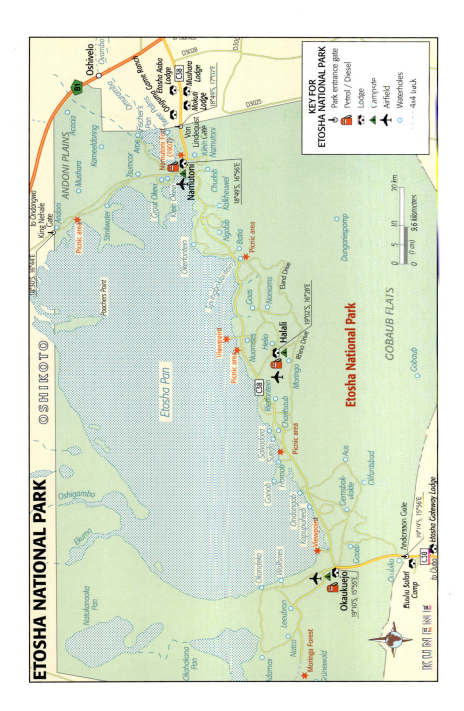

If you require room or bungalow accommodation, it is essential to book in advance – especially during school holidays or the popular months of August and September. Camping is a lot more flexible and there always seems to be place for just one more tent. Bookings for all camps in Etosha are made through Namibia Wildlife Resorts, Private Bag 13267, Windhoek, tel: 061-285-7200, fax: 061-224-900, e-mail: reservations@nwr.com.na, website: www.nwr.com.na.

Out and about in Etosha

We enter through Andersson Gate – you will be admitted, whether you have a booking or not – and slow down to the 60 kph general speed limit. You might see some game along this 20-kilometre tarred section to **Okaukuejo**, but for a better chance, take one of the gravelled loops. If you plan on staying at Okaukuejo, report to the office there and book in. You will be required to pay in advance for your accommodation, but remember to keep all receipts to show when you leave. The daily, per person, B&B rates (not including park fees) are N$650 sharing in a double room, and N$800 sharing in a chalet. Camping costs N$200 per site plus N$100 per person. All camps offer morning and afternoon guided game drives at N$500 per person, and night drives at N$600. Park entrance fees are an extra N$60 per person and N$10 per vehicle, per day.

Okaukuejo is the park's headquarters and largest of Etosha's three camps. It has a post office, shop, restaurant, bar, swimming pool, fuel, a waterhole floodlit at night, and the latest addition is an internet café (open 08h00–21h00 daily, cost N$30 per 30 minutes). Climb the spiral staircase of the old water tower to gain a good view of the sunset and to orientate yourself in this large camp. The floodlit waterhole is probably your best place to see black rhino, but all other animals, including elephant, also frequent it. The lucky few who are staying in the bungalows nearby can relax on their veranda, braaiing as they watch the game come to them.

Halali has a large, pleasant campsite with trees and ample ablution facilities, and the rooms and bungalows are similar in style and price to those at Okaukuejo. The booking-in procedure at the camp office is the same, and there is also a bar, restaurant, shop, fuel and pool. The floodlit waterhole is conveniently situated at the base of a hill. The slope forms a natural grandstand and the sunsets and game-viewing are no less spectacular than at Okaukuejo.

The roads in Etosha
are good enough. Sure, there are some potholes and fine white dust, but better roads make it easier to speed and invite more poorly equipped and ill-prepared tourists, who might be unappreciative of the real wilderness experience. So stick to the speed limit, keep your eyes peeled for animals and slowly cruise the 70-odd kilometres from Okaukuejo to Halali. The road skirts the pan with some alternative loops into the dense bush beyond to visit more waterholes.

The old German fort at Namutoni is now the park's main rest camp.

There's a track that leads out onto the pan near to Halali. Drive out to experience a little of the vast emptiness that the pan evokes, but don't stray off the track – even 4x4 traction might not get you out. Our road meanders ever eastward in Etosha to bring us to the Beau Geste-like fort of **Namutoni**. Looking like a foreign legion outpost (which it was), it even has tall palm trees waving in the wind.

The fort has been converted into tourist accommodation and offers a nostalgic base from which to explore the wild open spaces of Etosha. Like Okaukuejo and Halali, Namutoni also offers shaded campsites, shop, pool and restaurant. The floodlit waterhole is not as popular with game as the other two, but equally popular with tourists who enjoy wonderful sunsets sitting under the thatched shelter. Camping and bungalows are the same as at the other two camps, with the addition of the double rooms in the fort, which are N$900 per person.

Beyond the Von Lindequist Gate

Make use of your last opportunity for game-viewing when driving from Namutoni to the Von Lindequist Gate by taking a loop to the waterhole. On exiting the park, you will notice a few fine lodges just outside the gate, which offer more luxury and may sometimes have vacancies available when the park's accommodation is full.

The turn-off to **Onguma Private Game Reserve** is to your immediate left as you leave Etosha. About 9 kilometres down a good dirt road you will reach their bush camp. Quite small at the moment, they have a luxury tented camp, three twin-bed thatched bungalows, three twin-bed rooms and a family unit that sleeps four, starting at N$690 per person sharing, including

Etosha's Burchell's zebra populations are carefully monitored.

breakfast. They also have a pool, a thatched bar and dining area, and one of the nicest campsites in Nam. Away from the other accommodation, on grass and under shade, each site has its own power point and designer shower and toilet – at a cost of N$125 per person. Game drives are offered into Etosha or around their own private game reserve for N$420 per person. Contact Onguma on tel: 061-232-000, fax: 061-222-574, e-mail: onguma@visionsofafrica.com.na, website: www.ongumanamibia.com.

Mokuti Lodge is just off the road to the right as you exit Etosha. A large five-star resort in the prestigious Kempinski Hotel Group, it has 106 air-conditioned chalets, a swimming pool, tennis courts and hiking trails. Very smart and up-market, it feels like a well-run village. Doubles cost N$1 400, singles N$1 000 and game drives N$300. Contact central reservations on tel: 061-388-400, fax: 061-388-401, e-mail: reservations.mokuti@kempinski.com,

website: www.kempinski.com.

About 7 kilometres down the C38 from the Von Lindequist Gate is the turn-off to the best of the lot, **Mushara Lodge**. Impeccably decorated in chic African style and blessed with discreet, friendly and helpful staff, Mushara feels like an exclusive safari club. Spacious and luxurious bungalows shelter under the mopane trees around the lodge and, of course, there are game drives and a pool. Rates are N$1 100 single and N$2 200 double dinner, bed and breakfast. For the seriously rich, film stars and presidents, Mushara also offers two exclusive villas – 140 square metres of opulence in the bush, each with a private plunge pool, library, fireplace, bar and music selection. Rates include all meals, drinks, laundry and private morning and afternoon game drives to Etosha, and are understandably hefty at N$7 100 for two people. Contact Mushara on tel: 067-229-106, fax: 067-229-107, e-mail: mushara@iafrica.com.na, website: www.mushara-lodge.com.

Tsumeb, Otavi and Grootfontein 22

The good tarred C38 leads away from Etosha National Park to join the 31. Your choice here is to take either the route north to Ondangwa and on to Angola, or south to Tsumeb. Let's head south to the triangle formed by the three towns of Tsumeb, Otavi and Grootfontein.

Elephants still roam free in northern Namibia

About 24 kilometres before reaching Tsumeb, at S19°11.668 E17°33.044, turn off to the fascinating **Lake Otjikoto**. Formed by the collapse of the ceiling of a huge dolomite underground cavern, it was thought by early visitors to be 'bottomless'. Exploration by divers of the Windhoek Underwater Club has been dangerous and highly technical (see page 61), but has yielded some interesting finds. In 1915 the retreating German army dumped their weapons into the lake to avoid handing them over to the South African forces. Cannons, machine guns and an ammunition wagon have since been recovered, and some of these are on display in the Tsumeb Museum.

There is a charge of N$20 (N$5 for children under 12) to view the lake and a small farmyard zoo. For details, tel: 081-129-2421.

Tsumeb

Copper has been mined in Tsumeb for thousands of years. Damara and Owambo craftsmen worked the metal on a small scale until, in 1900, the Otavi Minen und Eisenbahn Gesellschaft (OMEG) started exploiting the mineral commercially and built a railway line to Swakopmund in order to export it. Mining operations were taken over by the Tsumeb Corporation Limited (TCL) and the town flourished as copper, zinc, lead, silver, germanium, cadmium and a variety of unique crystals were brought to the surface.

Unfortunately for TCL, the town and the miners, a 45-day strike in 1996 crippled the mine and it flooded, forcing it to close. It has not reopened since that time and, as a result, the town is struggling.

Entering town from the south on the B1 you will first encounter the **Tsumeb Cultural Village** on your right. There are 10 traditional huts and houses, each depicting the lifestyle of a different Namibian cultural group. Some traditional cultural activities are on show, as well as a good selection of handicrafts on sale at the small on-site museum. It is open 08h00–16h00 Monday–Friday and 08h00–13h00 weekends, and there is a charge of N$20 for adults and N$10 for children.

Pupkewitz Toyota (tel: 067-222-980) is across the road and then there's an Engen garage on your right. Carry on with Hage Geingob Drive to stay on the B1 and bypass the town. There are more petrol stations along this way, as well as a number of vehicle-repair workshops should you need them. But rather turn off here to enter Tsumeb via OMEG Allee. First up on your left is the **Pension OMEG Allee** in all its Austrian glory, down to the window boxes and mock balconies. The folk here run a tight ship and all is very neat and tidy. Bed and breakfast costs N$400 single and N$575 double, with back rooms a little cheaper and probably quieter. For details, tel: 067-220-631, fax: 067-220-821.

Just past the pension is the M-Web Internet Café, with the public library across the road. The **Travel North Bed & Breakfast** is next on the left. Here you will find air-conditioned en-suite rooms with TV, coffee, kettle, fridge and secure parking and braai spots at N$360 single and N$480 double. Travel North also offers friendly, knowledgeable tourist information, as well as an internet café, car hire and laundrette service for their guests – all-in-all a useful one-stop shop for all your tourist needs. Contact the B&B on tel: 067-220-728, fax: 067-220-916, e-mail: travelnn@namibnet.com, website: natron.net/tnn/.

The next block on the left, between 4th and 5th streets, contains the **Tsoutsomb Cottages**, a complex of bungalows with no bar, restaurant or pool – just good, solid, value-for-money accommodation. They have fully equipped kitchens and TV and cost N$180 single, N$325 double, N$500 for six beds and only N$700 for an eight-bed bungalow! For further info, tel: 067-220-404, fax: 067-220-592.

On the corner of 4th Street and OMEG Allee is the Tsumeb Nursery, coffee shop and beer garden – a good place for a light meal.

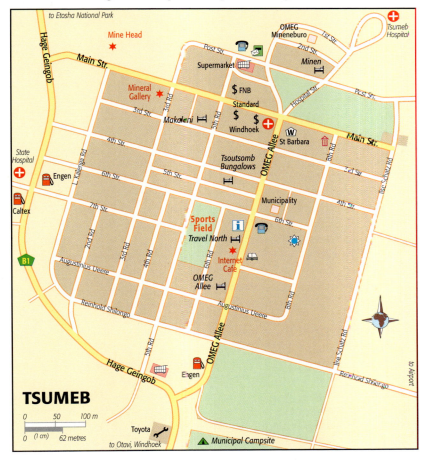

Turning left down 3rd Street off OMEG Allee brings you to the smart two-star **Makalani Hotel**. The 27 tastefully decorated rooms with en-suite bathrooms have air-conditioners, satellite TV and coffee/tea facilities. Secure parking, a pool in the central courtyard, and a thatched lapa bar all help to make this one of Tsumeb's best accommodation establishments. A single room costs N$430, double N$620, a double suite N$700 and a family room (four people) N$800. For reservations, tel: 067-221-051, fax: 067-221-575, e-mail: makalani@mweb.com.na, website: www.makalanihotel.com.

Tsumeb's other up-market hotel is across Main Street and through the small park to Post Street. The **Minen Hotel** reminds one of Tsumeb's heyday, when the mine and its bosses ran the town. This is a big old colonial-style African hotel, but it is well run and comfortable. The terrace, bar and dining area are popular gathering places for local businessmen, while the accommodation is secluded and overlooking a garden courtyard. Rooms each have TV and a fridge. Rates run between N$380 for a standard single and N$800 for a luxury double. For further info, tel: 067-221-071, fax: 067-221-750, e-mail: contact@minen-hotel.com, website: www.minen-hotel.com.

Back in Main Street you will find all the major banks, a pharmacy and various other shops. The interesting **Tsumeb Museum** is also in this street and you'll be able to recognise it by the old steam engine out front. The history of the region is comprehensively depicted inside and it boasts a display of the items brought up from the depths of Lake Otjikoto.

For **medical emergencies**, head up Hospital Street past the Minen Hotel to the private, church-run hospital, which also operates an ambulance service (tel: 067-221-001). There are doctors' consulting rooms next door to Tsumeb Pharmacy.

Otavi

Otavi, the smallest of the three triangle towns, is at an important crossroads. Coming up from the south, the B1 splits and you have the choice of either continuing north via Tsumeb or branching off east on the B8 to Grootfontein and the Caprivi beyond. There is a big Total service station at the turn-off, which is probably all you will need – it offers a bar and restaurant, shop, takeaway, ATM and puncture repairs.

Contact **Otavi Motor & Truck Repairs**, tel: 067-234-025 or 081-124-1034, for a 24-hour breakdown service.

The town is hardly worth exploring, but it does have a Spar supermarket, Standard Bank and post office.

If you need accommodation, you have two options. About 3 kilometres south of town is the pricey but admittedly up-market **Khorab Safari Lodge**. Comfortable bungalows set in a cool garden oasis and an à la carte restaurant serving local specialities make this a welcome stopover on the long road north. Well-appointed camping facilities are also available on the premises. Single B&B accommodation costs N$535 and double N$770. Camping is N$115 per person. Contact the lodge on tel: 067-234-352, fax: 067-234-520, e-mail: khorab@iafrica.com.na.

The other accommodation option is cheaper and more basic, but still comfortable. Follow the signs into Otavi to **Palmenecke Guest House**. Single rooms in this suburban home are N$195 and doubles cost N$350. For bookings, tel/fax: 067-234-199, e-mail: senotavi@iafrica.com.na, website: www.palmenecke.co.za.

Grootfontein

The B8 to Grootfontein passes large cattle and maize farms on its way east and, at S19°35.063 E18°03.059, 4 kilometres south of town, you will spot a turn-off onto the D2860 signposted to the **Hoba Meteorite**. If you have the time, make the detour to see this impressive chunk of metal. At 3x3x1 metres and weighing 60 tons, it is the largest meteorite in the world – awesome to think that it arrived here 80 000 years ago from outer space! It was discovered in 1920 and is 82% iron with 16% nickel. Follow the signs onto the D2859 (also accessible off the C42 from Tsumeb) to reach the grand entrance, office and small shop. There is an entrance fee of N$20.

You enter Grootfontein along Okavango Road, which carries straight through town to continue on as the B8 and eventually reach Rundu. A Caltex service station is first up on your left, with a sprawling taxi rank and bus stop across the road (transport north to Caprivi and south to Windhoek). There is also a turn-off down into the industrial area (where most vehicle-repair workshops are located). Staying on Okavango Road, you reach the **Meteor Hotel** on the corner of Hage Geingob. With a noisy bar and a run down look about the place, you'd have to be pretty desperate to stay here. Singles cost

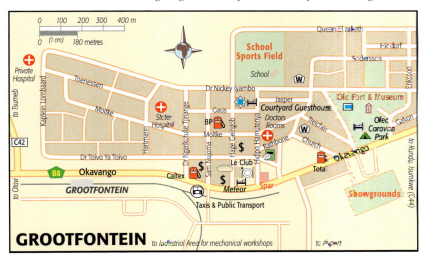

N$450, doubles N$700, and they throw in breakfast, so feel free to call on tel: 067-240-086.

Continuing on Okavango Road, you'll spot the large Spar supermarket on your left. They stock everything you may need and have a coffee shop, bakery and butchery.

Further on, also on the left as you are leaving town, is the **Olea Town Lodge and Campsite**. There are nine grassed, shady campsites with taps, electricity points and braai areas, and the ablutions are clean, with good wash-up facilities (N$120 a person). The four fully equipped self-catering bungalows can be subdivided into any size and cost N$395 single, N$600 double, N$795 triple, and N$895 for four people. Although the security does not look great, there is a guard on duty after 19h00. For more information, tel: 067-243-040, fax: 067-243-045.

The last place you pass before leaving town is the Total garage on your right – be sure to refuel for the long haul ahead – but there is more to Grootfontein than Okavango Road, so turn left at the Meteor Hotel into Hage Geingob, a pretty avenue lined with jacaranda and flamboyant trees. Here you will find the Standard and First National banks (with ATMs), the OK Grocer and Steinbach's Bäckerei, where you can stop and enjoy freshly baked sausage rolls, bread, coffee and cake.

Towards the top of Hage Geingob, turn right into Gauss Street to find the **Courtyard Guesthouse**. Here you will find safe covered parking, a swimming pool and air-conditioned

> **EMERGENCIES IN GROOTFONTEIN**
>
> ◆ State Hospital
>   (Dr Ngarikutuke Tjiriange Street)
>   067-248-150
>
> ◆ Private Hospital
>   (Captain Lombaard Street)
>   067-240-064
>
> ◆ Doctors' rooms
>   (corner Hidipo Hamutenya and Rathbone streets)
>   067-243-198 or 081-149-0338

en-suite rooms with TV and coffee-making facilities for N$425 single and N$605 double, including breakfast. For details, tel: 067-240-027, e-mail: platinum@iway.na.

There are two more budget accommodation options on the outskirts of Grootfontein. The **Lala Panzi Guest Lodge** is about 5 kilometres out of town when approaching on the B8 from the south (S19°35.496 E18°02.974). Rooms are basic, but are en-suite and have fans. Single rooms cost N$350, doubles N$500 and N$850 for four persons. Breakfast is included. For booking, tel: 067-243-648, fax: 067-243-749.

The **Maori Campsite** on the Andorra Citrus Farm sounds grand, but this small camp on the northern edge of town is very basic with a rugged campsite and saucer-sized rondavels. Accommodation costs N$195 per person in a rondavel and N$95 to camp (all sharing the same ablutions). For the lowdown, tel/fax: 067-242-351.

Rundu, Bushmanland and the Kaudom 23

The B8 between Grootfontein and Rundu is a long, straight stretch of tar that transports you from one world to another. You leave *'Suid-Wes'* behind and enter the Kavango, where Angola and Botswana are more real than Windhoek, and fences are a faded memory.

Birders may well have the hide – and sometimes the entire park – to themselves in the Kaudom area.

Approximately 56 kilometres from Grootfontein you will reach the turn-off left to **Roy's Camp** (S19°14.503 E18°30.107). Strategically situated for travellers heading north, south, east or west, Roy's Camp is perfect for a comfortable overnight stay or as a base from which to explore Bushmanland. There are grassed and shaded campsites, with clean and neat ablutions, a laundry area and communal kitchen for N$75 a person and bungalows for N$790 double. An atmospheric bar and restaurant serve three meals a day and there is a pool in which to wash the dust off. Guided tours to a San village are organised, too, and you can observe the culture and activities of this ancient people (half-day, full-day or two-day overnight walk in the wild). For more information, tel/fax: 067-240-302, e-mail: royscamp@iway.na.

There is one alternative to taking the B8 to Rundu: the C44, which turns off opposite Roy's Camp. This wide gravel road is the gateway into Bushmanland, the Kaudom Game Park and, for the adventurous, a backdoor into Botswana. But more about this later (see page 162) – let's first take the easy way north and get to Rundu.

Rundu

It is possible to bypass Rundu, but with distances around here being so great, you will probably need to refuel. There is a large Shell garage at the turn-off into town from the B8 (S17°55.976 E19°46.273), where you can also pick up public transport heading west, east or south.

To enter the town, turn in at the Shell station and drive down the Main Street. Cross a four-way stop (there's an Engen garage and Quickstop shop), and Drs Mostert and Van Schalkwyk have consulting rooms and a private clinic on the left, just past the discount builder's warehouse that looks like a casino. Also on the left is Ozzy's Beerhouse, Restaurant and Takeaway, always good for lunch specials and a noisy evening out. Next up is the obligatory row of South African clothing and furniture shops before you reach Standard Bank (with ATM) at the intersection with M Siwaronga Street. The public hospital is behind Standard Bank, Sparks Internet is across the road, and a little further on Main Street ends in a T-junction with Maria Mwengere Road.

> **EMERGENCIES IN RUNDU**
> ♦ Drs Mostert and Van Schalkwyk 066-255-048
> ♦ Public hospital and ambulance 066-265-500

Most of the shopping action takes place in M Siwaronga Street, so turn left out of Main Street opposite Standard Bank to pass Dunlop Tyres, Spar supermarket, the woodcarving co-op and OK supermarket all on your left. The **Shell/Toyota** garage (tel: 066-255-071) is opposite OK and Cymot motor spares (also gas refills and camping gear) on the left again. Rundu's outdoor market is further down and worth a visit as it has almost anything for sale, including a good selection of curios and handcrafts. If you need a tow or vehicle repair, call Gawie of **FDS Auto Electric**, tel: 066-255-760 or 081-298-6039.

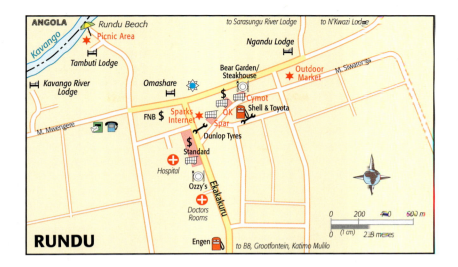

Back at the T-junction you will find the police station and the **Omashare Lodge**. A three-star, up-market option in Rundu, Omashare is centrally situated, with recently refurbished rooms surrounding a lawn and pool. There is pleasant indoor or outdoor dining and a large bar, all overlooking the Kavango River. Singles cost N$770 and doubles N$995. For details, tel: 066-256-101, fax: 066-256-111, e-mail: omashare@iway.na.

Just west of Omashare is the turn-off to Rundu Beach on the Okavango River and the **Tambuti Lodge**. The 'beach' is a sandy stretch of riverbank, with tables, benches, braai areas and a launching ramp for boats, but I'd be careful of crocs! Tambuti Lodge has one of the best positions in town but is dry and uninviting. Comfortable en-suite chalets cry out for a lush garden setting, but are cheap enough at N$400 a double, including breakfast. For more information, tel: 066-255-711, e-mail: tambuti@iway.na

As Rundu is perched on a ridge high above the Okavango River, there are some wonderful views of the plains below. The old-established **Kavango River Lodge** (drive to the end of Maria Mwengere and turn right) is situated at the most prominent point of this ridge and offers the best views, even if their bungalows are a little tired and dated. De luxe single rooms cost N$700 and doubles N$1 200. Contact the lodge on tel: 066-255-244, fax: 066-255-013 e-mail: kavlodge@tsu.namib.com.

The two most popular accommodation establishments in Rundu are east along Maria Mwengere. The first, **Ngandu Safari Lodge**, is situated at the turn-off down to the river and consists of 23 luxury, 12 semi-luxury and six standard units, all en-suite with air-con and telephone. There is a good à la carte restaurant, bar, swimming pool and neat grassed campsites with clean ablutions. Rates include breakfast and range from N$370 single in a luxury room and N$500 double to N$260 and N$400 in a standard room. Camping is N$35 per person plus N$35 per caravan. For further information, tel/fax: 066-256-723, e-mail: ngandu@mweb.com.na, website: ngandusafari-lodge.com.

Turn down at Ngandu to reach my favourite spot on the river, **Sarasungu River Lodge**. Comfortable, rustic cottages and a leafy campsite are set in the most beautifully lush gardens on the bank of the Kavango. The thatched bar/restaurant and pool area always seem to have a busy, friendly vibe and at night the muted sounds of Angola waft across the river. Sarasungu offers fishing excursions and a visit to a traditional village, and can even arrange day trips to Calai across the river in Angola. Their cottages are N$531 single, N$742 double, N$996 for three, and N$1 272 for four people, and camping is N$80 a person. For the lowdown on what's on offer, tel: 066-255-161, fax: 066-256-238, e-mail: sarasungu@mweb.com.na, website: www.sarasunguriverlodge.com.

On the way down to Sarasungu Lodge there is an evocative spot on the Kavango River where the locals from both sides (Angolan and Namibian) cross to trade. Turn left at S17°53.538 E19°46.750 and drive to the army post on the riverbank. This is not an official crossing point and only the locals can cross for short, informal visits, but the *mokoros* glide back and forth carrying basic foods and manufactured goods to Angola and bringing back cheap meat. The Angolan town of Calai across the river seems very rundown, but kingfishers dive for small fish, while women wash clothes and kids play in the water – a pleasant, peaceful scene.

A detour through Kaudom

The road east from Rundu into the Caprivi is a good, straight, tarred road, but I promised an interesting alternative – the rough 4x4 track through Bushmanland and the Kaudom Game Park.

Don't bother reading any further if you are not prepared for extremely harsh, sandy conditions. You need to be completely self-sufficient, take all your own food, water and fuel and be prepared to share the adventure with some very wild animals. But if this 'warning' has simply made you determined to tackle this route, read on ...

Assuming you will be coming up from the south, fill up with fuel in Grootfontein. You will not see another fuel station for days and at least 630 kilometres (to Divundu), so carry reserves. The big Spar on the way out of **Grootfontein** is a good place to stock up on food and drink, as there are no decent shops before Katima Mulilo (if you're heading east) or Rundu (if you're heading west).

Suitably stocked up and loaded down, hit the B8 north and travel 55 kilometres to the turn-off east onto the C44 opposite Roy's Camp (a good place to overnight – see page 160). The C44 is a good, wide, flat, straight gravel road for about 76 kilometres to the vet control gate, which is also your entrance into Bushmanland. The remaining 147 kilometres to Tsumkwe are

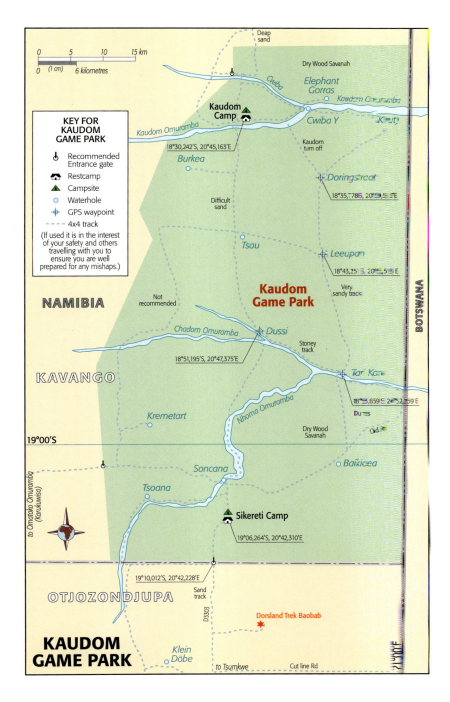

unfenced with wandering livestock and a few bad potholes.

Tsumkwe is not a town, it's not even a village, it's a crossroads in the bush (S19°35.490 E20°30.177). Turn left to Kaudom, carry on straight for Botswana and right to the Tsumkwe Lodge and on to Guru Pan. At the crossroads you will find a school, tiny general dealer, a new fuel station and a smart new government craft centre. The centre should, in fact, be a hive of activity, with San artists happily working at their ancient crafts, but in reality it is a white elephant and a waste of donor spending. There is not a San craftsman in sight and all you can buy is a warm Coke and some wilted fruit and veg.

Turn right here at the crossroads for the police station and the Savanna II supermarket where you can buy basic foodstuffs, but nothing fresh. The clinic is across the road, and about a kilometre down is the turn-off right (S19°36.032 E20°30.089) to the **Tsumkwe Lodge**.

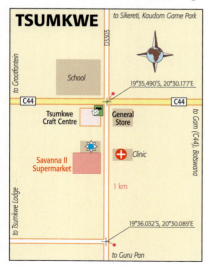

The bungalows are furnished with beautiful furniture made from local wood, lit by lantern and have donkey boilers for hot water. Singles cost N$495, doubles N$700 and camping N$65 per person. The lodge can organise day visits to San villages, overnight stays or evening dance entertainment. For particulars, tel: 061-374-750, fax: 061-256-598, e-mail: tsumkwe@ncl.com.na, website: www.namibialodges.com.

An exciting and difficult route in and out of Namibia is to continue straight at the Tsumkwe crossroads and head for the Botswana border at Dobe. The 55-kilometre road is rough and sandy, but the border is open 07h00–15h00 and you can cross to Gcangwa in Botswana. This is just north of Aha Hills and Drotsky's Caves – well worth a visit. You could then head north to view the San paintings at Tsodilo Hills and re-enter Namibia at Mohembo. Just a thought!

But there is no need to linger in Tsumkwe when wonderfully wild Kaudom beckons. Head north from the Tsumkwe crossroads up a rough sandy single track (rocky in parts, too). After 25 kilometres you will pass a rusty old Pepsi sign. Tracks lead off to the left and right, but stick to the well-used one heading northeast. After another 53 kilometres you pass through the unmanned gates of the park (S19°10.012 E20°42.228) and another 7 kilometres bring you to the small office of **Sikereti Camp** (S19°06.264 E20°42.310).

The thatched hut that serves as headquarters for the rangers here was so vandalised by elephants that a moat had to be dug around it. The staff are friendly and always pleased to receive

Brush up on your sand-driving skills for Kaudom, the wild elephant park.

visitors. As the camp accommodation has been abandoned by the NWR (elephants were trashing it faster than they could repair it), there is no charge for staying at Sikereti Camp, only the N$60 per person, N$10 per vehicle parks fee payable to MET. This must be one of the best bargains in Namibia!

The campsite is down to the right (south) of the office and consists of the abandoned bungalows and ablution block of the old NWR camp. The shower and toilets might still work (but only just!) and if you want hot water try the old donkey boiler. You're welcome to sleep in the broken-down bungalows, or even pitch your tent inside one, but one thing is sure, you will be visited by wild animals during the night. From mice to elephant and lion and hyena, you will hear them, see them or find their spoor the next morning. You will light your fire for the evening meal and hear nothing but the noises of the African night. Bliss!

Kaudom is not a large park, but it takes time to get around, and although it is only about 100 kilometres between the two camps of Sikereti and Kaudom, the stretch will take most of a day. There is a central route and an eastern one – ask the rangers which one is currently in favour. The drier months are best to view game, but the elephants can be aggressive then, so be careful. Deflate your tyres for the sand and be prepared to have your vehicle's paintwork scratched by the bushes and trees that crowd the track. Kaudom is only for 'proper' 4x4 vehicles and serious drivers who come well equipped and know what they are doing. For those who do venture into this wilderness, it is one of the last places where you have to fend for yourself and have the satisfaction of being self-sufficient. There are very few visitors and there's a stillness unsullied

Hides in Kaudom were built by Raleigh International volunteers.

by generators, swimming-pool filters and air-con compressors.

The tracks often follow the dry *omurambas* (Himba for 'vague riverbed') of rivers that hardly ever flow or churn through mopane forests, but there are no dunes like in the Namib or the southern Kalahari. This is a flat country. Some of the waterholes have hides raised on stilts, built by the volunteer organisation, Raleigh International, while others comprise little more than a few solar panels and a water trough.

Kaudom Camp is reached at S18°30.242 E20°45.163, where the office is similarly protected by a moat. Charges are the same as at Sikereti, but the bungalows and ablutions are in a worse condition. You can still camp in the bungalows, but the ablutions have been trashed and will never see water again. The elephants are even more aggressive here and care must be taken to stay out of their way at night when they go on the prowl.

On the up side, the chance of good game sightings is better up here as the camp overlooks the Kaudom *omuramba*, with waterholes and good grazing nearby. There is also a better system of tracks and game drives in the area and a couple of very pleasant days can be spent here.

Leaving the park via the northern gate requires you to navigate the worst sand in the area. If you've managed to get this far without deflating your tyres, now is the time to let them down to about 1 or 1.2 bars. The track out is deeply rutted, with a high *middelmannetjie*, the sand has been well churned up and, as the day heats up, it gets softer and fluffier, but eventually, after about 72 hard kilometres you reach the B8 at Katere. Turn left for Rundu (110 kilometres) or right for Divundu (88 kilometres).

The Caprivi 24

The B8 is the main thoroughfare through the Caprivi, running in an east–west direction from Rundu to Katima Mulilo and on to the Botswanan border at Ngoma Bridge. It is a well-maintained, wide tar road with little traffic and can be traversed quickly. The first 200-kilometre section between Rundu and the little settlement of Divundu, near Popa Falls, is featureless, except for the turn-off south to the Kaudom Game Park.

Popa Falls may be underwhelming, but these waters later become the impressive Okavango Delta.

An interesting alternative to the B8 is the gravel road that runs parallel with it to the north and links all the villages along the banks of the Kavango River. It is a good road and offers fine views of the river as it winds its way east. Travelling this route also brings you to the beautifully positioned **Shamvura Camp**.

Shamvura is a comfortable and convenient base to use before or after the rigours of Bushmanland, and a lovely introduction to the waterways of the Caprivi. The turn-off north from the B8 is conveniently situated opposite the road down to Kaudom, 110 kilometres from Rundu and 88 kilometres from Divundu. Two kilometres of good gravel brings you to a T-junction, turn right (east) and the gate to Shamvura is 9 kilometres further on at S18°02.447 E20°51.512.

Situated high on a ridge overlooking the Kavango, Shamvura offers spectacular views of the riverine forest and Angolan floodplains. There is a six-bed, self-catering family cottage, with fully equipped kitchen and veranda overlooking the river, and a number of permanent tents. The tents have en-suite bathrooms, wooden decks with views and a small garden area with a braai. There is also camping, with private kitchen and ablution facilities. Owners Mark and Charlie Paxton are nature lovers and specialise in boat trips on

WATERWAYS OF THE CAPRIVI

In a country as dry as Namibia, with so few constant rivers, it is quite shocking to find so much water as in the Caprivi. The Kavango River (as the Cubango) flows south out of the Angolan highlands to swing east and form the border between that country and Namibia. It flows strongly for 400-odd kilometres (augmented by the Cuito River at Katere) to Andara and then turns south again. Tumbling over Popa Falls, it cuts through Caprivi to enter Botswana around Mohembo, and by the time it reaches Shakawe it has already started fanning out into the wetlands of the Okavango Delta. Further east, the Kwando is a far more complex – and confused – river. It, too, starts life in Angola and is the border between that country and Zambia for a while before slicing through the Caprivi at Kongola, where it is renamed the Mashi. Swinging east, it becomes the border between Namibia and Botswana as the Linyanti River before spreading into lush, fertile swamps to reform as the Chobe and eventually join the mighty Zambezi at Kazangula.

The Caprivi can also claim the Zambezi as its own when it becomes the border between Namibia and Zambia from Katima Mulilo and flows east to Kazangula. Look at a map of the eastern Caprivi to see how the region is almost surrounded by rivers – the Kwando, Mashi, Linyanti, Chobe and Zambezi. Little wonder the wildlife is so prolific here!

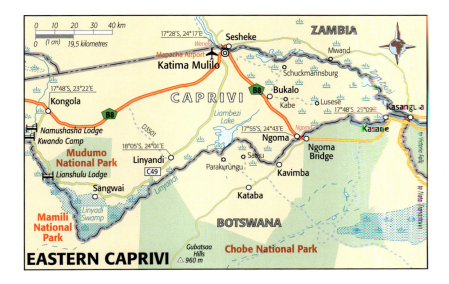

the river to fish for tigers or bream, or spot some of the wonderful bird life in the area. Accommodation costs N$400 per person in the cottage, N$300 in the tented camp and N$100 to camp. Contact the Paxtons for info on all other activities on tel: 066-686-055, fax: 066-686-054, e-mail: shamvura@iway.na, website: www.shamvura.com.

Divundu

Divundu is the village at the bridge across the Kavango River and is the gateway to the Caprivi (west of here is technically still the region of Kavango). The Engen garage on your right as you approach Divundu has closed, but the small workshop next door (tel: 066-259-167 or 081-128-0314) offers a breakdown service, mechanical workshop and puncture repairs. Fuel is available just before the bridge at the Shell garage, where there is also a well-stocked supermarket (including tyres, oil and filters).

The turn-off south to **Popa Falls** and on to the Mahango Game Park and Botswana is here at S18°05.966 E21°32.959. A small supermarket/bakery/bottle store at the intersection stocks fresh bread, ice and booze, and next door is the post office and another mechanical workshop. This is the C48 and at 5 kilometres you will reach the gates to the Namibian Wildlife Resort at Popa Falls.

There is a small, neat restaurant at the main office, and the accommodation is down by the river. Recently renovated and good value for money. Econo huts with four beds cost N$250 per person and camping is N$100 plus N$50 per person. Day visitors pay N$50, plus N$50 for a vehicle. (All bookings can be made through the NWR head office.) Popa is a pretty spot with riverside camp and picnic sites, but don't expect to be overwhelmed by the 'falls'. They are actually cascades over a series of rocks – but still impressive if you think that this water creates the huge Okavango Delta of Botswana. There is a better view of the falls and a quiet community campsite on the other side of the river (see also page 172).

Divava Okavango Lodge (formally known as Suclabo Lodge) lies just downstream from Popa Falls and offers exquisite views in a well-wooded setting. Dinner, bed and breakfast rates are a hefty N$2 780 single and N$3 960 double. Tel/fax: 061-244-558, e-mail: info@namibweb.com, website: www.namibweb.com/suclabo.htm. The **Rainbow River Lodge** is just a kilometre further on. Their 20 campsites are right on the river (with beware-of-the-croc signs!) and the chalets are on higher ground with great views. Accommodation and ablutions are all getting a little old now, but are still well kept, neat and spacious. The en-suite chalets are N$515 single and N$890 double, while camping is N$95 a person. For details, tel: 066-686-002, fax: 066-686-003, e-mail: rainbow@mweb.com.na.

The camp that everyone is talking about along this stretch of the river is **Ngepi**. To reach it, turn left at the Ngepi sign 10 kilometres south of the Divundu intersection and bounce down a not-quite-4x4-track for another 4 kilometres. They have a perfect site on the river, with huge trees, pretty gardens and lush lawns. The rustic tree houses are innovative and beautifully positioned among palms at the river's edge. The bush pub and restaurant are always abuzz with travellers sharing experiences over a cold beer, and they have funky open-air ablutions and a croc-diving cage. All sorts of activities are available, including *mokoro* trips, traditional dancing and drumming, and frisbee golf! Rates are N$300 in an en-suite bush hut, N$430 in the famous open-air tree houses and camping is N$85. All prices are per person and include breakfast (except camping). For further details, contact the camp on tel: 066-259-903, fax: 066-259-906, e-mail: bookings@ngepicamp.com, website: www.ngepicamp.com.

Another 5.5 kilometres down the C48 is the turn-off to **Mahangu Safari Lodge**. With solid brick-built bungalows, a comfortable thatched bar and restaurant and deck over the river – all set in park-like surroundings – this is an upmarket destination. On offer are luxury safari tents with own ablutions at N$520 per person and en-suite bungalows at N$740 per person – dinner, bed and breakfast. For reservations, tel: 066-259-037, fax: 066-259-115, e-mail: eden@mweb.com.na, website: www.mahangu.com.na.

> **An important point** to note when travelling through this region is that if you are on a motorcycle, you are not permitted to take the route through Mahango Game Park. No motorcycles allowed!

It is now just another 3 kilometres to the gate of the **Mahango Game Park**. This small park has good birdlife, some elephant and rare antelope such as roan and sable. There is no accommodation in the park, but it is possible to drive a circuit route of the entire park in a day. Other travellers pass through the park on their way to or from Botswana. Charges (not if you are passing through to Bots) are N$30 a person and N$10 for your vehicle.

On to Kongola and beyond

Back in Divundu on the B8, we refuel and cross the Kavango Bridge, heading east – the army roadblock on the other side is painless. Look out for the turn-off (S18°05.821 E21°33.966) right (south) down 3 kilometres to the best view site for Popa Falls at the lovely community campsite of **N//goabaca** (I can spell it but don't ask me to pronounce it!). Each site is in the riverine forest at the river's edge and has its own private ablutions with hot and cold running water. They also each have a kitchen lapa and wooden deck with a view over the papyrus reeds to the falls. It costs N$80 a person to camp and N$10 to picnic.

The road to the bridge across the Kwando River at Kongola is 200 kilometres of good, straight tar, but be careful of wild and domestic animals. Just before the bridge (at S17°47.031 E23°20.138) there is a turn-off to the right and left. Left takes you 1 kilometre to the excellent community campsite with the strange name of Bum Hill. It has great views of the river, good ablutions and high wooden platforms for game-viewing – a great overnight stop. Rates are N$80 a person. A right turn here, on the other hand, takes you down a 13-kilometre 4x4 track to Nambwa, another community camp. But first obtain a permit from the Susuwe Ranger station at Bum Hill as you will be entering the Bwabwata Game Park. On the drive down you will see quite a lot of game as the track follows the floodplain of the Kwando River.

Back on the B8, you cross the Kwando Bridge, pass through another army checkpoint and arrive at the intersection of Kongola. There is a fuel station, small supermarket and Mashi Crafts, where you can buy authentic, locally made crafts at reasonable prices. Here the B8 continues on its effortless way for another 100-odd kilometres, but the turn-off down the C49 via Mudumu and Mamili game parks is far more interesting.

The C49 follows the Kwando/Mashi/Linyanti River south through the game parks and then swings northeast to end at Katima Mulilo. A number of fine lodges grace the riverbanks along this stretch with the turn-off to the first, Namushasha, just 30 kilometres from Kongola. About 4 kilometres off the C49, you will reach this recently upgraded lodge in its fine position overlooking the river.

Namushasha Lodge offers luxury accommodation in finely fitted new bungalows overlooking the river and floodplains at N$1 000 single and N$1 430 double (inclusive of breakfast). It also offers camping on shaded, grassy sites at N$65 a person. The deck over the water presents one of the finest views in the Caprivi, with birds and hippo in the foreground and elephant grazing the floodplain beyond. Fine food and a great bar, together with activities such as game drives, boat trips and visits to a local traditional village, make Namushasha a prime destination. For further details, tel: 061-374-750, fax: 061-256-398, e-mail: namushasha@ncl.com.na website: www.namibialodges.com.

Just 5 kilometres further down the C49 brings you to the turn-off to

Camp Kwando. This camp offers canvas-over-pole chalets on the river's edge, with wooden decks built out over the water, at N$660 single and N$1 100 double (dinner and breakfast included). The site is very pleasant, with a swimming pool and basic but solid ablutions, for N$70 a person. As do all the lodges along this stretch, they also offer game drives, boat trips and traditional village visits. For more info, tel: 066-686-021, fax: 066-686-023, e-mail: reservations@campkwando.com, website: www.campkwando.com.

Mudumu and Mamili

You now enter the **Mudumu Game Park**, but there is no gate or entrance fee if you are just passing through. After about 12 kilometres you reach the turn-off to the Rolls-Royce of river camps, a game lodge that Brad Pitt and Angelina Joli would come to if they grew tired of the beach – **Lianshulu Lodge**. At Lianshulu you are welcomed with tea and freshly baked cake on a deck over the river that leaves you slack-jawed. The meals are prepared (not just cooked) by a gourmet chef and the staff are genuinely friendly and happy to look after you. The bungalows are perfectly positioned along the river and bigger than most people's homes. The maid runs a hot bubble bath for you and leaves a bottle of wine and two glasses within arm's reach! The sundowner boat trips and early-morning game drives are led by experts in their field and you never want to leave. And when you do, if you're not leaving by plane from the private airstrip, you'll find that your car has been cleaned for you. Dinner, bed and breakfast rates are understandably steep and range between N$2 300 single in off-season to N$5 200 double in the peak season. For reservations, tel: 061-274-545, fax: 061-239-455, e-mail: sabinak@safariadventure.com.na, website: www.safariadventurecompany.com.

The cheapskate option in Mudumu is to turn off 5 kilometres south of the Lianshulu road (at S18°08.294 E23°26.030) and camp at the official **Nakatwa Camp**. Also beautifully situated on the banks of the river, but with no facilities other than a long-drop toilet, this idyllic spot costs only N$30 per person plus N$10 for your car. The monkeys will steal from you during the day and the hippo will worry you at night, but what an unforgettable experience!

Mamili Game Park is south of Mudumu and even wilder. The turn-off to Sangwali is at S18°14.286 E23°39.685 and it is another 8 kilometres to the ranger's camp in the park at Sinsinzwe. There are two large islands in this swampland (Nkasa and Lupala) and three informal campsites (**Shivuma, Lyadura** and **Moaremure**). Mamili is very marshy during the wet season and resembles the Okavango in Botswana, so to avoid getting stuck, only visit from May to October. You will need a 4x4 as the conditions will be sand or mud all year and, like the Okavago, the flooding depends on rain far upstream in Angola. The fees here are the same as they are in Mudumu, and you must be completely self-sufficient. The C49 then loops around to rejoin the B8 just 8 kilometres before Katima Mulilo.

Katima Mulilo
25

Katima is a border town with quick and easy access to Zambia, Botswana and Zimbabwe (via Bots). Unfortunately, life has not always been peaceful for the town as the bomb shelters in many backyards attest. But, life in Katima Mulilo has settled down now and is even improving commercially as the Sesheke Bridge across the Zambezi has opened and trade with Zambia picks up.

The waters of the Zambezi at Katima Mulilo are legendary for boating and fishing.

Introducing Katima

Entering Katima Mulilo along the B8 from the Kongola side, you will first encounter most of the town's garages and vehicle-repair shops. There's a BP on the left, followed by **Katima Engineering Works** (tel: 081-262-7535 for 24-hour breakdowns) and **Truck & Tractor Repairs** (tel: 081-128-3216). Then there is an Engen garage with a Quick Shop for takeaways, and across from them, a branch of Trentyre for tyres and puncture repairs.

Mukusi Cabins is part of the Engen complex and your best bet for in-town accommodation. Basic, but clean and functional, wooden cabins are dotted around in a garden setting with good security. Standard rooms have air-con and cost N$380 single and N$480 double. All rooms share a communal ablution block, and there is an à la carte restaurant. For the lowdown, tel: 066-253-255, fax: 066-252-359, e-mail: mukusi@mweb.com.na.

The road continues on down past **Sharpe Engineering** (tel/fax: 066-252-450, e-mail: sharpe@iafrica.com.

A morning mist rises over a Zambezi houseboat at the Caprivi River Lodge.

na). Dick Sharpe is a 4x4 fundi, knows the area well and does vehicle and air-con repairs – a good guy to know. His wife, Katy, runs **Tutwa Tourism and Travel** from adjoining premises. Katy is a mine of information on travel in the region, runs a welcoming coffee shop where they also sell curios and maps, is the agent for Intercape bus services, offers safaris and day trips and is very knowledgable on local birds and birding. Contact her on tel/fax: 066-252-739, e-mail: tutwa@mweb.com.na, website: www.tutwa.com. There is a Total garage at the T-junction at the bottom. Turn left for the Zambian border (4 kilometres) or right for the town's river lodges and on to the Botswanan border (65 kilometres). The Total garage also houses the Cross Border Payment Offices where you must buy your permit if entering Namibia.

The centre of town is approached by turning right into Hage Geingob Drive just past Mukusi Cabins. Pass the Shell garage on your left before reaching the town's main intersection. A left turn here will take you past the big OK supermarket and on past the **hospital** (for an ambulance, tel 066-251-400) to the riverside drive. All the local and long-distance taxis stand at this intersection and there is a lively market here too. Continuing along Hage Geingob Drive you will find the post office on your right and then a tatty South African shopping centre housing the usual Pep Stores and Ackermans. Across the road on the left is a smart row of interesting businesses. First up is the smart new Baobab Bistro, a licensed restaurant for tasty breakfasts, lunches and snacks, which stays open late for dinners on Fridays.

Baobab Bistro is followed by the **Caprivi Pharmacy** (tel: 066-253-446), **Air Namibia** (tel: 066-253-191) and First National Bank with an ATM. The rest of Katima Mulilo is a town-planner's worst nightmare and not really worth venturing into. A new shopping area has opened about 100 metres down from Engen in Hage Geingob Street where Pick 'n Pay and Bank Windhoek have set up shop, along with Nedbank and an optitian.

Overnight in Katima

Back at the Total garage intersection, where the road turns left to Zambia, turn right towards Botswana. This is a continuation of the B8 and passes the town's river lodges on the banks of the Zambezi.

A couple of kilometres further (at S17°29.339 E24°17.142) is the turn-off to the Zambezi River Lodge, now run by Protea Hotels. Room rates (inclusive of breakfast) are N$637 single, N$934 double and N$1 376 for a family room. For info, tel: 066-253-149, fax: 066-253-631, e-mail: info@proteahotels.com, website: www.proteahotels.com.

The turn-off left to the **Caprivi River Lodge** is 5 kilometres out of town and takes you just a kilometre down to the best accommodation in the area. Smoothly and pleasantly run by owners Keith and Mary Rooken-Smith, the lodge is set in lush gardens overlooking the Zambezi. They have solid, brick-and-thatch en-suite chalets with ceiling fans, bar fridge and kettle, and sliding doors that open to the river. The rooms cost N$750 for a single and N$1 035 a double (B&B). They also have a comfortable en-suite wooden cabin that sleeps two for N$950 (B&B) and cabins that share ablutions for N$270 single and N$400 double (bed only). Mary cooks great meals and Keith runs **Hakuna Matata Adventures** for kayak and fishing trips on the Zam-

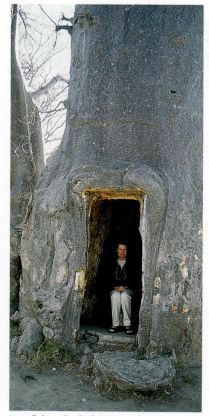

Not all the toilet facilities at Katima are as rough as this one carved into a baobab tree.

Wilderness areas of the north are home to black wildebeest.

bezi and guided tours into the neighbouring game parks. Great Landy lovers and bikers (Keith owns a Harley), they offer a discount to anyone arriving in a Land Rover or on two wheels. Contact the Rooken-Smiths on tel: 066-252-288, fax: 066-253-158, e-mail: mary@capririver lodge.net, website: www.capririver lodge.info.

Next along from the Capriri River Lodge is the once-lovely, but now rundown **Hippo Lodge**. It is presently closed for renovations.

On from Katima Mulilo

To Zambia About 4 kilometres northwest of Katima you pass through the Wenela border post into Zambia. You then have the choice of taking the new bridge across the Zambezi to Sesheke and west along an upgraded, tarred road to Livingstone, or keeping west of the Zambezi and taking the very rough, 4x4 road to Mongu. This latter road takes you past the Ngonye Falls on the Zambezi and across the ferry at Sioi.

To Botswana The 65 kilometres down the last stretch of the 38 to Ngoma Bridge border post into Botswana is good tar and should be uneventful. From Ngoma, it is another 55 kilometres to Kasane for access to the most remote and easternmost outpost of Namibia. This island paradise lies at the confluence of the Zambezi and Chobe rivers and is only (realistically) approached by boat from Kasane. **Impalila Island Lodge, Ntwala Island Lodge and Susuwe Island Lodge** are all close to each other and compete in the luxury stakes, although they are all run by Islands in Africa, tel: +27-(0)11-706-7207, fax: +27-(0)11-463-8251, e-mail: info@islandsinafrica.com, website: www.islandsinafrica.com (Impalila and Susuwe charge around US$500 per person per night in high season and Ntwala which is the most luxurious, charges US$750.)

Rundu to Ruacana 26

Having explored the region east of Rundu, let's take a trip across the top of Etosha, through the busy Owambo towns of Ondangwa and Oshakati to the wild Kunene River, Epupa Falls and Kaokoland.

The sun sets over Angola across the Kunene River at Rundu (above). Grey heron fishing (left).

The regular route from Rundu to Oshakati would be down the B8 to Grootfontein and then back up the B1 to the capital of Owamboland, but that's too easy – I'm going to suggest an alternative. The C45, which runs across the northernmost reaches of Nam, is a fairly good gravel road, shorter and takes one tantalisingly close to the Angolan border. It starts in Rundu, at the Engen four-way stop on Independence Avenue, or follow the signs to Nzinze off the B8.

The road follows the Kavango River (with nice views of the floodplains) for 90 kilometres to Nzinze where the D3405 forks off to the right – keep left here to stay on the C45 as it veers away from the river. The D3405 might look like nothing, but it follows the Kavango to Nkurenkuru (where fuel is available), which is a pedestrian crossing point to Cuangar on the Angolan side, and continues upstream to the border post at Katitwe. Katitwe is surprisingly busy, with heavily loaded trucks making their way there from the warehouses at Oshikango with supplies for the central-southern parts of Angola.

The road is long and featureless with a hassle-free army checkpoint at Mpungu, 80 kilometres from Nzinze. You will see very little habitation for the next 200 kilometres, except for the NPK B&B, close to Eenhana (at S17°28.403 E16°23.242). It's unlikely that you'll need a place to stay along this stretch, but if you do, the **NPK B&B** is a clean, comfortable refuge. Their rates are very reasonable at N$170 a room (single or double) or N$325 for a room with air-con (single or double, inclusive of breakfast). For more information, tel: 081-235-4343.

Eenhana has a bakery and mini-market at the turn-off, and a Shell garage and Bank Windhoek in the village. Another 48 kilometres brings you to the B1 – turn north for the Angolan border at Oshikango or south to Ondangwa. The short 13-kilometre section of B1 to Oshikango is lined with businesses of all sorts, but mainly vehicle-breakers' yards or small bars.

What's in a name?
The pokey little bars that line the highways in Owamboland make up for their simplicity by having fancy names. Club Shake your Body, Super Cool Bar or Super Sex Bar all advertise a pretty obvious type of joint, but what about the Back of the Moon Club or Let's Push Bar? See what you can list when you're up in these parts.

Oshikango is quite simply a street lined with shops and warehouses to supply Angolans with whatever they want. Trucks piled high with tarp-covered loads block the road and the closer you get to the border, the more chaotic it gets. Stay away if you don't have business there or want to cross the border! The **Oshikango Country Lodge** is the only decent accommodation here – you can't miss it on the western side of the road. It has a lively bar with pool tables and disco and a neat dining area, but the whole place is looking a little tired (but so would you if you lived in this town).

Rooms (single or double) cost N$500. For details, tel: 065-264-650.

Turning south from the C45 onto the B1 takes you 43 kilometres down to **Ondangwa**. A Shell garage and Shoprite supermarket welcome you on the right as you approach town, followed by an Engen and Pick 'n Pay. The **Ondangwa Protea Hotel** is at the intersection where you turn right towards Oshakati or left to reach the centre of Ondangwa. (Note that if you are travelling north up the B1, you will have to turn right here to stay on the main road to Oshikango.) The four-star Protea Hotel is the only upmarket accommodation in town and has comfortable rooms with air-con, TV and telephone for N$726 single and N$910 double, including breakfast. There is an à la carte restaurant and the offices of DHL are in the foyer. For reservations, tel: 065-241-900, fax: 065-241-919, e-mail: info@proteahotels.com, website: www.proteahotels.com/ondangwa.

If you are coming into Ondangwa from the south you will find most businesses on the left. The Standard Bank is up first, followed by a pharmacy and a doctor's rooms. A shopping centre with a well-stocked Shoprite is followed by a Shell garage and taxi rank, and then an industrial park and market, with an OK Grocer beyond that. Turn off right at the Bank Windhoek to reach two reasonable places to stay.

At the first right you will run into the compact **Ondangwa Rest Camp** situated around a small dam. It has three tents with beds and bedding for N$310 single and N$430 double, and four campsites where you can pitch your own tent for N$125 a person – all share cramped but clean communal ablutions. It's a popular spot with the locals to watch rugby and enjoy a dop. For more information, tel.fax 065-240-351, e-mail: restcamp@osh.namib.com.

Just outside their gate are two South African graves dating back to the 1917 conflict with King Mandume's forces, and across the road is the town's other medical practitioner, with a pharmacy and laboratory. Further up the road are the post office and police station, and off to the right is the neat and tidy **Ondangwa Town Lodge**. There's a fairly new block of comfortable rooms for N$425 single, N$585 double and N$695 for family room, breakfast included. For details, tel: 065-241-715, fax: 065-241-717.

Oshakati

You will pass many motor-repair workshops as you enter Oshakati. The first accommodation establishment on the right (at S17°47.160 E15°43.274) is the **Santorini Inn**. With a large, secure parking area and most rooms set in a pretty garden with swimming pool, this is a place to relax and recuperate or gird yourself for the rigours ahead. They have a car-hire service and also offer angling tours on the Kunene River, into Angola, or down to the coast around Henties Bay (e-mail: angling@iway.com.na). Single rooms are N$380, doubles N$600. For further information, tel: 065-221-803, fax: 065-220-437, e-mail: info@santorini-inn.com

Next up on the left is the unfinished Rochas restaurant and the **Eluwa Hotel**. The Eluwa Hotel is a large concrete building set in unkempt gardens, but has reasonable rooms with TV and air-con for

The once mighty Ruacana Falls are now starved of water by Angola's Calueque Dam.

N$400 single and N$600 double. Rooms without TV and air-con cost N$250 and N$400. **Rochas** is a popular Angolan/Portuguese restaurant in the same complex serving tasty food and cold beer. For details, tel: 065-222-038, fax: 065-224-282, e-mail: rochas@iway.na.

On the left-hand corner, just past Rochas, is an Engen garage with attached Wimpy, and behind is a shopping centre with a Kentucky Fried Chicken and Shoprite supermarket. On the left at the next intersection, Robert Mugabe Street, is another small business centre with a Standard Bank and ATM, as well as a Primary Health Centre (tel: 065-222-522). Across the road, at 749 Main Road, is the large **Oshakati Pharmacy** and a medical complex housing GPs, a dentist, laboratory, X-ray facility and an ambulance service. To contact the medical centre, tel: 065-225-500, fax: 065-221-775, e-mail: oxis@mweb.com.na.

Turn left into Robert Mugabe to reach the town's top hotel, the **Oshakati Country Lodge**. Like so many accommodation establishments in Namibia, the Oshakati Lodge consists of a large thatched main building with a great bar and public areas furnished with lovely polished wood. Outside is a pool surrounded by the well-appointed rooms, all set in pretty gardens. Rates are N$666 single and N$1 010 double. The lodge is also the agent for **Ovambo Car Hire**. Contact them on tel: 065-222-380, fax: 065-222-384, e-mail: countrylodge@mweb.com.na.

Follow the signs down Robert Mugabe into Kwame Nkrumah Street to get to the comfortable and secure **Oshandira Lodge**. All rooms have coffee machines, air-con and TV and cost N$550 single, N$725 double and N$950 for a four-bed family room. A new wing has been built and the rooms here are slightly more expensive. The management are friendly, efficient and professional. For information, tel: 065-220-443, fax: 065-221-189, e-mail: oshandira@iway.na.

Back in Main Street, you cross the bridge and then pass Cymot on your left (for motor spares and camping gear), more garages and both the First National Bank and Standard Bank. Towards the end of town, on your right, is a big, secure Engen fuel station with clean toilets, and next door a smart new Spar supermarket with coffee bar for light meals or take-aways. There is a post office and the Izone Internet Café in the same building.

Finally, on the left as you exit the town, you will find a laundry and across the road is **Northern Auto Repairs**. They repair 4x4s (Land Rover specialists) and operate a breakdown service. For particulars, tel: 065-221-802 or 081-127-3836, e-mail: nar@iway.na.

Ruacana

The C46 heading west to Ruacana carries you away from the commercial activity of Oshakati and the border towns, into the wide-open spaces of the Namibian far northwest. The road is wide and tarred, with little traffic, and the countryside is dotted with *makalani* palms and *oshanas* (small vleis or lakes that fill with water after the rains, but later dry into dusty depressions). Donkeys and goats wander around as if they own the road, so be ready to brake.

The small town of **Outapi** is reached after 155 kilometres, where you will find a couple of garages, general dealers, banks and a busy taxi rank. On the west of town you'll also find the smart new **Outapi Town Lodge**, a large motel-styled complex with good security. Their charges are N$425 per night single and N$600 double (including breakfast), and they also serve lunches and dinners For more information, tel 065-251-029 fax: 065-251-032.

The turn-off into **Ruacana** town is after 68 kilometres (at S17°24.822 E14°21.267), and another 5 kilometres off the C46 brings you to a BP garage and mini-market on your right and a bottle store across the road. This is about all there is to Ruacana, except for the comfortable **Eha Lodge** a short distance down the road This new lodge is the ideal base from which to tackle Kaokoland or Angola, or a nice touch of luxury after you have done so. Single rooms cost N$640, doubles N$875 (breakfast included) and shaded camping with spotless ablutions cost N$55 a person. They also offer accommodation in huts for N$185 a person, a good à la carte dining room and visits to the nearby Ruacana Falls and hydroelectric power station. For further information, contact the lodge or tel: 065-271-500, fax: 065-270-095 e-mail info@ruacanaehalodge.com.na website: www.ruacanaehalodge.com.na.

The only other accommodation in Ruacana is around the other side of town at the **O'Sheja Guest House** and **Sunset Camp**. Rooms in a suburban house cost N$200 per person and the rough-and-ready campsite across the road charges N$55 per person.

Kaokoland 27

The tarred C46 continues for another 17 kilometres past the town of Ruacana and drops down through the hills to the turn-off (at S17°23.727 E14°14.380) to the hydroelectric power station and the Angolan border post.

The picturesque Warmquelle spring (above) at Ongongo Camp.
A young Himba herdsman (opposite) poses defiantly in northern Kaokoland.

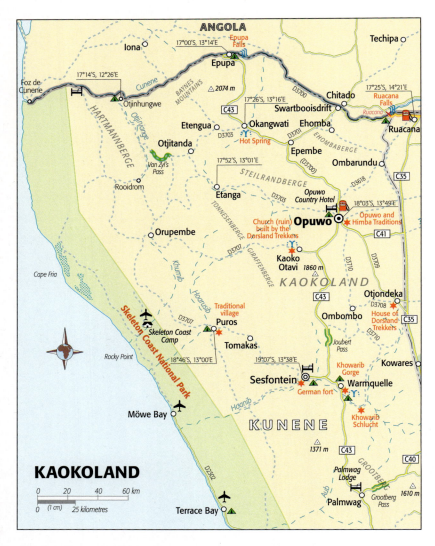

KAOKOLAND

Take the turn-off, drive 1.3 kilometres and turn right again – it is another 12.5 kilometres to the border. There is a good view of the **Ruacana Falls** at the highest point where the radio and water towers are (S17°23.831 E14°13.288), but unless it has rained very heavily you will be disappointed as almost all the water is diverted through the turbines of the hydroelectric plant.

The fine tarred surface of the C46 lasts a little longer as it winds down to the **Hippo Pools Communal Campsite** on the Ruacana River. This is an attractive site under trees at the water's edge, but listen out for the siren that warns of sudden rising water levels. New ablution blocks have been built, with solar water heating and modern long-drop toilets – charges are N$60 per person.

The road now deteriorates and becomes a rough gravel road. Speeds of 50 kph can sometimes be reached, but at other times you will have to slow right down to 5 kph. You will not require 4x4, but a vehicle with high ground clearance is necessary. Travel with two spare wheels and more than enough fuel – the next fuel is only available at Opuwo. Where the road splits into different tracks, choose the one that will take you closest to the river as it will

THE HIMBA

The Himba are a seminomadic group that trek with their cattle and goats in search of good grazing. They are a tall, strikingly attractive and photogenic people and live an independent and traditional lifestyle. The men wear leather aprons and sandals. Unmarried youths shave their hair into a strip across the top of their heads, ending in a ponytail that hangs down into their necks. Only when they marry will they be allowed to wear large turbans of softened sheepskin over unshaven heads. They all wear bulky necklaces, while the youths sometimes have wedges of leather cut from the ears of cattle given to them on initiation. The men's lives revolve around the herds – cattle are their status and wealth and they protect their herds with their lives. The women follow the men and their cattle, carrying the food, water and babies. Strikingly beautiful, they rub their almost-naked bodies with a mixture of red ochre, animal fat and fragrant herbs. Their only clothing is a multilayered skirt – they don't even wear sandals. But, they do like to adorn themselves, the main item being a large cone-shaped shell worn around the neck. Copper bangles decorate the wrists, ankles and neck, and to signify their married status, Himba women wear their hair lengthened with hair shaved from their brothers' heads into many long, thin braids and drawn backwards over their shoulders. They also wear the headdress of marriage, the *erembe*. The young unmarried girls wear smaller aprons, fewer adornments and have their hair in two plaits draped forward over the face. You will come across Himba kraals all over the mountains and plains of Kaokoland. Conical huts of sticks and branches covered with a layer of mud, often seem to be abandoned. Skulls and horns of cattle slaughtered in funerary rites stand forlornly, impaled on poles. As families trek with their cattle in search of grazing, these kraals are used regularly, so please don't go poking around these places, thinking that they'll never be used again. You're in their land and these are their homes. Tread lightly.

also take you through some interesting Himba kraals.

It is 74 kilometres to the **Kunene River Lodge** (S17°21.283 E13°52.855), a cool oasis along this stretch of the river. You will pass Omunjandi Restcamp and Onduuzo Himba Community Restcamp along the way, but rather press on to the Kunene River Lodge. Here you will find a comfortable, well-run establishment with huts, bungalows and camping in park-like surroundings on the banks of the Kunene.

The management here are very knowledgeable birdwatchers and also offer river-rafting excursions and sundowner cruises. The huts are small, solid and comfortable and cost N$465 single and N$740 double. The newer bungalows are luxurious, with sliding doors that open to the beauty of nature and cost N$660 single and N$1 100 double (all inclusive of breakfast). Camping is N$80 a person and there is a swimming pool. For bookings, tel: 065-274-300, fax: 065-274-301, e-mail: info@kuneneriverlodge.com, website: www.kuneneriverlodge.com.

You now have the choice of either continuing along the D3700, which follows the river to Epupa Falls, or swinging away from the river on the D3701 to join the C43, which runs up from Opuwo via Okangwati to Epupa. The road along the river is 100 kilometres of difficult 4x4 driving and should take about six hours; the other route is longer at about 160 kilometres, but is a far better road and will take half the time. The turn away from the river is at S17°20.470 E13°50.950, but before you head south drive 3 kilometres beyond the turn-off to reach the historic settlement of **Swartbooisdrift**. This was the main crossing point for the Dorsland Trekkers and became a far-flung trading post between South West Africa and Angola. The old buildings are now in ruins, but there is a new clinic and police post and the Himba come to 'town' to buy their basic necessities at the small store there. It's one of Africa's stranger sights to see a Himba woman, wearing nothing but a leather skirt and smeared with red fat, talking on a public telephone.

If you carry on along the river, enjoy the next 100 kilometres of bump and grind, or return to the D3701. From the turn-off, climb the hill and stop at the **Dorsland Trekkers' graves and monument**. Graves of a Roberts, Van Eck, De Klerk and Prinsloo, among others, have been hacked into this harsh, stony ground and the monument commemorates this unfortunate group's return from Angola in 1928.

You join the C43 at Otjivize and swing north again. You are now deep into Himba territory and traditionally dressed men and women will flag you down to visit their village, take their photos or buy their handicrafts. Many want lifts to the next town, so if you have room on the back of your bakkie, offer some a lift. They will really appreciate it and give you the opportunity of chatting to them informally and taking a couple of photos.

After 32 kilometres you will reach the small settlement of **Okangwati**, where there is a clinic, general dealer, bottle store and police station. In the village (at S17°26.075 E13°16.560) the road forks – keep right to cross the dry, sandy riverbed to continue on to Epupa, bear left to tackle the spectacular Van Zyl's Pass to the Marienfluss. The final 75 kilometres swoops down to the Epupa Falls through spectacular mountains and over boulder-strewn koppies. If the sun is dropping low in the sky, the landscape will assume the beautiful shades of the Himba people, while the baobab trees stand silhouetted against the sky. There is a hilltop on your left as you approach the falls and it offers a fantastic view of the sunset over the falls – don't miss it!

Epupa Falls

Epupa is a difficult destination to reach, but your first glimpse of the falls makes it all worthwhile. The mighty Kunene River squeezes down a deep narrow gorge in a flurry of mist and spray. Tons of water tumble down over rocks and boulders past baobab trees clinging to the canyons. Swallows swoop overhead while *makalani* palms sway in the background. And the best part is, you can camp right there.

The **Epupa Community Campsite** (S17°00.137 E13°14.637) would have to be in the water to be closer to the falls. It nestles beneath palm trees on the banks of the river, with the roar of the falls in your ears and rare birds flitting overhead. It is well run by the local community, with good security, hot-water showers and individual braai spots, taps and washing-up facilities. Obviously popular, it can fill up during the busy months of July and August, but it must be one of the greatest bargains in Namibia at N$80 a person. For bookings and information, tel: 065-695-102.

The Epupa Falls campsite is one of the most spectacular in all of Namibia.

Shades of blue as the sun sets behind Baynes mountains in northern Kaokoland.

Next door to the community camp, but still just a stone's throw from the falls and on the banks of the river, is the privately run **Omarunga Camp and Tented Lodge**. They have 10 comfortable furnished tents, each with their own shower and toilet at N$1 000 single and N$1 800 double (dinner, bed and breakfast), and five shady campsites at N$76 a person. You can enjoy a cold drink in the bar and a hot meal at the open-air restaurant. Guided tours are offered to a Himba village (N$390) and punctures can be repaired (N$100). Booking information is available from Camelthorn Safaris, tel: 064-403-096, fax: 064-402-097, e-mail: camtrav@iafrica.com.na, website: www.natron.net/omarunga-camp.

Another community camp, **Hot Springs**, is next along, with the same amenities and prices as the first, but less popular. Then, a short way upstream, you will find the luxury option of the area, **Epupa Falls Lodge**. This luxury tented camp offers personalised service and excellent food, a swimming pool (the only one at the falls) and a suspension bridge to take you across to a private island where you can hike the lush riverine wilderness of baobabs, wild figs and makalani palms. Daily tariffs per person sharing are N$1 200 including accommodation and three meals. Contact them on tel: 061-232-740, fax: 061-249-876, e-mail: epupa@islandsinafrica.com, website: www.epupa.com.na.

Opuwo

Retracing our steps back down the C43 for 182 kilometres brings us to the capital of Koakoland, Opuwo. Along with fuel, food, accommodation, a bank, cellphone reception and motor-repair shops, it offers a lifeline to visitors and locals of the area. Here Himba meets Herero meets overseas tourist and the images are quite startling – a bare-breasted Himba woman passing a Herero woman in full-skirted Victorian dress being videod by a skimpily clad Italian holidaymaker!

The main intersection in town (S18°03.743 E13°50.385) is where the C41 from the east joins the C43 from Epupa Falls in the north and continues down south to Sesfontein and Palmwag. Just east of this intersection is a shopping complex that consists of the First National Bank, an internet café, BP garage and OK supermarket with wines, tyres and a coffee shop. Driving north from the intersection up Opuwo's main road, turn left to find the **Ohakane Lodge**. This small, comfortable and affordable lodge is also centrally situated and boasts good security. Air-conditioned en-suite rooms are N$505 single and N$880 double (rates are lower during the hot summer months of December to April). Breakfast is included, and there is a restaurant, and Himba excursions are offered. For more information, tel: 065-273-031, fax: 065-273-025, e-mail: ohakane@iway.na.

Further up the main road is the Opuwo supermarket and across the road a tyre repair and motor-spares shop. The police station is next up on the left, followed by the Kunene Pharmacy on the right. Turn off at the next left and drive 1.5 kilometres over the hill to the breathtakingly beautiful **Opuwo Country Hotel**. This stunning new lodge boasts a main building that contains a mock Himba kraal under the largest thatched roof structure that I have ever seen. The dining room spills out onto a deck with a swimming pool and a view of the valley and mountains far in the distance, and the bar is one of the most attractive in the country. The accommodation is, not suprisingly, very luxurious and pricey at N$1 235 single and N$1 740 double. Meals are reasonably priced at N$79 for breakfast and N$160 for a buffet dinner. There is also an all-new terraced campsite overlooking the valley, where you can enjoy some of the lodge's luxury for only N$85 per person. Central reservations and information are at tel: 061-374-750, fax: 061-256-598, e-mail: opuwo@ncl.com.na, website: www.namibialodges.com.

Dragging ourselves away from this hilltop splendour, we head south out of town on the C43. After 24 kilometres keep left to stay on this road; straight on will take you via Kaoko Otavi to Orupembe, Rooidrom and or into the Marienfluss. At about 30 kilometres you will pass through a short, shallow valley filled with a collection of beautiful baobab trees, but keep your speed down as there are some deep dips and sharp curves in the road. The short but steep **Joubert Pass** is reached after 110 kilometres and is a rude reminder of how rough conditions can get.

About 13 kilometres after the pass you will reach an intersection, leading right to Sesfontein (10 kilometres) and left to Palmwag. **Sesfontein** is the southern gateway to the real Kaokoland – the Kaokoland of Puros, Rooidrom, the Marienfluss and Van Zyl's Pass. It is also the ideal base from which to explore the Hoanib River and its desert-adapted wildlife. So, although our route is south to Palmwag, let's go have a look and maybe stay over at Sesfontein. This dusty little settlement has little to recommend it beyond a few puncture repairers, a shop and, of course, a bottle store. But it does have fuel, the last for a long way if you are heading to Puros and north, and it does have quaint accommodation and camping, both at the old German **Sesfontein Fort**. The fort has been tastefully restored and has a genuine old Beau-Geste, foreign-legion look and feel about it. Luxury rooms are built into the walls and open onto the palm-treed and pooled courtyard (rates N$1 000 single, N$1 560 double). Private and protected campsites suffer a bit from inadequate ablutions but are still comfortable (N$80 a person). For information, tel: 065-275-534, fax: 065-275-533, e-mail: info@fort-sesfontein.com, website: www.fort-sesfontein.com.

On to Kaokoland

To experience Kaokoland as it was before the roads were improved and tourists with hired cars took over, head down Van Zyl's Pass through the Otjihipa mountains into the Marienfluss. Camp on the banks of the Kunene where the overlanders can't drive their trucks and head down to Sesfontein via Orupembe and Puros. But, take note, this is a very rough and difficult route and should only be tackled by experienced off-roaders who are well equipped.

At S17°26.000 E13°16.334 in Okangwati, turn southwest to take the rough track towards **Van Zyl's Pass**. The small village of Etengua is passed at 27 kilometres and then it's another 32 kilometres to the next village, **Otjitanda**. If you want to bail out now and head around in a loop back to Opuwo via Etanga, then swing left just beyond Otjitanda, but we hang tough and keep right and on to Van Zyl's. Another 21 kilometres takes you to Otjihende (S17°38.550 E12°45.470), and if you left Epupa this morning then you might want to start looking out for an overnight camp spot soon. You will not make it from Epupa over the pass in one day, so don't push it.

The following 13 kilometres are really rough as the pass is approached and the top reached at (S17°39.339 E12°41.720). This is an unimproved track over steep mountains in the middle of nowhere and you will need low ratio and sometimes diff-lock to negotiate the rocks and boulders. From the top of the pass there is a wonderful view of the valley and a scary view of the final 3-kilometre drop down the pass. This descent is very steep and it will be with feelings of relief and achievement that you will level out onto the soft, forgiving sand of the **Marienfluss**. Keep right (north) for another 65 kilometres to reach the campsite on the **Kunene River**. I know all the books and maps say you can tackle Van Zyl's Pass only from east to west, but it has been done the other way and it's not impossible.

There is an up-market, private camp on the Kunene. Pass it with an air of superiority – you've driven there, its guests probably only flew there – and head for the communal campsite. There are some shade spots, toilets, showers and taps, but nothing else. Be sure you arrive completely self-sufficient with everything, including drinking water and firewood. A couple of laid-back, pleasant days could be spent relaxing and checking over your vehicle, but don't be tempted to swim where there might be crocs lurking.

Heading south again, it is 45 kilometres to the fork to Van Zyl's Pass (S17°33.312 E12°33.234). Keep right and drive 28 kilometres to **Rooidrom**. A red drum marks this intersection – right (west) takes you to Hartmann's Valley, so left (south) is the one we want and will take us through more rugged mountains to another intersection after 50 kilometres. Keep right here (left goes to Etanga and on to Opuwo) for another 15 kilometres to reach the windmill at **Orupembe** (S18°09.367 E12°33.634). The road improves now for the 105 kilometres to the little settlement of **Puros**. This whole area is dotted with 'fairy circles', room-sized patches of ground where nothing grows. Scientists still debate the cause of this fascinating phenomenon and can't figure it out. Maybe fairies do have something to do with it!

There are some good campsites around here and the chance to spot the famous desert elephants. Alternative tracks and canyons in the Hoarusib and Hoanib rivers also beckon, but it remains for us to tackle the final 100 odd kilometres to Sesfontein and enjoy the decadent luxury of clean linen and a comfortable bed at the Fort Sesfontein Lodge.

On to Sesfontein

If you want to camp in the Sesfontein area and have a 4x4 vehicle, head south from the C43 intersection for 11 kilometres to **Warmquelle** and then turn off (S19011.090 E13°48.339) to follow the signs for another 6 kilometres to

The old German fort at Sesfontein is now a comfortable lodge and camp.

Ongongo Campsite. I would rate this secluded and picturesque site under a sky filled with rosy-faced lovebirds as one of the best in Namibia. Hidden down a steep, stony track (hence the need for 4x4) are a couple of levelled sites, and at the top of the gorge is the real reason for coming down here – a hot-water spring tumbling down a waterfall into a clear natural swimming pool below. Lanterns light the way at night and donkey boilers heat the showers in the rustic ablution blocks – no generators, no overlanders, just beauty, peace and quiet. Rates are N$75 per person and you can contact Liana Greeff on tel: 081-314-0216, e-mail: ongongo.campsite@hotmail.com, website: www.ongongocamp.co.za.

Back on the C43 you will start noticing a subtle difference in your surroundings – you are leaving Kaokoland and entering Damaraland. After 11 kilometres, you'll reach the turn-off left to a few community campsites in the Khowarib Schlucht canyon. This narrow canyon offers a spectacular shortcut eastwards to the C35, with the added bonus of maybe seeing desert elephants, but check with locals before tackling this route. The first site is just a kilometre from the main road (at S19°15.714 E13°52.061), situated on a ridge overlooking the narrow canyon. Others further up the canyon are all pretty similar. There is not always water in the river and when dry the area can be very dusty. This is one of those sites that can be either very good or very bad, and sometimes even deserted.

Further down towards Palmwag you will pass signposts to other community campsites. Some are quite far off the main road and although they might not be great destinations, they do give you the opportunity to venture into these wilderness areas legally and with some confidence. **Palmwag Lodge** (S19°52.868 E13°56.386) is about 7 kilometres north of the C40 intersection and just north of the veterinary control gate.

Palmwag lies on the usually dry Uniab River in a large concession area. Desert elephants often drink in front of the lodge, black rhinos can be found on game drives and a leopard has been spotted lurking around the swimming pool at night. Other than the popular morning and afternoon game drives, day tours to the Hoanib River or a Himba village can be arranged. Accommodation is in comfortable bungalows clustered around the main building (N$1 385 single and N$2 270 double). The campsite is well positioned overlooking the dry riverbed and has individual lapas with a braai and good ablutions (N$105 a person). They also operate the fuel station down the road at the vet gate. For more information, tel: 064-416-820, fax: 064-404-664, e-mail: enquiries@namibia-tracks-and-trails.com, website: www.namibia-tracks-and-trails.com.

Leaving Palmwag, we pass through the vet gate and a couple of kilometres later reach the intersection with the C40 from Kamanjab. Keep right to stay on the C43 and 40 kilometres later you will join the C39. A right turn here would take you down to the Skeleton Coast at Torra Bay. But keep left, and the C39 swings east and brings you into the heart of Damaraland and the first of many wonderful sights to see.

Damaraland 28

What is today a desert wilderness must have been a hunter-gatherer's paradise as far back as 5 000 years ago. Twyfelfontein, Brandberg and Spitzkoppe all display fascinating evidence of the previous inhabitants and their culture. While the rest of Namibia is steeped in colonial and precolonial history, this relatively small area contains the ancient background to the modern state of Namibia.

The caves at Spitzkoppe once sheltered groups of San.

Coming from the west along the C39, look out for the turn-off to the right onto the D2612. There is a small shop and puncture-repair place here, as well as a track leading off to the left for 2 kilometres to **Camp Xaragu** (S20°35.379 E14°20.534). Nicely hidden from view and road noise, Xaragu is behind a hill in an isolated valley and offers the best budget accommodation in the area. A little shop, bar and pool form the focus for this camp, which consists of chalets (N$620 single and N$780 double), furnished tents that share ablutions with the campers (N$375 single and N$460 double) and campsites (N$75 a person). Breakfast is included in chalet and tented accommodation, and lunch costs N$75 and a full dinner buffet (usually braai or potjie) N$120. There is an interesting menagerie of orphaned or injured wildlife roaming the premises and a collection of snakes in glass tanks. For bookings and info tel: 067-687-037, fax: 067-687-037, e-mail: xaragu@africaonline.com.na, website: www.xaragu.com.

Turn down onto the D2612 and after 11.7 kilometres look for an unsignposted track leading off to the right for 0.6 kilometres to the **Wondergat** (S20°30.864 E14°22.345). Legend has it that this dangerous, unguarded hole in the ground is bottomless – divers made it down to 100 metres before running out of oxygen. Tread carefully, you could just tumble straight down into hell! Turn off the D2612 at S20°31.444 E14°23.821 and cross the dry Aba Huab riverbed for access to the ancient rock engravings of Twyfelfontein, the strange rock formations of the Organ Pipes and the dark mass of the Burnt Mountain.

Just across the river is the locally owned and run **Aba Huab Camp**. Rather exposed and dusty campsites cost N$125 a person and fully equipped tents cost N$315 single and N$550 double. The bar serves dinner at N$65

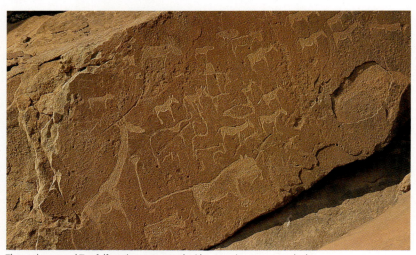

The rocks around Twyfelfontein are covered with engravings, or petroglyphs.

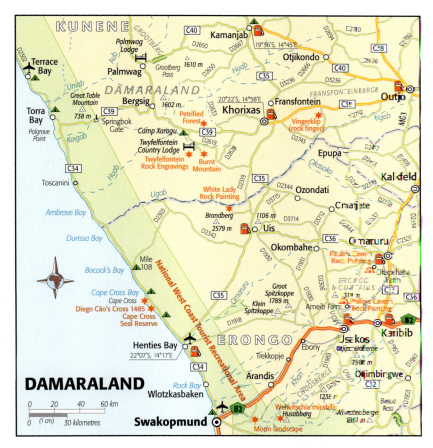

a plate. For details, tel: 065-331-104, fax: 067-331-749.

Three kilometres further is the turn-off (S20°34.529 E14°24.053) to Twyfelfontein, straight on to the Organ Pipes and Burnt Mountain.

Along the short 5-kilometre road to the Twyfelfontein engravings is a turn-off right to the **Twyfelfontein Country Lodge**. Not far off the road but well tucked away among giant rock formations, this three-star establishment is the best in the area. The open-sided dining room and bar, swimming pool and 56 en-suite rooms, all in earthy colours and built of natural materials, blend in beautifully with the surroundings. Although there are some magnificent rock engravings in the lodge's grounds, guided excursions are offered to the other sites nearby. Magnificence does not come cheap, though, as their rates are N$1 250 single, N$1 740 and N$282 for dinner. For information and reservations, tel: 061-374-750, fax: 061-256-598, e-mail: twyfelfontein@ncl.com.na, website: www.namibialodges.com.

Park in the guarded area (S20°35.454 E14°22.308) and walk to the new Twyfelfontein visitors' centre. This award-winning little building is made entirely out of recycled material and houses an interpretive display on the engravings and their history. Buy your tickets here (N$50 per person, plus N$15 per car) and wait for a guide to conduct you over the half-hour Dancing Kudu route or the one-hour Lion Man route. Whichever route you take, you will be astounded by the prolific artwork cut into the rock faces of the boulders strewn around the mountainside. Over 2 500 engravings of animals and humans have been discovered – elephant, rhino, lion, antelope and their hunters. Inhabitants of the area have been carving and chipping away at the rocks since 300 BC and only stopped during the 19th century. After your hike you will be grateful for the kiosk at the visitors' centre selling snacks and cold drinks.

Retrace your tracks for 5 kilometres to the road, which takes you on to the next fascinating site, the Organ Pipes. Four kilometres brings you to the parking area (S20°36.767 E14°24.920), which overlooks the shallow dry gorge that contains this strange formation of rocks. Dolorite columns, some 5 metres high, pack the side of the gorge-like organ pipes in a church – perhaps not the most exciting sight in the world, but amazing to think they were formed 120 million years ago. There is no visitor's charge.

Nor is there a charge to view the Burnt Mountain, and rightly so, because it is hardly worth driving the extra couple of kilometres to see a dark ridge of stone that, to the imaginative among

Hunters and their prey – San paintings in the caves at Spitzkoppe.

us, might look burnt. Please don't confuse this pile of black gravel with the magnificent and awesome Brandberg, which is about 200 kilometres south.

Make your way back to the C39 again to visit the Petrified Forest, 58 kilometres west of Khorixas, but beware of many unofficial and rip-off sites along the way. The 'real' one is at S20°26.435 E14°36.470 and costs N$35 per person and N$15 per car. As at Twyfelfontein, a guide escorts you around a trail that takes in many large and lengthy petrified logs and a great number of rare welwitschia plants. The logs are a mind-boggling 200–300 million years old, while some of the welwitschias have 'only' been around for 1 000 years. There is also a selection of authentic handcrafts, minerals and crystals on sale here that would make excellent souvenirs.

Khorixas

Khorixas is one of those awful little towns close to major tourist sites where the locals hustle and hassle the 'poor' traveller who has to stop and refuel there. It does, however, also have a supermarket, Standard Bank with ATM, and a choice of two accommodation establishments. Actually there is no choice, as the privately owned and run iGowati Lodge is so much better than the Khorixas Lodge, run by Namibia Wildlife Resorts.

iGowati Lodge is centrally and securely situated opposite the Total garage and Multisave supermarket. A pleasant, thatched main building with patio and swimming pool fronts a row of 29 comfortable en-suite rooms that can sleep up to four people (N$380 per person B&B). Camping is under shade on grass, with electricity points and

The looming Pondokberge.

braai facilities for N$50 a person. For more details, tel: 067-331-592, fax: 067-331-594, e-mail: igowati@mweb.com.na, website: www.igowatilodge.com.

Khorixas Lodge is on the western outskirts of town and has a rundown look and feel. A large selection of accommodation ranges from campsites (N$100 plus N$50 per person) to standard bungalows (N$600 double) to luxury bungalows (N$800 double). Contact NWR for bookings.

From Khorixas take the C39 east out of town towards Outjo for 8 kilometres to reach the intersection with the C35 (S20°22.120 E15°02.413). North will take you to Kamanjab, but we head south towards Uis to visit the mighty Brandberg. About 112 kilometres from Khorixas turn right onto the D2359 at S21°07.065 E14°51.351. Approximately 15 kilometres down this good dirt road is the turn-off to the **Brandberg White Lady Lodge**, the most accessible and best accommodation in the area. It is 11.5 kilometres down to the lodge on the banks of the dry Ugab River. They offer chalets at N$704 single and N$1 210 double (dinner, bed and breakfast), en-suite furnished tents at N$330 single and N$495 double and camping at N$60 per person. Desert elephants are regularly seen strolling through the camp and the lodge boasts stunning sunset views of the Brandberg and what must be the weirdest nine-hole golf course in the country – I first mistook it for a 4x4 obstacle course! Contact the lodge on tel: 064-684-004, fax: 064-684-006, e-mail: ugab@iway.na, website: www.brandbergwllodge.com.

For the remaining 7 kilometres from the lodge turn-off to the Brandberg visitor's centre (S21°05.621 E14°40.566), this huge mountain massif looms larger and larger, until it seems to engulf you and your car. Namibia's highest peak, Königstein (at 2 572 metres), is here, as is the famous San painting of the White Lady. Pay your N$35 per person to the National Monuments Council of Namibia, which administers this site, as they do at Spitzkoppe, the Petrified Forest and Twyfelfontein, and your guide will lead you up the valley on a fairly strenuous hour-and-a-half hike to the site of the San paintings. Try to time your hike for the cooler early morning or late afternoon (last tour leaves at 16h00) and take drinking water with you. There are many large trees to rest under, and the birdwatching is rewarding, so don't rush. The guides point out interesting flora and fauna along the way, and will also tell you that the White Lady is now believed to be a male, probably a *shaman* conducting a ceremony. Linger a while at the sites and try to absorb some of what must have been going on in the artist's head as he (or she?) created these timeless masterpieces. Wild animals race across the rocks while human figures dance in joyous celebration – and the fact that we might not be interpreting the paintings correctly only adds to their mystique and beauty.

On to Spitzkoppe

Back on the C35, it is just 13 kilometres to the turn-off into **Uis**. Between 1951 and 1990 tin was mined here on a large scale and the town was built. It died when mining ceased, but now tourism is breathing new life into the area. People are moving back and recycling the old mine houses and buildings into lodges and restaurants. Turn down into town and drive to the four-way stop. Most of what you will need is clustered around this intersection – the Montis Usti B&B and restaurant, the Koenigstein Restaurant and Guest House, Brandberg Rest Camp, Brandberg supermarket and Engen fuel.

Montis Usti is a new establishment that offers five rooms at N$300 per person B&B, a restaurant and takeaway. On the opposite corner, you will find the **Koenigstein Restaurant and Guest House**. The welcoming bar and restaurant offer tasty food, cold drinks and home baked cakes, and accommodation consists of five air-conditioned rooms for N$350 per person B&B, and camping at N$75. For further information, tel/fax: 064-504-120.

Next door to the Koenigstein is the old mine recreation club that has now been transformed into the **Brandberg Rest Camp**. The huge 25x12-metre swimming pool has been maintained, badminton can still be played in the hall, and I swear I heard the ghosts of miners drinking in the big old pub. Poolside en-suite rooms cost N$350 single and N$600 double (B&B) and camping N$80 per person. There are also a couple of well-equipped self-catering flats at N$500 for two persons and N$1 000 for four per night. Trips are offered to the old mine as well as geology and desert elephant excursions in a Landcruiser. For details tel/fax: 064-504-038, e-mail: brandberg@africaonline.com.na, website: brandbergrestcamp.com.

Continue past the Brandberg Rest

Camp and turn left to reach the other accommodation in town, the **White Lady Bed & Breakfast and Camping**. A neat and tidy operation with a sparkling pool and comfortable en-suite rooms that cost N$410 single and N$678 double (including breakfast). The campsite is too small for overlanders and is shaded with good ablutions – at N$70 per person. They also run mineral tours and desert trekking. For more details, tel/fax: 064-504-102, e-mail: whitelady@iway.na.

Monty van der Smit, the local expert on all things mineral and crystal, lives next door and has an amazing selection of semiprecious stones for sale. He also conducts mineral and adventure tours and is a mine (geddit?) of information. Contact him on tel: 064-504-096, e-mail: monty@iway.na.

From Uis there is a wonderful backroad shortcut to the **Spitzkoppe**. Head east out of Uis on the C36 for 5 kilometres, then turn south onto the D1930, a good swooping, dipping gravel road. After 75 kilometres turn right onto the D3716 at S21°44.868 E15°15.612 and you will be driving straight towards the magnificent peak of the Spitzkoppe, the highest point of which is 1 728 metres. About 11 kilometres down the D3716 brings you to the turn-off and gate into the protected wilderness area of these great inselbergs (S21°50.507 E15°12.377).

Day visitors pay N$25 per person, plus N$10 a car, and to camp costs N$45 per person. The many San paintings found in these mountains attract most travellers, but many also come to climb the difficult rock faces. Finding your way around can be confusing, but to reach Bushman's Paradise, the best paintings in the Pondokberge, keep right and around the front of Gross Spitzkoppe. You pass some wonderful campsites under sheer walls of granite to reach the parking area at S21°49.654 E15012.896. Above you will see the slippery path up the smooth rock face with chain railings to assist you. Keep right until you see a small valley below, then climb down into it and hike to the overhang on the left to find the longest gallery of San paintings you are ever likely to see. Human and animal forms race across the walls and one can only guess at the groups of hunter-gatherers who congregated in this hidden valley, feasting, telling stories and painting on the walls of their caves so that we can drive our 4x4s in for a quick half-hour digital photoshoot. Modern man's graffiti and vandalism are a shame and, to be honest, an embarrassment.

The rough tracks around this wonderful group of mountains lead you to idyllic hidden campsites, but be prepared – there are no facilities at all and water is only available at the main gate. Check out the website: www.natron.net/nacobta/spitzkoppe.

To get back onto the main B2 highway that runs between Swakopmund and Okahandja, return to the D3716, turn right and drive through the village of Grootspitskop and on for 12 kilometres. Don't forget to look back at the Spitzkoppe – it looks magnificent from this angle. You will reach the D1918 that comes up from Henties Bay, turn left here for 17 kilometres to reach the B2.

Well-laid-out routes lead to the rock engravings at Twyfelfontein.

Index

Aba Huab Camp 196–197
accommodation 21–26, 41–45, 65, 170
Aus 90–92
Bushmanland 164
Caprivi 168–169
Damaraland 196–203
Divundu 170–171
Etosha 148–152
Grootfontein 157–158
Kaokoland 186–194
Katima Mulilo 174–177
Kaudom Game Park 164–166
Keetmanshoop 83
Lüderitz 95–96
Mariental 86
Oshakati 181–183
Otavi 156–157
Otjiwarongo 143
Outjo 144–145
Ruacana 183
Rundu 161–162
Sesriem 06–107
Sossusvlei 106–107
Tsumeb 155–156
Walvis Bay 115
Windhoek 72–75
activities 60–65, 115–116, 126–127
Ai-Ais 12, 23, 28, 79, 99–102
Hot Springs 101
Ai-Ais Richtersveld Transfrontier Park 22, 26, 99
Alexander Bay 28, 52

Alte Brücke Resort 123
Alte Feste 68, 71
Alte Kaserne 124
Andara 168
angling 60, 131 (see also fishing)
Annie's Cottage 80
Aranos 133, 136
Arebbusch Travel Lodge 74
Ariamsvlei 28, 52
Auas City Hotel 73
Auob Lodge 136
Aus 90–92
Aussenkehr 100
Automobile Association (AA) 37

Bahnhof Hotel 132
Bay View Hotel, The 95
Bed-and-Breakfast Association 42
Beira Mar 96
Benguela Medical Centre 130
Big Five Central 134
birding 60, 78, 94, 117, 22–26
Blue Note 76
Bogenfels 94
border crossing 53, 55, 80, 164, 175, 177
Bosua Pass 132
Brandberg 195, 200
Rest Camp 201
Brandberg White Lady Lodge 200
Bucks Camping Lodge 130
Buitepos 52

Bullring Sportsbar 85
Büllsport Guest Farm 107
Burnt Mountain 198–199
bus travel 54–56, 57, 155, see also transport
Buschveld Park Lodge 144
Bush Pillow 143
Bushmanland 12, 19, 159–166
Bwabwata 171
Byseewah Guest House 130

Calai 162
Camel Lodge 81
Camp Kwando 171–172
Camp Xarago 196
camping 43 (see also accommodation)
Camping Hire Namibia 78
Cañon Mountain Lodge 102
Cañon Roadhouse 102
Canyon Hotel 83
Cape Cross Lodge 131
Cape Cross Seal Reserve 22, 131
Caprivi 10, 12, 29, 62, 162, 167–172
Game Park 22
Caprivi River Lodge 176
car hire 62, 72, 116, 127
Cardboard Box Backpackers 74

Central Lodge 84
Chameleon Backpackers' 74
Chameleon Safaris 58
Christuskirche 71
communications 38, 63, 78, 127
Courtyard Guesthouse 158
Courtyard Hotel 114
currency 11
customs 18–20, 63, 80
Cymot 77, 97, 183

Daan Viljoen Game Park 22, 75
Damara 10, 14, 18–19
Damaraland 195–203
Dare Devil Adventures 118
Desert Festival 107
Diaz Coffee Shop 96
Diaz Point 93
diving 61
Divundu 169
documentation 36
Drostky's Cave 53
Duine Hotel, De 130
Dunedin Star Guest House 124
Dunes Backpackers 124
Dylan's Bar 77

Eco Marine Kayak Tours 116
Eenhana 180
Eha Lodge 183
Elisenheim 75
Elizabeth Bay 94
Eluwa Hotel 181–182
embassies 36–37, 64

204 | Index

Epupa Community Campsite 189
Epupa Falls 12, 179, 189–190
Epupa Falls Lodge 190
Etosha National Park 12, 18, 22, 49, 139–145, 147–152
  Garten Hotel 144
  Gateway Lodge 145
  Pan 22, 148–149
  Safari Camp 145

Felix Unite River Adventures 100
festivals 78, 107, 128, 131
Fish River Canyon 12, 23, 26, 28, 61, 79, 89, 99–102
Fish River Hiking Trail 101
fishing 126, 131, 173, 176–177
food 20, 43–45, 49
Friedenskirsch 140

Garub Pan 92
Gathemann House 71
Gathemanns 76
Giants' Playground 138
Gobabeb 110
Gobabis 49, 57, 62, 133–138
Gochas 133, 137
Goerke House 93
golf 126
Gourmet Tours 72
GPS 37
Grootfontein 10, 19, 153–158
Grünau 28, 52, 81–82
Grünau Country

House 82
Hakuna Matata Adventures 176–177
Halali 150
Hansa Haus 95–96
Hardap Dam 86–87
Hardap Reserve 23
health 47–50, 130, 144, 156, 158, 160, 175
Henckert Tourist Centre 132
Henties Bay 60, 129–132
hiking 61, 108
Hippo Lodge 177
Hippo Pools 186–187
Homeb 110
Horse and Bell Internet Café 85
horse-riding 126
Hospitality Association of Namibia (HAN) 42, 65
hospitals 49
Hotel Cela 73–74
Hotel Europa Hof 120, 122, 125
Hotel Prinzessin Rupprecht 120, 122
Hunsberg Conservancy 26
hunting 61, 65, 78

Igowati Lodge 199–200
immunisation 48
Impalila Island Lodge 177
Izone Internet Café 183

Joubert Pass 191

Kalahari 23, 26, 28, 52, 133–138
Kalahari Sands Hotel 72, 76

Kalkfontein Hotel 82
Kamelruhe Guest House, The 137
Kaokoland 12, 29, 177, 185–194, 19
Kapps Hotel 95, 96
Kaserne 120
Katere 166
Katima Mulilo 10, 22, 28, 29, 49, 168, 173–177
Kaudom Camp 166
Kaudom Game Park 23, 159–166
Kavango 10, 18
Kavango River 22, 23, 60, 162, 168, 179
Kavango River Lodge 161
Keetmanshoop 10, 49, 56, 57, 81, 84, 90
Kegelbahn 93
Kgalagadi Transfrontier Park 133, 137
Khomas Hochland 22, 67
Khorab Safari Lodge 157
Khorixas 199
Khorixas Lodge 200
Kiepie's Dance Bar 77
Klein Windhoek Guesthouse 73
Koenigstein Restaurant and Guest House 201
Koës 133, 138
  Hotel 138
  Pan 138
Kokerboom Motel 80
Kolmanskop 12, 92, 94
Kongola 171
Kreplin House 93
Kristall Kellerei 132
Kücki's Pub 125

Kuiseb Canyon 24, 112
Kuiseb Delta Adventures 115
Kuiseb River 25, 110
Kunene River 60, 179, 192
  Lodge 188
Kwando River 22, 23, 171

La Vida Inn 86
La-di-das 76
Lafenis Lodge 83
Lagoon Chalets and Caravan Park 115
Lagoon Lodge 114
Lake Oanob Resort and Game Reserve 87
Lake Otjikoto 61, 154
Lala Panzi Guest Lodge 158
Langnorm Hotel 114
LevoTours 116
Lianshulu Lodge 172
Long Beach 118
Long Beach Leisure Park 118
Lüderitz 10, 12, 14, 20, 24, 28, 62, 80–87, 91, 92–97
  Museum 93
  Nest Hotel, The 95
  Yacht Club 97
Lüderitz Safaris and Tours 97

Mahango Game Park 23, 170
Mahangu Safari Lodge 170
Mainliner Intercity Bus Service 155
Masalani Hotel 156
malaria 50
Maltahöhe Hotel 87

Mamili Game Park 23–24, 172
Mangetti Game Camp 24
Maori Campsite 158
maps 8
  Damaraland 197
  Eastern Caprivi 169
  Etosha 149
  Gobabis 135
  Grootfontein 157
  Kaokoland 186
  Katima Mulilo 174
  Kaudom 163
  Keetmanshoop 84
  Lüderitz 91
  Namib-Naukluft 105
  Otjiwarongo 142
  Rundu 161
  Southwestern Namibia 81
  Swakopmund 119
  Tsumeb 155
  Tsumkwe 164
  Walvis Bay 113
  Windhoek 69
Marienfluss 192
Mariental 10, 23, 62, 86
Mariental Hotel 86
Masonic Hotel 80
Mata Mata 26, 28, 52, 133
Mesosaurus Fossil Site 138
Meteor Hotel 157–158
Minen Hotel 156
Mirabib 110
Mitzi's Medicine Depot 77
Moaremure 172
Mokuti Lodge 152
money 53, 63,
Montis Usti 201
Mpungu 180

Mudumu Game Park 23, 172
Mukusi Cabins 174
Mushara Lodge 152
Musikwoche 128

Ngoabaca Camp Site 171
Nakatwa Camp 172
Namaqualand 80
Namib Desert 79
Namib i 121
Namib Shore B&B 130–131
Namib Wüste Farmstall 132–133
Namibgrens Guest Farm 109
Namibia Professional Hunting Assoc. 65
Namibia Tourism 65
Namibia Wildlife Resorts (NWR) 20, 22, 42, 65, 78, 97, 120, 169
Namibian Craft Centre 77
Namib-Naukluft Park 24–25, 28, 61, 103–110
Namibnet Internet Café 78
Namushasha Lodge 171
Namutoni 151
National West Coast Tourist Recreation Area 25
Nauchas 109
Naukluft Hiking Trail 108
Naukluft mountains 24, 25
Neuras 108
Ngandu Safari Lodge 161–162

Ngepi 170
nightlife 76–77
Nkurenkuru 180
Noordoewer 26, 28, 29, 52, 79–87
Norotshama 100
Ntwala Island Lodge 177
Nujoma, Sam 12
Nzinze 180

O'Portuga 75
Ohakane Lodge 191
Okahandja 10, 26, 132, 139, 140–141
Bridge 140
Lodge 141
Rest Camp 140
Okangwati 188–189
Okaukuejo 150
Oktoberfest 78
Old Breweries 76
Olea Town Lodge and Campsite 158
Olive Trail 108
Omarunga Camp and Tented Lodge 190
Omashare Lodge 161
Omaue Namibia 143
Ombinda Country Lodge 144
Omunjandi 188
Ondangwa 180, 181
Hotel 181
Rest Camp 181
Town Lodge 181
Onduuzo 188
Ongongo Campsite 185, 194
Onguma Private Game Reserve 151–152
Opuwo 62, 190–192
Orange River 26, 28, 52, 62, 79
Lodge 81

Organ Pipes 198
Orupembe 193
Oshakati 10, 180, 181–183
Oshakati Country Lodge 182
Oshandira Lodge 182–183
Oshikango 29, 180
Oshikango Country Lodge 180–181
Otavi 153–158
Otjitanda 192
Otjiwarongo 10, 26, 49, 62, 141–143
Outapi 183
Outjo 144
Owambo 18
Owamboland 49, 180–183

Paaltjies 60, 112–114
Palmenecke Guest House 157
Palmwag Lodge 194
Pappot, The 87
Pelican Bay Hotel 114
Petrified Forest 199, 201
Platform One 125
Pleasure Flights and Safaris 127
police 49
Pomona 94
Popa Falls 12, 167, 169
Protea Hotel 114–115
Provenance Camp 100
Puccini House 74
Puros 193

quadbiking 61–62, 126
Quiver Tree Forest 138

Red Dune 137
Rehoboth 87
Remhoogte Pass 108, 109
Rhenish Mission 140
Richtersveld 99
River Chalets and Camping 86
River Rafters 100
Rooidrom 193
Roy's Camp 160, 162
Ruacana 179–183
Ruacana Falls 182, 186
Rundu 10, 22, 49, 62, 159–166, 179–183

Safariland-Holtz 77–78
San 14, 19–20, 198–199, 201, 203
sandboarding 126
Sandwich Harbour 24, 25, 60, 112, 116
Sarasungu River Lodge 162
Seagulls Cry 124
Seeheim Hotel 90
Sendelingsdrif 28
Sesfontein 191–192, 193–194
Sesfontein Fort 192
Sesriem 12, 24–25, 28, 104
Sesriem Canyon 104–105
Shamvura Camp 168
Shivuma 172
Sikereti Camp 164–165
Skeleton Coast 14, 18, 26, 131–132
   Park 22, 25–26
   Safaris 131
Skubbe Bar, The 130

skydiving 127
Solitaire 107
Sossusvlei 12, 24, 28, 105–106
   Lodge 106
Speed Week 62
Sperrgebiet 28, 92, 94
Spitzkoppe 195, 198–199, 200, 201, 202
Spreetshoogte 109
Stampriet 136
Station Grill 125
Stiltz, The 122
Stony's Hotel 137
Sunset Camp 183
surfing 62
Susuwe Island Lodge 177
Swakopmund 10, 20, 25, 49, 57, 58, 62, 112, 117–128
   Brauhaus 125
   Hotel and Entertainment Centre 121
   Municipal Restcamp 124
   Museum 121
Swakopmunder Apotheke 121
Swartbooisdrift 188

Tambuti Lodge 161
Tandala Ridge 145
telephones 62 , 63,
Terrace Bay 26
Thüringerhof Hotel 73
Tiger Reef Beach Bar 125
Torra Bay 26, 131
Tour and Safari Association 65
tour operators 127
Town Hoppers 57
Tranendal Farm 137

Transkalahari End Resort 134
Trans-Kalahari Highway 10, 28, 131–132
Trans-Namib Museum 71–72
transport 51–58, 116, 128
Travel North Bed & Breakfast 155
Treasure Trail, The 94
Tsauchub River 24, 105, 108
Tsoutsomb Cottages 155–156
Tsumeb 10, 19, 49, 57, 153–158
   Cultural Village 154
   Campsite 154
   Museum 156
Tsumkwe 164
Tug Bar and Restaurant 119–120
Tutwa 175
Twyfelfontein 195, 201, 203
   Country Lodge 197–198
   Visitors' Centre 198

Ugab 144
Uis 201

Van Zyl's Pass 192
Vioolsdrif 52
visas 12, 53
Von Bach Game Reserve 26
Von Lindequest Gate (Etosha) 151

Walvis Bay 10, 14, 16, 20, 49, 57, 60, 62, 110, 111–116

Warmquelle 185, 193–194
Waterberg Plateau Park 22, 22, 26, 141
Waterkloof Trail 108
watersports 62
Weltevrede Guest Farm 102
Welwitschia Trail 24
West Coast National Recreation Area 60
White House Guest Farm 82–83
White Lady Bed & Breakfast and Camping 202
Wika Carnival 78
Wilderness Safaris 58, 131
wildlife 21–26, 148, 152
Windhoek 10, 12, 16, 28–33, 49, 57, 62, 67–75, 79–87
Windhoek Country Club 76
Windhoek Underwater Club 51
Wine Bar, The 75, 75
Witvlei 134
Wondergat 196

Zambezi River 60, 168, 173, 175, 176, 177
Zambezi River Lodge 175
Zebra Pan 110
Zum Wurzelsepp Restaurant 75

Other titles in this exciting series

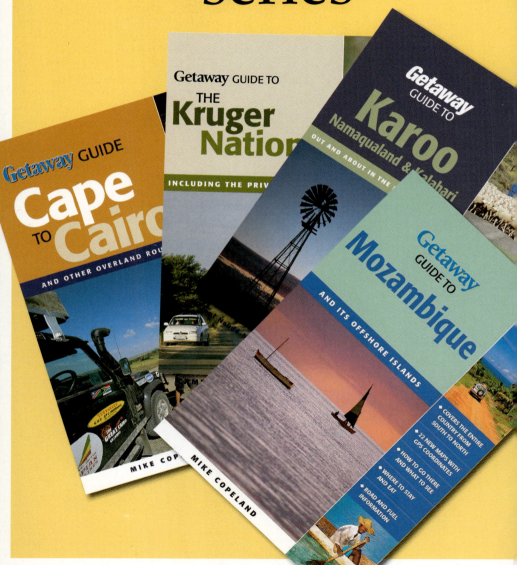